KAREN ANN

The story that sent shockwaves around the world

"This is a book which could break your heart . . . Besides the obvious heroes here—Karen's parents, brother and sister—we find others who move us by their dedicated help to the sufferers."

—*Publishers Weekly*

"This book reveals the intricacies behind the facts of the Karen Quinlan story . . . Karen Ann's hauntingly psychic poetry . . . the parish priest whose wholehearted support deepened the Quinlans' faith . . . the intelligent young lawyer who worked without pay . . . The participants are vulnerable and very human and immediately grasp and hold our sympathies."

—*Library Journal*

"This is the story of one family's devotion and courage in the face of tragedy . . . Told with quiet eloquence, Karen's plight touches all of us, as do the courage and faith of her parents."

—*Argosy Magazine*

KAREN ANN

The Quinlans Tell Their Story

by Joseph and Julia Quinlan
with
Phyllis Battelle

*This low-priced Bantam Book
has been completely reset in a type face
designed for easy reading, and was printed
from new plates. It contains the complete
text of the original hard-cover edition.*
NOT ONE WORD HAS BEEN OMITTED.

RL 7, IL 7+

KAREN ANN:
THE QUINLANS TELL THEIR STORY

*A Bantam Book | published by arrangement with
Doubleday and Company, Inc.*

PRINTING HISTORY

*Doubleday edition published September 1977
2nd printing .... September 1977
Literary Guild of America edition September 1977
Readers' Digest serialization September 1977
Bantam edition | September 1978
2nd printing*

ISBN 0-553-11738-6

Published simultaneously in the United States and Canada

*Bantam Books are published by Bantam Books, Inc. Its trade-
mark, consisting of the words "Bantam Books" and the por-
trayal of a bantam, is registered in the United States Patent
Office and in other countries. Marca Registrada. Bantam
Books, Inc., 666 Fifth Avenue, New York, New York 10019.*

PRINTED IN THE UNITED STATES OF AMERICA

TO KAREN

*Whose life was God's gift to us
and whom we will lovingly return when it is time
with the hope that our story will be an
inspiration to others who struggle with life and death.*

Acknowledgments

Although it would be impossible to acknowledge the generous assistance of everyone who helped us throughout the last two years, we wish to express our special gratitude to the following:

Our families, especially Karen's grandparents, Robert and Bertha Duane

Paul and Maria Armstrong

The Most Reverend Lawrence B. Casey, Bishop of Paterson, New Jersey

The Reverend Paschal Caccavalle

The Community of Our Lady of the Lake Church

James M. Crowley

Joseph Fennelly, M.D.

John M. Fox and the members of the Morris County Sheriff's Department

Milton Helpern, M.D.

Institute of Society, Ethics and Life Sciences

Kennedy Institute, Center for Bioethics

Julius Korein, M.D.

Morris View Nursing Home

New Jersey Catholic Conference

The Reverend John Quinlan

The Reverend Monsignor Frank Rodimer

Shearman & Sterling

The Supreme Court of New Jersey

The Reverend Herbert Tillyer

The Reverend Thomas Trapasso

Warner-Chilcott Laboratories, especially Ralph Amato and David Shafer

Richard Watson, M.D.

Charles P. Young Company

To the institutions and their staffs who have ministered to our daughter, Karen—and particularly to all of the nurses who not only provided exceptional care but were a source of comfort to the family.

*time is endless, therefore what does
today, tomorrow and now mean?*

These lines were written
by Karen Ann Quinlan
on January 7, 1975.

The Beginning

Landing, New Jersey, is a quiet, casual summer resort town that outgrew its best season and went year-round during the suburban sprawl of the 1960s.

Once a spa for the very rich from New York City, fifty miles directly to her east, Landing had 3,064 residents by the year 1975. These diligent middle-class families had replaced the mansions and terraced gardens of the 1920s with modest, proudly maintained houses strewn alongside, and up the sloping hills from the south shore of Lake Hopatcong—a state-owned tourist lure that quadruples the population on hot, boisterous summer weekends, and often shrouds the town in silence and thick, scudding fog during the colder months.

The boating and swimming on usually tranquil Hopatcong, and a small and ancient amusement park called Bertrand's Island, provided the principal local interest until the autumn of 1975, when a young Landing resident, Karen Ann Quinlan, became famous.

Many people here knew Karen. She lived in the same house in Landing all her life; directed the softball team, taught swimming and lifesaving, led skiing expeditions to the nearby Pocono Mountains—she was a leader. For nearly twenty of her twenty-one active years, Karen was almost a fixture at the lake. She lived only about six hundred yards back and up from the sandy beach which is now the Country Club. You turn right, off the lakefront road at the yellow cement Shore Hills Market, go straight up the two-lane incline, past the softball field, make a left on Ryerson Road, looking out for children on tricycles and bikes or carrying plastic surfboards in summer, and the Quinlans' is the gray frame two-story with the white statue of the Virgin Mary in the front yard.

It was only a four-room one-level bungalow when Joseph Quinlan built it in 1952 as an investment in the family he and his wife, Julia, planned to have. Landing was rustic in those days. There wasn't another house in the area—only immense oak trees—and they could visualize bringing their babies here for healthy summers away from the cramped fifth-floor walk-up apartment in West New York, New Jersey, where they lived as newlyweds. Then, in quick succession, Julia suffered miscarriages and a stillbirth.

This series of traumas was so devastating that the Quinlans found themselves moving here to Landing—not, as they had planned, to benefit their children, but to escape from the city where their son had died in his mother's womb, and Julia had been advised that she would never bear a live child.

There were only 702 unfamiliar faces in Landing then. It seemed a mournful place, especially in fall and winter when the fog rolled up off the lake. They set about making new friends, joining "Our Lady of the Lake," an old stone Roman Catholic Church built high on a bluff above Lake Hopatcong. It was there, encouraged by their pastor, that the Quinlans decided to adopt a baby.

Thus came Karen.

As Fate or God (the Quinlans knew it was God) so often arranges life's marvels, Julia then confounded the doctors by giving birth to two natural children, a delicate dark-haired girl, Mary Ellen, and a husky boy they named John.

But it was around Karen that most of the family activities revolved. Funny, athletic, mischievous, she seemed the extrovert who set the pace. Beneath the outgoing surface, however, Karen Quinlan was a young woman with extraordinary perceptions of herself, and of her place in history. During the last months of her cognitive life, before she fell into a coma which would affect the world, she predicted her fate to friends.

And on January 7, 1975, she wrote a poem—it lay undiscovered for 18 months—in which she prophesied precisely that pathetic comatose condition in which her body soon would be trapped.

"A gift of God," the nun at the maternity home for adoptive infants had said, as she placed Karen in Julia's arms.

The Quinlans were never to forget that.

Chapter 1

April 11, 1975, was the last ordinary day.

Looking back, Julia Quinlan sees herself driving along the shore road as usual to her job at the Rectory, watching the morning sun sparkling and rippling across the lake—the perfect day to begin a suntan. Then at three o'clock, heading home and noting, frustrated, that the lake had gone flat and steel gray. It was Friday, so she stopped at the Acme supermarket for weekend groceries and, as she pulled the car into the garage, she heard the phone ringing. She remembers fumbling with the house keys, juggling an enormous shopping bag, and then hurrying into the kitchen, hoping it was the call she had been waiting for.

—And it was. It was Karen.

"Hi, Mom." she said. "How are you doin'?"

"Oh, fine, honey," I had to catch my breath. "How about *you*? How's your new place?" I tried to keep my voice happy. On Monday, she had moved into a house over on Cranberry Lake, and Joe and I were upset about it. Karen knew how we felt, and there was no point belaboring it.

"It's terrific. You're really going to love it." She sounded elated. "It's your kind of place. You know, rustic and quaint. Almost like one of those converted barns you've always wanted."

"Sounds charming."

"That's it. Exactly the word. There's a huge outdoor stone fireplace and a patio surrounded by great old trees. My room is on the second floor, with windows that look out on this real forest—"

She was obviously excited, almost singing, and as she rambled on about the house, I could feel my muscles begin to relax. Everything was going to be fine. Dear

1

Lord, we had been so concerned when she suddenly told us she was planning to rent a room in a house ten miles away. Joe, trying to act stern and looking only stricken, saying, "But why should you pay rent when you have your own room here at home?" Karen surprised, then indignant, moaning, "I'm twenty-one, Dad. If you can't make it on your own at twenty-one, you'll never make it." No rational comeback. Karen reassuring, "Don't be so overprotective—I'll only be there two weeks." She was driving to Florida in May with a girl friend. "And don't worry because the house happens to belong to two guys. I assure you they're harmless, and couldn't care less about me. I'll be safe." A reluctant giving-in, a kiss and a hug, and she was gone.

And now, on the phone, Karen was saying, "When can you drive up and see me?"

"Gee, let's see." I had to think for a moment. "What about Sunday after mass?"

"No good. I'm busy Sunday. Can you come Monday?" she said.

I reminded her that Monday was my Rosary meeting. I was president of the Rosary Society this year.

Finally, after some rather giggly analysis of our respective social obligations, we agreed on Tuesday afternoon, after I got off work. Karen gave me instructions on how to get to Cranberry Lake, about a ten-minute drive, then needled, "Knowing you, you'll get lost. But I'll send out the St. Bernards." It was typical Karen.

We must have talked for an hour and a half. She said she was saving her money to send Joe and me to Hawaii for our thirtieth wedding anniversary in September 1976. That was typical Karen, too—all-out generous, and very naïve. I doubt if she had any concept of the plane fare. And she mentioned that she was starting on a "starvation diet" to slim herself back into her size seven bikinis for Florida.

I resisted the mother's instinct to urge her to eat sensibly. Moderation is not a word in Karen's vocabulary. Once she sets her mind to do something, she wants instant results.

"And, by the way," she was saying, "I've been thinking that if I like Miami, maybe I'll look for a job there and stick around in Florida for a few months."

"I think that would be fantastic," I said, and I meant it. Karen and I are alike in our love for travel and independence. If I were her age, I'd do the same thing exactly. "Do it now, honey. Once you're married and have babies, you won't have the chance," I said, and she hooted.

"That'll be the day!"

It was after 5:30 when we finally hung up.

"Don't forget Tuesday," she said. It occurred to me that perhaps she was homesick, but she would never admit it.

"And give my love to Dad."

They were the last words I ever heard her speak.

Joseph Quinlan remembers dinner that evening as the usual rousing family get-together:

—Julie told us about Karen's call, and that she seemed very happy. I felt relieved to hear that, but I still didn't like the idea. I said, "I wish somebody could tell me why she moved into that place with those two fellows."

Julie sighed and said, "Honey, she hasn't 'moved in' with anybody. She's just rented a room, and these young men happen to be the landlords."

Then Mary Ellen, who is nineteen and knows everybody in all the surrounding counties, said, "You've seen one of them, Dad. He's Bill Zywot—he grew up just down the road from us. The other fellow, Tom French, I don't know anything about, but don't worry, Dad, they're definitely not her type."

"Who *is* Karen's type these days?" I said. "What happened to Tommy Flynn?" Tommy was a nice kid, amateur wrestler. He and Karen went together all through high school.

"He's in college down in St. Petersburg," Julie said. "Maybe Karen will see him next month when she goes down. By the way, changing the subject, Karen is going to send us to Hawaii for our thirtieth anniversary."

John let out a howl when his mother said that. John is seventeen, and he idolizes Karen, but he is going through the cynical age. "Karen?" he erupted. "Save that kind of money? What's it cost?"

"John, shame on you." Julie pretended to reprimand him, but she was smiling. "I wish you were half as generous as she is."

"You're evading the issue. How much does it cost?"

"I have no idea," Julie said, "but if Karen sets her mind to it, she'll do it."

"Mom's right," Mary Elen said, "and I'll tell you how she'll do it. Along about July, Karen will call a little conference. She'll say, 'Listen, you kids, we're going to send Mom and Dad on this little anniversary cruise. I've saved seventy-five bucks—how much can you kick in?'"

"Mary Ellen, you're terrible!" Julie was smiling. She loves it when the kids needle each other—and they're always needling. It's something they picked up from Karen.

"I wouldn't count on that trip if I were you," John said.

"Thank goodness you're *not* me," Julie informed him, standing up. "You wouldn't appreciate Hawaii!"

We realized it was 7:45, and Julie had a Cursillo Prayer Meeting at church. After she left the house, John asked me if he could borrow the new Datsun and drive over to Netcong, pick up a boy friend, and bring him back to the house. They wanted to play pool in the basement.

I tried to talk him out of it. There was a heavy layer of fog out there, and John had only had his driver's license for three months. But it was just a five-mile drive to Satch Romano's home, and John was so eager to show off the new car.

"Okay," I said finally, and flipped him the keys, "but be back within an hour."

After he left, I felt uneasy. I sat down and turned on the TV and there was nothing showing that I cared about, and I kept thinking to myself, "Relax. Everything is fine." Two hours later, I found I was dead wrong.

At 9:15 P.M. on April 11, John and his friend were driving up a hill a few miles from the Quinlan home, when suddenly another car came ripping over the top from the other side.

The other car was in the center of the road. John

swerved out onto the shoulder to avoid a collision, and the
new green Datsun flipped into the air and spun over three
times before it smashed into the ground.

Julia, who was at the prayer meeting when the accident
occurred, felt afterward that "it was a miracle those
boys survived":

—The car was totally demolished. Not a fender, not a
door, nothing wasn't crumpled.

The hood rolled forward like a window shade and
smashed right through the front windshield, pinning
John and his friend in the front seat.

John was stunned. He was unconscious for several
seconds. When he came to and realized what had happened, he managed to crawl out the shattered front
window, cutting himself terribly. The other boy made
it out through a hole in the back of the car, God knows
how. Both of them dreadfully bruised and their faces
and bodies covered with blood, but no bones were
broken.

Some neighbors heard the crash and rushed out.
When they saw gasoline spurting out of the car, they
quickly pulled out a wire, disconnecting the ignition.
Then they called an ambulance, which took the boys to
a hospital emergency room.

John was afraid to call home. He knew that I would
still be at the church, and he didn't want to talk to Joe.
Not that he was afraid because of the new car. He was
frightened because one of his hands had been severely
cut, and John sensed that this would terrify Joe. It
happens that my husband lost his left arm during the
war. He also lost a finger on his right hand. Naturally,
he is unusually sensitive to the children's injuries, and
John feared that if his father saw how seriously his own
hand had been injured—well, he was sure that Joe
would imagine the worst.

Finally, because there was no other way out, John
did call, and of course Joe drove to the hospital immediately, in Mary Ellen's car, and brought him home.

Usually I am calm in emergencies. I think that's the
way most mothers are. So I behaved quite efficiently
that night. John was alive, that was the important thing.
But as so often happens, the emotional reaction was
delayed. The realization of what had happened seized

me the next day. Our only son, and he had come within inches and seconds of being killed. I could feel every nerve end in my body. I could barely let John out of my sight.

I wouldn't go when Joe said he was visiting the garage where the car had been towed. When he came home, that Saturday morning, Joe's face was gray. He said, "All we can do is thank God. It was a miracle that those boys got out of that car alive."

And then Joe made a strange statement. He said that he had visited the scene of the accident and that, as he stood there looking at the skid marks in the road and the shattered glass still lying, like weapons, in the dirt, "I got this awful feeling—that this is not the end. That something else terrible is about to happen."

I felt chilled. Joe had never spoken before of any kind of premonition. He had never said anything even remotely like this. If it had come from Karen, I could have taken it more casually. Karen is extremely intuitive, and so am I. We often kid each other about which of us has a stronger "tenth sense." But coming from my husband, it was frightening.

Joe never mentioned it again. In fact, a few weeks afterward, when I reminded him of this feeling he had had, Joe looked completely blank.

"I don't remember anything like that at all," he said.

Joe had suffered for thirty years from a hiatus hernia, a condition that his doctor said was worse than an ulcer, because it was chronic. There was no way of permanently curing it. With a bland diet and periods free of tension, he was comfortable, but any outside pressure brought on painful attacks. After John's accident, Julie knew "he was feeling that hernia, like a fist twisting in his stomach":

—He never complained, but it was obvious from the tight expression on his face, and he could scarcely eat at all.

John was caught up in his own nightmares. He's always been a quiet boy. Takes after his father; neither of them talks very much, but both of them feel everything deeply. And John was quieter than ever now. He told me later that he kept seeing himself going over and over in that car, reliving the accident for weeks.

On Monday, when Joe and I went back to our jobs, we found it a relief. Work is therapy for me, and I was happy that my boss, Father Tom Trapasso, kept me busy with letters to type. That night, I went to my Rosary meeting. By the end of the day I was so exhausted that I felt if I could just make it up those twelve steps to the bedroom, I would fall asleep the moment my head found the pillow. Joe felt the same way. By eleven o'clock, for the first time in four days, we were deeply asleep.

The telephone rang at two in the morning.

Jolted awake, Julie remembers groping in the darkness toward the table beside her bed.

—My first thought was "Where is John?" It was pitch-black, and I was trembling, and all I could think of was John has crashed.

Then suddenly I remembered no, it couldn't be John. He can't drive. He's still bandaged, he's in bed—it must be my mother. My mother is eighty-one, and I thought, "Oh, Mama, she's had a stroke."

Joe had turned on a light, and finally I found the phone and said hello.

"Is this Mrs. Quinlan?" A woman's voice.

"Yes."

"I'm sorry to tell you, but your daughter is in the hospital. She's in serious condition, unconscious."

Dear God. "Do you mean Karen?"

"Yes. Karen Ann. The doctor asks that you and Mr. Quinlan come here as soon as you can."

"We'll be right over. What hospital?"

"Newton," she said. "I'm sorry, this is Newton Memorial. I'm a nurse. Karen is being treated right now in Intensive Care."

I managed to hang up the phone and then, all at once, I felt I couldn't move. Joe was coming around the bed, and I could hear him asking questions, but I couldn't answer. First John, now Karen. Cars spinning out.

Joe says it was almost a minute before I said anything and, when I did, all I told him was "Karen is very sick. We have to go to Newton right away."

He pulled me up and off the bed. Mary Ellen wandered into our room. She was half asleep still, and frowning. I remember reaching out and helping her tug her long black hair out from under the robe she was fumbling to pull around her shoulders, and saying, "You go back to bed, honey. We'll call you as soon as we know something more."

Mary Ellen looked at me as though I was crazy. "More about *what?*" she said. "Who called? What's happening?"

That's when I began to cry and, as though the tears splashed the confusion out of my head, I also started to think and function. All at once, I felt quite calm and controlled.

"There's been some kind of accident," I said. "Karen's in the hospital. She's unconscious."

"Don't worry too much," Mary Ellen said. "There's nothing that serious about being unconscious."

She was so casual about it, so positive, that I felt a little better. Of course, Mary Ellen was right. These things do happen quite often. Even Mary Ellen herself was unconscious for three long days once, following an appendectomy. It was frightening, but all at once she just woke up. She came out of it beautifully.

Joe was already dressed.

He told Mary Ellen to go back to bed. "Karen's going to be okay," he said quietly. "People are often knocked unconscious, and they come right back."

Trying to reassure her, he had duplicated her own words, almost precisely—without realizing it. I don't think Joe had ever heard Mary Ellen say them.

His mind was already fifteen miles away. Emotionally and spiritually, I think Joe was already with Karen.

Chapter 2

They assumed that Karen had been in an auto accident. That she had suffered a concussion, and it had left her unconscious.

As Joe maneuvered the dark and winding back roads toward the hospital, Julie thought, "What can parents do?"

—You talk to your children. You warn them not to drive too fast, you give them lessons, make sure that they take the driving courses, and then all you can do is pray.

We kid Karen a lot about her having a bit of a heavy foot on the accelerator but she always laughs about it and kids us back, saying she's the most competent driver in the family. And perhaps, except for Joe, she is. Karen probably has put in more mileage in the three years she's had her license than I have in twelve years of driving. It's nothing for her to go hundreds of miles a day in her little Volks—visiting a friend in college, or taking another friend through the Poconos for a weekend. If anyone wants to ride anywhere, they just pick up a phone and call Karen, and she's ready. It doesn't matter where. If Karen likes somebody, she takes off.

But she likes to drive fast and, when she's alone, she takes chances. One night last year she was by herself in her car, and she miscalculated a turn in the road, and her car veered off the edge of a cliff and slid at full speed down a ravine into a valley of rocks. The car was almost a total wreck, but Karen walked out of it without a scratch.

She hitched a ride home and, when she told us about it, Karen acted as though it had been some kind of funny adventure instead of a dangerous accident. She seemed almost proud of herself, that she'd come

9

through it unhurt. As though it proved how indestructible she is.

Joe was shaking that night. I have never seen him angry with Karen, but the realization that she could have been killed, and that she wasn't taking it seriously, was too much. He talked to her sternly for a long time, and Karen wasn't accustomed to that. Dad was always tolerant, Dad never lectured. I think seeing her father in such anguish for the first time finally brought her to her senses. She cried. She said she was sorry.

Later I wondered if perhaps the accident had really frightened her and she didn't want to show it, if instinctively she had tried to cover up her fear by pretending to be strong and proud of herself. It's quite possible. Because Karen always had to appear strong. She never wanted anyone to think she was vulnerable.

The accident didn't hold her down for too long. She went rummaging around a junk yard and found parts for her car and, with the help of a boy friend, she rebuilt it. The axle had been broken, the carburetor was cracked, and the fenders were destroyed, but Karen replaced them with her own hands. It took a few weeks, but once she'd fixed up that Volkswagen she was happy. The accident slipped out of her mind.

It didn't leave mine. In the back of my mind, I was always afraid that if there is such a thing as a law of averages, it might catch up with Karen.

It was about 2:50 when we reached Newton Memorial Hospital. Dr. Paul McGee, the physician who was in charge of Intensive Care that night, was waiting for us. And he wasted no time telling us that Karen had not been in an automobile accident. "Your daughter is in a coma, in critical condition," he said, "and we don't know what caused it. I hope you'll be able to help us. I'm going to need some kind of medical history of Karen, and hopefully it will help evaluate her condition.

"You cannot treat coma," he told us, "without any clues to the cause."

He was talking so quickly I was bewildered.

"Can we see her?" I pleaded. That's all we wanted to do now. We could go into the medical history later.

"Yes, Mrs. Quinlan, but be patient with us a moment first."

Coming up behind Dr. McGee was a dark-haired young man, accompanied by a girl with a dazed look about her. The young man introduced himself as Tom French, so he was one of the boys who had been renting a room to Karen. And when the girl came out of his shadow I saw it was Terry O'Neill, whom I'd met a long time ago when her family lived up the street from us.

Dr. McGee said, "These are the people who brought Karen in. They can tell you what they told me."

Then Tom French informed us that they had been out with Karen that night, celebrating Terry O'Neill's birthday. They'd gone to a roadside tavern near their house called Falconer's, he said, "and Karen began to act kind of strange, as if she was about to pass out. We thought she was drunk, so we all went out to the car and drove back to the house. Karen kept nodding out in the back seat, and when we got home we took her up to her room and put her on the bed, thinking she could sleep it off."

After that, it seems, Terry and Tom French, and the other boy at the party, Bill Zywot, all went downstairs for a while. Then, when they went back up to check on Karen, she wasn't breathing.

"I quickly tried mouth-to-mouth resuscitation," French said, "while the others called the rescue squad. But she wouldn't start breathing again. She was turning blue. A few minutes later a policeman came, and he ran up the stairs and pulled her off the bed onto the floor, and when he gave her the mouth-to-mouth, that's when she started to breath again, and her color came back."

I stared at the French boy, dazed. It wasn't his fault that he didn't know the proper procedure. I wouldn't have known what to do either. But he couldn't look at me. Perhaps he was sorry that he couldn't do more.

"What was Karen drinking that could have caused something like that?" I asked him. "She doesn't usually drink that much."

"Oh no." He seemed eager to answer. "She didn't drink that much tonight, Mrs. Quinlan. She couldn't have had more than three gin and tonics. And it was like she was so *drunk* from it."

"That brings us to a question," the doctor said. "Mr.

and Mrs. Quinlan, do you know if your daughter took drugs?"

My immediate reaction was anger, real revulsion. I looked at the doctor and I thought, "This man is unfair. Why should he suggest that she took drugs—just because she is young? Why is it that when a young person gets sick, everybody assumes they're on drugs? If someone my age would go into a coma, they'd assume it was a heart attack. They pigeonhole people." I wanted to tell him that, but I couldn't. I was struck dumb.

"That would help us a lot, if we knew—" he began.

"Dr. McGee, Karen would never take drugs," I said coldly. "She never took anything in all her life. Not even aspirin."

The doctor said, "Well, I'm sorry if my question disturbed you, but I'm just trying to find some reason for this coma. If we're going to bring her out of it, we have to know everything. And we did find almost a full bottle of Valium in her handbag."

"But that's only a tranquilizer, isn't it?"

"It's a tranquilizer. But the combination of Valium and alcohol are notoriously dangerous," he said.

I felt caught in one of those nightmares where you want to run and your legs are riveted and you know there is no escape.

Joe Quinlan was not surprised by Dr. McGee's question.

—I know that plenty of young kids are taking a lot of crazy things these days, and it was natural that he would jump to that conclusion—since there didn't seem to be any easy answer to Karen's trouble. But I wasn't concerned that Karen might have taken anything, because she was too health-minded. Even marijuana—I know some of her friends smoke it, because Karen told us they did. And she tried it once, but she hated it. Karen said she would never try it again, not because of any objections we might have, but because, as she said, "It slows you down." And anything that slowed her down was not for Karen.

I told Dr. McGee that. "Karen's athletic, she always has been. People like Karen stay away from drugs."

A few minutes later, when this Tom French and the

girl Terry left, Dr. McGee told me that Terry O'Neill
had been telling him a lot of wild stories: that Karen
had taken a whole list of drugs—methadone, heroine, co-
caine—you name it. The doctor discounted the things
she said, though, because she was half hysterical.

And because it didn't make sense.

The way he saw it, if Karen had taken the drugs
Miss O'Neill told him about. "She wouldn't be in a
coma now. She'd be dead. They'd have killed an ele-
phant," he said.

Remembering the phone conversation with Karen,
Julie informed Dr. McGee that Karen was on a "starvation diet."

"She may not have eaten anything at all since last
Friday," Julie said. "Maybe that explains why she had
the Valium. To calm her nerves. And if she took those
drinks on an empty stomach, they could have hit her
very hard."

Dr. McGee conceded that a heavy diet, plus alcohol,
might have been a factor. But obviously he was still
thinking in terms of drugs. The next day he asked Mary
Ellen and she was indignant that he was asking questions like that.

"She never took anything in her life like a drug,"
Mary Ellen said. "And she didn't drink that much,
either. She'd have a beer, and sometimes a 7&7 [Sea-
gram's Seven and Seven-Up]. But Karen wasn't the
type to go out and get bombed."

It was difficult for everybody, being asked questions
like that.

No parent likes to hear even a suggestion of their
children being on drugs.

But the way the doctor put it—that if Karen was
taking drugs, that it wouldn't be so serious, because
they could treat her for it—Julie and I found ourselves praying that it *was* drugs that caused the coma.

But it wasn't. All the drug tests turned out to be
negative.

Shortly after three in the morning, on April 15, Dr.
McGee led Joe and Julie Quinlan into the Intensive Care
Unit.

Karen was stretched out on a bed, lying on her back.

A black mouthpiece, with a tube connected to a small respirator machine, was inserted in place. She appeared to be sleeping quietly. Julie was reassured.

—She looked very pale, and this breathing device made a pumping sound, but otherwise Karen seemed normal. As though she were just sleeping deeply. I kissed her on the forehead, and she seemed to be cool and dry, and as frightened as I was, it was hard to believe that she wouldn't wake up in the morning and be fine.

Dr. McGee urged us to talk to her, to try to pull her out of the coma. I said, "Honey, it's me. Wake up. Try to wake up." Joe kept holding her hand and saying, "Karen, you're going to be all right. We love you." But there was no reaction. The only sound was the pumping-pumping of the machine.

The immediate problem was not the coma, but her breathing. Dr. McGee said the critical situation was her breathing, and that if it couldn't be stabilized, he was afraid pneumonia would set in. He said that what often happens with people in a coma is that they attempt to throw up, they swallow it, and it goes right into the lungs while they're unconscious.

"This is what may have happened to your daughter," he said.

When I remember the rest of that long night, I see doctors and nurses coming in and out of the room, asking us please to leave so they could take tests, telling us we could come back in, Karen gagging on the black mouthpiece, Joe and I walking up and down the corridor saying little to each other because there was nothing to say. And through it all, we were talking to her, pleading with her, and I was thinking, "Karen, don't do this." Because some instinct was telling me that she wasn't going to make it.

Shortly before dawn, Joe Quinlan walked down to the lobby of the hospital and found a cigarette machine. He stood there for several minutes, staring at it.

—Karen was always nagging me, since she was nine years old, to stop smoking. Even after she took up the habit herself, she kept after me. So last New Year's

Eve right at midnight, I had tossed a half-pack of Winston's to her and said, "Okay, I've had my last cigarette in this lifetime." The whole family cheered. I was a hero. And I'd stuck with it, too, until tonight.

When I walked back upstairs, and into that corridor, smoking a cigarette, I saw Julie looking at me. She had been crying and I thought, "Oh my God, this will just upset her more, seeing me smoking."

But she knew. Karen would understand, too.

"You need that," Julie said quietly. I did.

Promptly at 6:15 A.M., Julie Quinlan called her parish priest, Father Thomas Trapasso.

—I knew Father Tom would be waking up, getting ready for seven o'clock mass, and I needed to talk to him. Joe was my rock of Gibraltar, but Father Tom was my link to God. I needed his support and his prayers. All her life, Karen had been such a good little fighter, but maybe she wasn't going to win this time. Do mothers know something that other people don't see?

I was in control when I placed the call. But when Father Tom answered the phone, I said, "Hello, this is Julie—" and then I was crying so hard I couldn't go on.

Joe took the receiver and asked Father to come to the hospital. As soon as he could after mass.

Father Tom, the fifty-year-old pastor at Our Lady of the Lake, has a round, compassionate face lined with the confessed cares of his twelve hundred parishioners. After talking to the Quinlans, he was disturbed on two levels:

—First, I knew it must be a terribly serious situation, for Julie to break down. She is a strong woman, with a naturally optimistic outlook on life. It was unbelievable to me that she was so emotionally overwrought.

And I was very fond of Karen. She was a sensitive girl, a thinker, and—sometimes a rare trait in young people—totally honest. One night, shortly after I came to the parish four years ago, I wanted to go skiing and didn't know the slopes, so Karen said she would take me. She was reticent at first, as she always was with

older people, and then suddenly she said, "The trouble
with religion is—it's dull." The way she said it, not to
shock me but to inform me exactly what she thought,
was lovely. I began to laugh, and after that we got
along beautifully. She sang at some of our masses. She
had a pretty voice.

And I admired her. She was blunt, and generous, and
she reached out for people. I felt she was religious in
the deepest sense of the word. If she had lived in a big
city, Karen might have joined marches to help society,
but in a small town she did whatever she could, by giving everything she had to the people she liked.

That morning when I arrived at the hospital, Julie
had control of herself, and she immediately took me in
to see Karen.

It looked as though she was simply sleeping, peacefully. Not knowing about the seriousness of her condition, I was frankly relieved.

But then Julie said something that took me completely by surprise. She said, "I hope to God she either
makes it, or she dies."

Later I thought how remarkable that was. She could
already visualize Karen living on and on, in a coma.

But at the time—maybe I'm a chauvinist, but I didn't
think of a woman like Julie, who has always been so
devoted a mother, looking upon such an emotionally
charged situation with logic. And yet, even in her logic,
she was crying.

She said, "Karen wouldn't want this, Father. She
would hate this."

I didn't know quite what to say. I just felt that we
all had a lot of praying to do.

Mary Ellen Quinlan arrived at Newton Memorial Hospital at eight o'clock that morning. When she saw her older
sister, Mary Ellen became unusually quiet. She picked up
Karen's hand and held it. She thought, "Well, she looks
okay. Only her hair is dirty. Karen's going to hate that
when she wakes up—that her hair's dirty."

One of the nurses told Mary Ellen, "Talk to your sister.
The more you talk to her, the quicker she might come out
of the coma."

Mary Ellen tried, "I said, 'Hi, Karen. Can you hear? It's me.' "

—But when she didn't show any signs of hearing me, I just started stroking her hair.

I kept thinking about the time when I had pneumonia, and Mother put me in Karen's room because the heat came up in there, and it was always warmer than mine. Karen wasn't supposed to come in, because she might catch my germs, but every night she'd sneak in anyway, and sit on the side of my bed and tell me stories, and rub my head until I went to sleep.

My parents always thought she would make a fantastic nurse and she really would, except she had such fear of doctors. And fear of cancer. Karen wasn't scared of anything or anybody, except that one thing—being sick and dying of cancer. If she would get a little bump on her face, she was sure it was cancer. If she had a sore throat, it would have to get so bad that she couldn't swallow before she would tell Mother, because that would mean she had to go to see the doctors. One time in high school, she told Mary Lou McCudden, "I'll bet you I'll die of cancer," and when Mary Lou laughed about it, Karen said very seriously, "You'll see." She had such fear.

Some people thought that was odd, because Karen was always so strong and healthy, but she had this feeling always that she'd better live fast, because she might not live long. Everything was now, now.

I thought, when she wakes up and sees where she is, it'll be awful for Karen. She'll think it all came true, and she's dying.

Throughout the morning, doctors and nurses ran blood tests—then X rays and a lumbar puncture. Julie and Joe signed authorizations for every test, hoping each time that there would be a new clue to the reason for the coma. There was nothing.

In the afternoon, it was confirmed that Karen had pneumonia. She was struggling for breath. She was running a high fever.

Julia and Joe were in the corridor outside Intensive Care, discussing their son, John. Julie remembers:

—John had come in after Mary Ellen's visit, and when he saw Karen, his color drained away as though someone had slapped him across the face with whitewash. He was physically ill. He rushed out of the room.

We were still standing by the bed, wondering whether Joe should go after John, when the doctor said we had a new emergency. He gave us a paper to sign, giving them permission to perform a tracheotomy. They would have to make an incision in Karen's throat and insert a tube connected to a much larger respirator.

As they described what they were about to do, I felt I would pass out. I couldn't bear to watch that. So while Joe signed the authorization, I went down to the waiting room and put my head between my knees to keep from fainting, and prayed.

Mary Ellen was shocked:

—They had to do the operation right there, in the ICU, because there was no time to move her. They cut a hole in Karen's throat, and the whole bed was covered with blood. I never saw anything like that, and they inserted a plastic tube into the incision. It was attached to a respirator.

When it was all over, I watched the respirator work. It pumped air into Karen's lungs, then it would stop so that she could take a breath by herself, and if she didn't, then it pumped again. But sometimes she would take a breath and the machine was pumping at the same time, and then she would choke and a buzzer on the machine goes off with a loud blast. The first time that happened, Karen raised way up in the bed and her arms flew out and her eyes popped open, and she looked like she was in so much pain I was scared out of my mind.

I screamed, "Nurse!" and the nurse came running. She adjusted the respirator and Karen fell back.

When I recovered, I thought, "Boy, when Karen wakes up I'll tell her about that, and she'll laugh. She likes stuff like that—when people are worried out of their minds and then everything comes out all right."

Late on the evening of April 15, Joe Quinlan finally agreed to leave the hospital and go home for a few minutes.

There were people who should be informed about Karen's condition, which, at the moment, was relatively peaceful. Mary Ellen and John had already told the relatives, and the word had begun to circulate among Karen's friends.

Joe wanted to stay, so Julie could go home and get a few hours of sleep. But she refused. She said, "Honey, I have to be here. I couldn't sleep anyway, I couldn't bear it, thinking of her possibly waking up alone in that place. Mothers are selfish, I suppose, but if she opens her eyes, I want it to be my face she sees."

On his way out, Joe was stopped by a nurse. "Would you like to take these with you, Mr. Quinlan?" Karen's clothes—her old blue jeans and the gray print shirt.

Well, sure. "She'll need fresh clothes anyway," he thought.

Just like Karen, wearing jeans and a shirt to a party. She was such a tomboy always; she never seemed to feel comfortable in dresses.

As he tucked the limp little bundle of clothes under his left arm, Joe remembered her first Holy Communion Day, when she was eight:

—Julie had bought her a pretty white dress, and Karen knew that was what she had to wear to church, but when she came stomping down the steps that morning, you could tell that she wasn't too happy about it. But she went through the mass and didn't complain. Didn't say a word. But after the ceremony, when we had a family party to celebrate, Karen couldn't stand it any longer. Just as people started arriving, she suddenly spun out of the house, and took off like a bullet, and climbed the highest tree in the back yard.

Chapter 3

At first, the change was almost imperceptible. Karen's head began to move, rotating slowly, almost methodical-

ly, from one side to the other. Sometimes her neck would
arch, forcing her head back into the pillow, as though she
were straining to pull away from the respirator tube in her
throat.

Julie was excited.

—It was as though her body was immobilized, but her
head was trying to escape. We couldn't know whether
it was the fever making her restless, or if the surgery
might be irritating to her—but the simple fact that she
was moving at all seemed encouraging because it might
be a prelude to her fighting her way out of the coma.
"Karen, come on, Karen." We were like a whispering,
macabre sort of chorus, trying to pull her up, out of
that other world.

Once that night, while I was holding her hand, I
squeezed it hard, hoping some of my energy would
flow into her, and I thought I felt a slight pressure
from her hand in return. I squeezed again. "Karen,
do you hear me?" But she never again gave me a
sign.

Maybe I was hallucinating. Perhaps I had imagined
it. But I'll always feel that at that time, she was aware
I was there.

Joe returned to the hospital shortly after he had left it,
and spent all of his time that night standing beside
Karen. He, too, sensed that she was trying to come back—
and he wanted to help her:

—I would lean down close to her, and say, "I love you,
Karen." Then I would repeat aloud the names of
everybody she knew, each time hoping she might recognize and respond. I named every member of the family. I would repeat the names of each of her friends.
Then I'd go over places where we had gone camping,
or she had been skiing. I even named the Broadway
shows she liked best, like *Pippin* and *Grease,* and when
I ran out of those, I started on her favorite songs—
"Für Elise," the piece she always played on the piano,
and "Bridge over Troubled Water," a song she sang so
beautifully.

Just any name or place she might recognize, I kept
saying it. Over and over, all through that night.

But if Karen heard me, I couldn't know. There was no reaction at all.

By morning, the heavy doses of penicillin had done their job, and her lungs were less congested. The pneumonia crisis seemed to be passing.

The nurses had tied her to the bed so that, if she should wake up suddenly, she couldn't thrash around and hurt herself. They used a soft, gauzy material which Julie thought might be cotton blankets cut into strips for the purpose. They wrapped these restraints around Karen's ankles and wrists, and then knotted them around the metal frame of her bed. That alone was encouraging.

I can't remember exactly when it happened. But sometime during that second or third day, Karen opened her eyes.

"Karen!" I half-shouted it.

Julie was there—she saw it, too—and she leaned forward and kissed Karen. And then the nurses came hurrying over, and there was all kinds of excitement. For just a few minutes, we thought it was all over, and that she had come back, and I prayed harder than I have prayed in years and years.

But she didn't recognize us. She was staring right through us. A nurse placed her open hand a few feet from Karen's face, and slowly moved it forward until it almost touched her nose, and Karen blinked. But when the hand moved to one side, Karen's eyes didn't follow it. She just wasn't focusing.

In a way, that was the most disheartening development of all, watching her eyes look into space, or move all around the room, as though she were looking and looking for something—and finally forcing ourselves to realize that she couldn't see.

Joe and the nurses were momentarily away from Karen's bed.

Julie lifted the sheet draped over her daughter's body. . . .

—I don't know why I did it at that particular time. And I saw that Karen's left foot was twisted inward at the ankle, in an awkward position. And her left elbow was drawn up tight against her side. Her left hand was cocked at the wrist, in that same strange position that her foot was in, and her fingers were bending inward. It looked as though the fingernails were digging into her wrist. This was only on the left side. The right side looked normal.

I thought that she must have had a stroke.

When I asked the doctor about it, he said there was no way of telling whether or not she had suffered a stroke. But her posture was undoubtedly an indication of some brain damage. He could not be sure yet how extensive the damage was.

In retrospect, it seemed incredible to me that there had been no preoccupation with brain damage earlier, or even any discussion of it. We had been through thirty hours of testing and emergency procedures, and only now did this subject come out in the open. Not that anything could have been done about the brain damage. Joe and I were told that—from Tom French and the policemen's experience—it appeared that Karen had stopped breathing for two periods of about fifteen minutes each.

The EEG [electroencephalograph] test, we discovered, had been abnormal—had registered slow brain wave patterns—but apparently that is always true of people in comas. And doctors say that it is almost impossible to get an accurate EEG in a hospital, because of interference from so much other electrical equipment, especially in the Intensive Care ward. So that wasn't conclusive.

I didn't know what to think. I was bewildered. Now that her eyes were open, my early feeling—that she couldn't make it—was not so strong. Not strong at all.

I thought now that she could pull through this and come out of the coma, and that if she did, Karen might be like a baby again, helpless, leading some kind of halfway existence. And when I visualized this, the possibility of Karen coming home with us again, suddenly I couldn't bear the thought of losing her.

My emotions turned completely around, and I prayed, "Dear God, bring her back to us. We'll take her any way we can have her. Just bring her back."

Mary Ellen stopped in at the hospital on her way to Centenary College for Women.

As she was stroking Karen's forehead, "Suddenly Karen opened her eyes, as though she was just waking up":

—She blinked once, and she looked right at me, and I was sure she recognized me. I will always think she recognized me. It was a totally different look than the blank look she had before.

I skipped my classes, and I stayed around the hospital until ten o'clock that night, waiting for her to look like that again. But Karen just returned right away to that blank stare. She never ever did look like she recognized me again.

I think then I realized she might die. And I remembered a nightmare I had not very long ago. In my dream, I was getting married. I was standing in the back of the church, and I kept looking around for Karen, and she wasn't there. Everybody else was—Mom and Dad, Grandma and Grandpa and Cousin Bobby—but Karen wasn't in that church, and I ran down the aisle, desperately looking, and crying, "Where's Karen? I can't get married without Karen." But I couldn't find her anywhere.

When I woke up, I was really scared. I sneaked in to Karen's room, and there she was in bed, sleeping, and I was so relieved.

I never told Karen about the dream, because she might have been frightened. I wondered if maybe she dreamed something like that, too. Because she was very sensitive. I remember when a good friend of the family, Bill Birch, died of cancer, Karen was terribly depressed. She loved him a lot, and I felt she could just sort of see herself fading away, the same way he did.

Karen's friends had been telephoning the house, asking for news.

The nurses urged the family to encourage friends to visit, hoping some face or voice could startle Karen back to consciousness. So John, who was home and took most of the calls, told people to stop by Newton Hospital anytime. "My parents will be there. Ask for them at the information desk."

One of the earliest visitors was Tommy Flynn.

Julie felt exceptionally hopeful when she heard Tommy was coming:

—He meant a lot to Karen. She dated other boys, but when she started going out with him, she didn't bother with anyone else. He is a handsome boy who liked sports, and he was an amateur wrestler, and of course Karen was immediately attracted to that. Tommy comes from a large family—five boys and one girl, Michelle, who was a friend of Karen's—and the whole family was very active, very sports-minded, so Karen fit right in. The Flynns had an extremely close family, like ours, and they loved Karen very much. Even after they broke up, Karen and Tommy would talk on the telephone for hours. They were still attached to each other, and I thought if any of her friends could bring her back, it would be him.

Tommy Flynn didn't know what to expect.

He hadn't seen Karen in more than a year, but she called him often—sometimes phoning him in Florida, where he was a sophomore at Eckerd College—to tell him what she was doing, how she was feeling, what was on her mind.

—The last time we had talked was on her birthday two weeks ago. I was home on winter vacation, and she was telling me about something that was very important to her, but I had to cut off the conversation that day because I had to start back to school. So Karen asked when I'd be home again, and I told her I'd be back on Monday, April 14.

"Are you sure you'll be home that day?" she said, and I told her, "Definitely. I'll be here." And I was, and I waited around the house all day, looking for her call, and she didn't phone. I was very surprised, because that wasn't at all like Karen.

Then the next day, or the day after, I heard she was in a coma.

I talked to some of our friends, and nobody seemed to know what it was all about, but when I arrived at the hospital and saw Mr. and Mrs. Quinlan I knew it was bad. Mrs. Quinlan looked very upset. She was crying. Then when I went into the room and saw Karen, I stood in a state of shock.

There was so much expression on her face, and I just couldn't believe that there was no inner recognition at all within her being. Karen was always sensitive to everything that went on around her—more than anybody I have ever known—so I felt that she must know I was there. She must feel that energy beside her, almost like a life force you can't stop. She must have recognized a type of communication with someone outside of herself.

And yet her eyes were moving so rapidly, and they didn't seem to focus on me or on any one place. You can see something in a person's eyes when they are recognizing you, and I saw nothing in Karen's. They were almost like not attached.

I remember thinking something really, really sad has happened. Because Karen was a real vital type of life force, with an incredible amount of energy. A really, really funny and loving girl that you just enjoyed being around. And now, her eyes—it was like the light had been taken out of them or something.

Julie sat on a leather couch in a waiting room. She had a view of the entrance to Intensive Care, and she never moved her focus from that door.

—When Tommy came out, after seeing her, I knew from the way he walked that he hadn't gotten through. He looked beaten, and I felt sorry for him. We didn't talk much. He said he'd be back. Tomorrow probably, he said.

Other friends of Karen's came in. There was a whole procession of them—Karen had so many. I remembered on her sixteenth birthday, one of the girls, Ginny Roche, even hired the American Legion Hall over at Indian Lake for Karen's surprise party. There were more than one hundred youngsters there, and Joe and I went, too, and it was beautiful—all in honor of Karen.

Karen would hate the emotions I went through that

afternoon. Maudlin. I sat there in that waiting room thinking about her, tears running down my cheeks, going over in my mind what an imp she was, and how joyous. The reason everyone was drawn to her is that she always enjoyed life to the fullest, and she'd have this instinctive urge to make others do the same. From the time she was twelve, she almost never came in the kitchen when I was there without grabbing me around the waist and swinging me in circles till I'd have to laugh. She could never just walk down our stairs—she had to grab hold of the spindles and sail through the air, landing with a crash. Over the years, Joe had replaced the fourth spindle five different times. But you could never actually get angry with her, because when Karen did something wrong she did it with such exuberance that it was funny, rather than aggravating.

The one time when she really did get in trouble—she was in grammar school, and she sneaked into the chapel of the parish church with one of her girl friends and took a swallow of the sacramental wine—even then, the pastor and the principal didn't punish the girls.

Karen confessed immediately.

"Well, why did you do it, Karen?"

"I was curious what it tastes like."

It is possible to be guilty and innocent all at once. Karen couldn't bear dishonesty, and she couldn't bear seeing people suffer. If anyone needed her, and she liked them, she would do anything in the world until they were happy again. This is why people loved her and depended on her—because she would turn herself inside out until they were able to laugh again. She wanted happiness around her, and she dreaded pain and gloom. "There's nobody like Karen," my mother always said. "She lights up rooms." And Cousin Bobby Duane, when he came to visit her, almost broke my heart when he came out of Intensive Care.

"The terrible thing, Aunt Julie," he said, "is if it was me in a coma, Karen would bring me out. I don't know how, but she'd do it. And here she is and I can't do anything."

Mary Lou McCudden, one of Karen's closest friends throughout high school, arrived in late afternoon. Like

Tommy Flynn, Mary Lou was unprepared for the sight of Karen:

—Whenever I thought of a person in a coma, I'd thought they would just lie there very quietly, almost as though they were sleeping. Karen's head was moving around, as if she was trying to pull away from that tube in her throat, and she made little noises, like moans. I didn't know if she was in pain, but it seemed as though she was. And I thought—if Karen could ever see herself like this, it would be like the worst thing in the world for her. It would be so hard for her to accept being so dependent on all these doctors and nurses, and the equipment and everything.

Karen was the most independent person. She was a different sort of person than anyone you ever met, more outgoing and spontaneous. We didn't even know each other very well in our freshman year in high school, but one day she just came over to my house and she knocked on the door and asked if I'd like to come to her house for dinner. That's the way she was. So I did, and Mrs. Quinlan made her famous baked ziti with sausage, and ever since that night we've been friends. That was the special thing about Karen. She didn't plan ahead. She'd decide to do something and she'd just up and do it. One time we were driving in her car to the mountains to go skiing and on the way she saw a billboard that said, "Fly the Poconos." She turned that car around and took me on my first airplane ride. I got sick.

She didn't get sick, of course. You could never imagine her sick. She was always in control. The one who took care of everybody. Nobody could take care of her. She wouldn't let you. Karen wanted everyone to think she was strong. That's why it didn't seem right, her being down like this.

But I tried to convince myself she'd be all right. She was pale but she looked pretty. I remember she still had her nail polish on. I told myself, "Oh, well, she's strong. She's going to come out of this. I've heard of comas that last a week or maybe even a month, but the patient finally comes out."

I thought that was the way it would be.

Among the other visitors that afternoon was Father John Quinlan, a six-foot-five, gangling thirty-year-old associate priest at a nearby parish of Star of the Sea. No relation, in spite of bearing the identical name, Father Quinlan had been close to the family—especially Karen.

—When I first met her, the only thing we had in common was our name, and Karen didn't know how to react to me. She was basically a quiet sort of person with adults, and the fact that I wore a clerical collar probably didn't help. Young people don't ordinarily look on priests as being particularly with it.

But one day I went over to their house in a sports car, and Karen was real curious about it. When she discovered I was into loving cars—that made all the difference. We became friends. I took her for her first driver's test when she was seventeen, and the following year I tried to use a little pull to get her a summer job as a camp counselor. We kidded each other a lot and she was always a warm person, but there was a very serious, introspective side to Karen. She would sit in the back of the church on Sundays, contemplating. I often wondered what she was thinking about so deeply, but on the subject of serious things—she never let me in the ring with her.

When I saw her lying there, I felt helpless. All I could do was just pray for her.

There were three friends of Karen's who were unable to appear at Newton Memorial Hospital during that first stage of Karen's coma.

Lee Swart, a towering twenty-three-year-old artist who had loved Karen until their relationship ended the previous summer, was out of the state. Gloria (known as Little Lori) Gaffney, an almost lifelong friend, was in school. Nanette Foit, who had been a lifeguard with Karen at Lake Hopatcong, made nightly phone calls to the Quinlan home but couldn't bring herself to visit the hospital.

These three shared, but never discussed among themselves, a discomforting bond. Karen had told each of them that she would die young, and she would go down in history.

Sixteen months later, when Julia Quinlan learned of Karen's earlier predictions, she sat silently at the breakfast table for several minutes.

Then she said, "I don't know how to explain that":

—Karen was extremely intuitive. She was also almost incapable of telling a lie. From the things she said to me over the years, maybe she had an insight.

She often talked to me, for example, about not wanting to be kept alive by machines if something terrible should happen to her. And she asked me to be sure to donate her eyes to an eye bank if she died. And on her first day on the job when she worked at the Microy Plastics Company, she took out a five-thousand-dollar life insurance policy with Mary Ellen as beneficiary, and she came home that day and told her sister about it.

"If I die," she told Mary Ellen, "you'll be all right."

It's unusual for young people to think of things like that, but Karen did.

Yet it's strange—only a week before the coma, Karen went to see a palm reader. She came home very excited. She held out her palm and showed me the way her heart line curled all the way down around her wrist, and she said, "You know what, Mom? I have one of the longest life lines the palmist ever saw. I'm going to live forever." Oh, she was so happy about that.

I don't suppose we'll ever solve these mysteries of the human mind, just as I don't think we'll ever know the cause of the coma—only Karen could tell us that.

But the truth is that Karen was a special person, and maybe she *did* know something that the rest of us were not privileged to know.

She was a gift from God. That was made very clear to us, from the day she came into our lives.

Chapter 4

It had never occurred to Julia Quinlan that she would adopt a child—that a doctor would warn her she was "too small" to give birth to a baby.

She *was* small. At physical maturity Julie barely reached five-one, weighed less than ninety pounds, and had to search for size three dresses in the "petite department" of specialty shops.

—But I was extremely healthy. We were good Catholics, and there certainly was never any question that I would have a family, as soon as I met the "right" man. My father, Robert Duane, who is the typical Irishman and the life of every party, could hardly wait to indulge his grandchildren in wild stories about leprechauns. And my mother, Bertha Duane, just plain could hardly wait.

Joe came into my life when I was fourteen, and he was sixteen. He was extremely shy and serious, and all I wanted was fun. We lived in a three-family house in West New York, New Jersey, an old community just across the Hudson River from Manhattan, and I would dream of traveling, and living in New York City. Joe was much too settled for my taste.

He was the youngest of his family of six children, and all of the others—except one sister—were at least twelve years older than he was. So every one of them ordered him around. One of his jobs was taking care of his sister May's children. May lived with her husband and two little babies in the same house with us, so that's how we met—when he was baby-sitting, and I was dreaming of better things.

Mrs. Quinlan and my mother became friends, so when Joe asked me to go out to the movies, my mother said it would be fine. If it was Joe, I could date when I was fifteen. If it was any other boy, I'd have to wait for my first date till I was sixteen. So of course I went with him, and we'd see the movies and then stop in at ice-cream parlors with juke boxes, and I felt quite smug because he was tall and handsome, and my girl friends envied me. But still, he was too mature, and I was too independent. Practically the minute I turned sixteen, I would go out to high school socials on Friday nights and meet other boys, and go steady with them for a month or so. But Joe and I contined to date occasionally.

On his seventeenth birthday in April 1942—right after World War II began—Joe wanted to enlist in the Army. But his mother refused to sign the papers because she was a widow, and she needed him. Never wanting to hurt anyone, particularly his mother, he didn't try to join up again, but waited until he was drafted when he was eighteen. Then he was in the infantry, and they shipped him to Europe—and only four months later he was hit by artillery. And he lost his left arm.

When his mother called to tell us, I remember my mother shaking her head and saying, "Poor Joe, he works so hard all his life, and the first time out, he gets this."

I felt deeply sorry for him and I wrote letters to the rehabilitation hospital in Atlanta, but I was still so wrapped up in my dreams that it didn't touch me personally until the day he came home. Not until—without letting me know he was coming—Joe knocked at our door.

He was standing there, looking taller than when he went away, and so good-looking in his uniform. Not saying a word.

I couldn't keep myself from looking first at his arm. There was nothing to see. He had his new artificial hand pushed into his pocket.

Then I looked up, and I saw he was smiling, and all at once his face seemed the most beautiful I had ever seen. I sort of fell apart emotionally. All that had happened to him, and Joe was smiling. Not complaining, and not bitter.

I guess he could see that I was almost shaking, not knowing what to say, and he stepped toward me and very gently put his right arm around my waist and pulled me toward him. And while I just leaned against him, knowing I was going to cry, he said, "Don't be sad,

Julie, I'm really lucky. God has been very good to me."

I grew up very suddenly that day. I also fell in love.

We became engaged on my nineteenth birthday and were married seven months later, on September 22, 1946. I had a good job at a bank and Joe worked and was taking college courses at night, but we decided to start a family. We couldn't wait for children. We planned to have four. As we saw it, that was an ideal number—enough for a happy family, but not too many to put a strain on our finances.

We tried to plan our future carefully. Since we lived in a fifth-floor walk-up apartment in West New York, we knew we wanted to find some property out in the country, so that the children could get away and lead a healthier life in the summertime. We read all of the real estate advertisements, and one Sunday in 1951 in the New York *Daily News* there was an ad for country land near Lake Hopatcong that sounded so enticing we got in the car and drove out immediately to see it. That's how we discovered Landing. That day, the developer showed us an empty lot with huge, wonderful trees on high land above the lake, and it seemed to be exactly what we wanted. Joe put five dollars down on it, and it was ours. Joe commissioned a builder to lay a foundation and put up the structural "shell" of a four-room house. Then he was going to build our first home himself.

We spent almost every weekend after that driving to the site, working at building the home. Joe did it all himself, brick by brick, one wall at a time. He hooked up the wiring and the plumbing, laid the floor and tiles —everything himself. My family and our friends thought it was amazing that he could be so dextrous and powerful, but they don't know Joe as I do. Building had become his hobby and he enjoyed the challenge of it, but there was more to it than that. My husband is a man who is totally dedicated to providing for those he loves, and he loved me and he loved the children he knew we would have, and he devoted himself totally to preparing for them. To him, at that time, it was a mission. And he became so skilled that I have often thought Joe could do more carpentry with one hand than any other man with two hands and a full construction crew.

When I conceived, there was great excitement. I was the first person in my family to marry, and of course my parents could hardly wait for their first grandchild. Joe and I didn't even try to be calm and casual about it. I had never been giddier.

But at three months, I miscarried. I felt guilty and couldn't figure out what I might have done wrong. Nobody else was that concerned. After all, there was plenty of time. I was still only twenty-one.

But the next time I became pregnant, I miscarried again. At three and a half months. The doctor made the usual explanation—that this was nature's way of protecting us from producing an imperfect child. Still, I felt that it must be I who was imperfect, not my baby. Joe just thanked God that I was well. "That's all that matters," he said. You can bear almost anything if your husband supports you as mine did.

During the third pregnancy, I hardly left the apartment. I took a leave of absence from my job and spent a great deal of time in bed. Which was difficult for me. When I'm worried or upset, I can usually lose myself in keeping busy. Work is therapy for me, but I forced myself to let Joe do a great deal of the housework. A healthy baby was the most important thing.

At five and a half months, I had my third miscarriage, in spite of all the precautions. And, at that stage in your pregnancy, you can tell what the baby would have been. We lost a boy.

I was frantic now, and Joe very calmly, but firmly, confronted the doctor and asked him for an explanation.

This doctor said that my womb was tipped; that there are three different positions for the womb possibly to tip into, and that mine was in the worst position. He said that I probably could never carry a baby full term, under the circumstances. He was very businesslike about it and didn't offer us any solution, except the possibility of a Caesarean—if we wanted "to try again." Later, I learned that surgery could have corrected a condition like mine, but this doctor never mentioned that possibility, and Joe and I were too young and naïve to ask questions.

When the fourth pregnancy was confirmed, both of us were frightened. Frightened is too soft a word. Petrified is more appropriate.

We located a different obstetrician, in a bigger metropolitan hospital. He gave me some medication which, he assured us, would help me through the first few months. "If the fetus is just allowed to become large enough," he said, then I would pass through the danger period and hold on to the baby.

The medication worked beautifully. This time, I went the full nine months.

On July 28 [1953] I went into labor, and Joe rushed me to a maternity hospital. For that reason, because it is only for babies and mothers, I expected it to be so nice—but when we walked in, it was like going into a factory. Cold. I'll never forget.

They put me on an icy-cold table, and I jumped, just feeling it under me.

Then the doctor and the nurses kept coming over and listening to my stomach for a heartbeat. For almost three hours, while I was in labor, they kept searching and searching, and finally the doctor said, "You've got to do all the pushing and the work now, Mrs. Quinlan—everything on your own now. We think the baby is dead."

Of course, I became hysterical, and they put a mask over my face and I went under. When I woke up, I remembered what had happened. I looked around for Joe and saw that I was no longer in the labor room. I was in bed, and the first thing I could see was a mother, in the bed next to mine, nursing her baby.

I was so weak, and I was too deeply sad even to cry. I lay there thinking. "We finally have our baby and it is dead." And as I drifted in and out of sleep, wishing I could see my husband—at least they could have given me that—Joe was sitting downstairs in a waiting room, wondering what was happening.

For most of the day, he sat in that waiting room. No one could answer his questions. Until finally, ten hours later, a nurse informed him that I had given birth to a stillborn son.

Our baby weighed 6½ pounds. We named him Joseph Quinlan, Jr. The hospital said we must get a cemetery plot for him—that this was Joe's responsibility.

So Joe made the arrangements, and the funeral di-

rector told him, "The way we handle cases like this is
that we bury the baby, and we don't tell even the husband where the baby is buried, because you might be
tempted to tell your wife. And believe me," the under-
taker said to Joe, "it's best that Mrs. Quinlan never
goes to the cemetery. I've seen women with stillborn
children who spend all their time going to the cemetery,
and mourning, and it becomes even more of a tragedy
than the stillbirth itself."

So neither of us ever saw our son.

When it was time for me to leave the hospital, the
doctor came to see us.

"Mr. Quinlan," he said to Joe, "your wife is very
small. If she becomes pregnant again, in view of her
history, I would strongly recommend birth by Caesarean
section. Even then, there is no guarantee that she will
bear a live baby."

For the first time in my life, I felt like jumping out a
window.

There was a choice to be made: whether to live in the city
apartment or move out to the little house in Landing, even
without children.

Joe and Julia decided on the country. Away from the
memories.

They settled into the bungalow, and Joe quickly found
a new position, in the Accounting Department of the
Warner-Chilcott Pharmaceutical Company, in Morris
Plains, a nearby community.

Joe refused to let his wife dwell on her unhappy memories:

—And I didn't want Julie even to consider trying again
to have another baby. At twenty-three years of age, she
had been through more physical and psychological pain
than most women have in a lifetime. So we joined the
nearest Catholic parish, Our Lady of the Lake—a pretty
stone church that stood on a bluff above Lake Hopatcong—and found some new friends.

But of course we still wanted children, so we began
to talk about adoption. We went through long discussions about getting a baby from overseas, about maybe

getting one from Ireland. We were considering all the possibilities. But then at the church, the pastor, Father Duffy, suggested that we go to Catholic Charities in Paterson [N.J.]. So in February of 1954—almost a year after we had moved to Landing—we drove to Paterson and spoke to a Miss Reed, who was in charge of adoptions. She came to see our house, which had only four rooms at the time—the living room, two bedrooms, and kitchen. We pointed out to her that we didn't need the extra bedroom, and that would be a baby's nursery, between the kitchen and our bedroom. She was very impressed—that we could provide a separate room for a child. And we had a front yard and a back yard. "That's wonderful," she said. "These things are very important when you're applying for a baby."

After we passed Miss Reed's approval, she sent us to a Sister Naomi at St. Joseph's Maternity Home, in Scranton, Pennsylvania. This nun sat and talked to us for four hours, and taking notes all the time—I don't know how many pencil points she wore down in the process. She was like a psychiatrist, asking questions all the way back, from our childhoods on. At that time there was a shortage of babies, so it was the prospective parents who were carefully screened.

When she finally finished with us, Sister Naomi said, "Well, I want to thank you for coming. I had a beautiful letter about you from Father Duffy at your church, telling me that you are a couple with deep religious faith. That means a great deal to us here."

Joe and Julie prayed. Made novenas. Julie remembers:

—I didn't decorate the bedroom, because that might have been bad luck.

But in my mind, I knew exactly the way it would look as a nursery.

On April 27, during the afternoon, Sister Naomi phoned.

"Mrs. Quinlan, we have a baby for you—if you can come up tomorrow?"

I felt giddy. Dear God, what do you say when you're offered the greatest gift? I said, "Of course, Sister. We could come up tonight. Should we come tonight?"

But she said no, that wouldn't be necessary. "Tomorrow will be just fine."

Joe was in his office, and when I called, he couldn't believe it.

"It's only been two months. Adoption agencies don't work that fast," he said.

"This time they certainly did."

"Is it a boy or a girl?" Joe asked.

Oh, my Lord—I'd forgotten to ask.

"Does it make any difference?" I said. Then I started to laugh.

The next morning they attended eight o'clock mass at Our Lady of the Lake, then drove to Hackettstown to buy a white layette, a safe color for either a boy or girl. Even with that delay, they arrived at St. Joseph's Children's and Maternity Hospital in Scranton, Pennsylvania, before noon.

Sister Naomi met them and took them into a small chapel at the hospital. She walked directly to the altar and told them to please wait there, that she would be gone for only a moment or two.

When she returned, she placed a baby, wrapped in a blanket, in Julie's arms.

"This is what I want you to remember," Sister Naomi said, "that although this baby comes to you through us, she is a gift from God."

Julie looked down and saw "this beautiful, perfectly round face with the tiniest nose and ears you ever could find."

Joe was stunned by the turned-up nose, the largest, bluest eyes he had ever seen—"even the whites were blue"—and a dimple in the baby's chin, just like the dimple in his own. It made her seem, from the beginning, to be his own.

Catholic Charities has rules on how much information may be offered to adoptive parents, and Sister Naomi adhered to them strictly.

"Your blessed infant," she said, "was born on March twenty-ninth, in Scranton. Her birth weight was seven pounds, two ounces, and she was named, by her mother, Mary Ann. I cannot give you any more details, except to assure you that the baby's natural mother is both Irish and Catholic, like yourselves, and a very good woman, active in her church."

Joe began to ask questions, but the nun shook her head, smiling. "Now, Mr. Quinlan, if there is anything else you want to know about your baby's heritage or her special traits, you just watch your child. She'll tell you. She'll develop on her own." On the drive home, Julie sat in the back seat with the baby, unable to take her eyes off the passive little face:

—She was quiet, sometimes sleeping and other times looking up at me with those huge, wondering eyes—but never crying, never whimpering.

We decided to name her "Karen Ann," because I love the name "Karen," and I felt we should keep the "Ann" in deference to her natural mother. I wondered how that woman could bear it, holding a precious infant like this in her arms, nursing her, seeing her every day for four weeks, and then suddenly having to give her up.

I couldn't think of any torture more cruel.

When we finally pulled in the driveway, my mother and sister, Alberta, ran out of the house to meet us and to see Karen, and even then, with all the excitement, she didn't cry. She was a perfect baby.

But the next morning I realized she was ill. Her eyes were not bright, as they had been the day before, and she had spent the night flailing and stretching her legs, as though she had pain. I thought it must be the change, or the long trip, or that perhaps St. Joseph's had given us the wrong formula. She quickly grew worse. Developed diarrhea and a high fever. By the second morning, Karen was so dehydrated that I called Joe at work and asked him to come home. "When you touch her," I told him, "it's like you're touching the skin of a ninety-year-old woman."

That frightened Joe, and he drove right home and we bundled her up and took her to Dr. Morley P. Wells, who was considered a fine pediatrician in Dover. When Dr. Wells saw her, and weighed her, he was alarmed. She had lost almost a pound from her birth weight. He immediately telephoned St. Joseph's, and they reported an epidemic of dysentery among their babies. One of them had died. But they were sure, they told him, "that the Quinlan baby got out in time."

Dr. Wells knew that she hadn't, and he rushed Karen to St. Clare's Hospital in Denville which was a brand-new, modern facility in northern New Jersey. He placed her in isolation. A revolving battery of pediatric nurses began watching her. She was given water and food intravenously.

Joe and I sat in the corridor outside her room, not wanting to talk about this, even between ourselves. It was too incredible. We finally had our baby and maybe now we were going to lose her. Our gift from God—where was He? Would He really take her away again?

For three days we waited, helpless. Karen looked completely lifeless.

"I can't give you any hope," Dr. Wells said finally. "I'm afraid the illness has gone too far."

We had been expecting that.

It was a Sunday, the Sunday when Joe was scheduled to receive his confirmation at Our Lady of the Lake, and we didn't know what to do. Stay with Karen, or go to church. I made the decision. I decided it was vital that Joe make his confirmation, which is the receiving of the gifts of the Holy Spirit. There was nothing we could do for Karen here, and Joe needed the strength of his religion now more than ever. He didn't want to go. I had to convince him. All the way to church we prayed, and all through the service, and immediately after confirmation we rushed back to the hospital.

Dr. Wells was waiting at the door of Karen's room, and he said, "I don't understand it, but she has passed a crisis. She seems to be perking right up."

Her eyes were bright again, and she was wriggling around in the bed, and as I reached down to pick her up, Joe said, "It has to be a miracle."

Three days later, we were bundling our baby up for the trip home when Dr. Wells came in the room.

"You don't need to worry about *this* little girl," he said. He was laughing, and so were we, and Karen almost seemed to be dancing in my arms. "She's so full of life," he said, "she's going to give you both a hard time."

Chapter 5

After her infant flirtation with death, it was as though
Karen knew she must make up lost time. She would climb
over the sides of her crib. Julie would be in another room,
"and I'd hear a thud—and I'd rush in":

—And there Karen would be, on the floor, looking up
at me with those huge eyes that seemed to be saying,
"Look—I'm amazing. I did it again." She rarely cried.
She seemed to be as shockproof as a good watch.

We didn't buy a play pen. It would have been like
trying to confine a tiger in a carton. Karen never
crawled. She would just grab hold of tables or chairs
and pull herself up, standing perfectly straight. When
she was five months, Miss Reed from the adoption
agency dropped by unexpectedly to check on us. Adoption agencies do that. It was a summer day, and I had
Karen outside. While Miss Reed and I were talking,
Karen pulled herself up and stood erect and beautiful,
like a model. Miss Reed was overwhelmed. She said,
"I've never seen a baby who's so strong and lively."
That was a considerable relief, especially to Joe. He
was always conscious that the agency could take her
back anytime during the first year, if they decided to,
and that would have just destroyed us.

Karen began walking at seven months. Nobody could
believe it, and I read in Dr. Spock's baby care book
that walking at even ten months is a sign of unusual
precociousness. I always felt that Karen needed to walk
early, because she had places to go. And as soon as she
could walk, she ran—she raced. She was always toting
around a toy gun, or her plastic baseball bat. We had a
swing in the back yard, and one of our neighbors
couldn't bear to watch Karen swinging, because she

thought sure she would go over the top of the bars.

One day Joe looked out the kitchen window and suddenly yelled, "Good Lord—look at her now!" He raced out the back door, and I ran to the window. There was Karen, hanging from the top bar of the swing by her legs. And laughing. No concept whatever of danger.

She never played with dolls. It was always clear Karen would be an athlete. Down at the lake, she would race along the beach, darting in zigzags in and out of the water, as though daring it to come up and attack her. She'd climb to the top of trees, and it wouldn't occur to her to ask for help in getting down. If Karen was ever intimidated, she would never let you know it. All through her childhood, whenever she found herself in a precarious situation, she'd get herself out of it—her way. She was just an adorable, curly-haired blond little girl, full of mischief. Joe would say, "You should have been a boy, Kari—you'd make a fantastic little boy." Karen loved that. She agreed with her Daddy one hundred per cent.

When she was completely exhausted—even then she had to be doing something. To avoid going to sleep, because sleep always seemed a waste of time to Karen, she would pick up a book and sit down and "read" it aloud. Long before she knew how to read, she would make up stories, pretending they were in the book. It was so funny to watch her, sitting on the couch with the book in her lap, seriously "reading" me a story. Often as not, the book was upside down.

Joe and I were sure she was going to be a genius.

When Karen was a year old, Joe and Julie Quinlan applied for another adoptive baby from Catholic Charities. As often happens, Julie became pregnant before the application had been processed. She was frightened, because of the Jersey City doctor's warning.

—When I told Joe I was pregnant, he hurried over to Boonton, a nearby town where they have a top gynecologist, Dr. Emile Hornick. Dr. Hornick sent away for my medical records, and took several tests, and then he said, "Do you realize that you have an RH factor, Mrs.

Quinlan?" We were astounded. Can you imagine going through three miscarriages and a stillbirth, and nobody ever told me I was RH?

But the doctor said he thought with the new hormonal drugs, I should be able to hold the fetus and deliver naturally. "However," he said, "it is quite probable that you will have a 'blue baby.'" He assured us even that shouldn't be a critical problem; but as I neared full term, he prepared the hospital for emergency blood transfusions for the baby, if that should be necessary.

On May 3, 1956, Dr. Hornick induced labor. Realizing how worried I was, he gave Joe permission to stay in the labor room with me, and I looked forward to having him there for emotional support. But Joe was so terrified, he just sat in a corner saying his Rosary. Once between contractions, I panted, "Boy, Joe, you're a big help." He didn't even look up from his beads.

I was still hazy from the anesthesia when Dr. Hornick said, "You've given birth to a beautiful girl. Eight pounds, two ounces."

I didn't believe him. "No," I cried. "You're lying to me. The baby's dead."

Only after he put Mary Ellen on my stomach, and I could feel the weight of her, did I know. It was a beautiful moment.

We thought Karen would be thrilled to have a sister, but she was decidedly unimpressed. Not that she was jealous. We never had a sibling rivalry problem. Karen simply just thought Mary Ellen was a bore—so quiet, so feminine, so little. Not Karen's type at all.

After a few weeks, I became concerned about Mary Ellen. She stayed in her crib, lay perfectly peaceful on my shoulder when I'd pick her up. I thought perhaps she wasn't normal, and I took her to Dr. Wells. He laughed at me. "Don't worry," he said. "She's normal. You're comparing her with Karen, that's all, and Karen's overactive. Just never compare these two little girls. They're two entirely different personalities." And that's the way they always were in their little-girl days. If Mary Ellen couldn't do something sitting down, she wouldn't do it. If Karen had to sit, she'd rebel. They had nothing in common.

It was totally different when our second natural-born

child came along. John was born on September 28, 1957—a robust baby, nine pounds, five ounces. A few minutes after he arrived, Joe called home to tell Karen about it, and she went wild. My parents were staying with the two girls, and they said Karen went slamming out of the house and raced all around the neighborhood, banging on doors like some rowdy Revere, yelling, "I have a brother, I have a brother!"

Karen was just about three and a half then, and from the day we brought John home, she took him over. This was *her* baby. She never wanted a doll, but John would do nicely. She'd hoist him from his crib and carry him around the house like a prized quarry she'd found. She taught him how to paddle in our plastic back yard pool before he could crawl. She wrestled with him, taught him to swing, "kilt" him a million times with her toy gun, and, when he was a bit older, always took him to the beach or the softball field with her. Mary Ellen sometimes tagged along, but it bored her—and Karen was bored having her.

John was Karen's alter ego. They were close buddies, always.

When Karen was five, Joe Quinlan decided to add a second story to the house, and a family room off the kitchen. "It was a long project," he remembers, "but there were a lot of laughs."

—Julie's dad helped me with the major construction, but Karen was the one who did the dirty work. She liked to get her hands stuck in the mortar, and nagged me to let her carry the bricks. When the new second floor was completed, Julie and I took the biggest of the four bedrooms, and of course Karen got the second largest. Oh, she loved it—her own room.

There was a three-foot ledge running along outside the bedroom windows, and Karen loved to climb out on it and perch there. When she was about eight, one night we heard Mary Ellen shrieking upstairs, and we ran up to see what happened. Karen had crawled across the ledge and banged on Mary Ellen's window, then jumped back out of sight.

Karen loved to scare people. She was forever leaping

out from behind doors to startle you, and when the children got to the age of slumber parties, she was the one who made up the ghost stories.

Anyway, when she had her first room, Julie wanted to paint it pink, but of course, Karen would have none of that. She insisted on turquoise.

Much later, when she was in her teens, Karen came to me one night and said, "Dad, I want to paint my room—will you get me the paint, whatever color I want?" I thought oh-oh, we were in for it now. But we'd always made it a policy to let the children choose how they wanted to decorate their bedrooms, so I said, "Okay, honey, but I just want to warn you in advance that there are two colors that are almost impossible to paint over if you get tired of them. Those colors are black and red."

Karen looked delighted and cried, "How did you guess?" Then, helped by a couple of friends, she painted her room in flat black, with white streaks of lightning flashing down the side of one wall, and then, because she asked for it, we bought bright red carpeting. Karen put up special lights, and when she was finished with the room, Julie and I were surprised. It was wild, but it was attractive. And Karen was so proud of the results. She got the idea from Christ House, which is a Catholic retreat house with special programs for teen-agers where Karen and her friends liked to go because they had folk masses, and a recreational area down in the basement—painted in psychedelic colors, like Karen's room.

So we survived her "psychedelic period" very nicely, and after two years she tired of it and went back to blue walls. "See, Dad?" she said, "black isn't that hard to paint over."

Since she was so bright and creative, we always expected that she would get all A's in school. The teaching nuns thought so, too. And at first, in the early grades, Karen really sailed along, learning to read quickly and write well. She was composing little poems in the early grades, not for school assignments but just because she loved to make words rhyme.

But as she went along into the higher grades of grammar school, she didn't continue to get the top marks in all her classes. Maybe there wasn't enough of a challenge. She despised mathematics, which was typical of most of her girl friends, too, so we weren't concerned about it. And she didn't particularly like the books she was assigned to read. That was sort of typical of Karen —being so independent and not particularly liking to be given orders.

She didn't exactly rebel against authority, but she felt that just because someone was in a position of authority didn't mean that they were necessarily always right.

So she didn't particularly take to being given orders. For instance, when we gave her piano lessons, Karen quickly decided to give them up. She didn't like the teacher. Mary Ellen started lessons from the same teacher at the same time, and Mary Ellen didn't like the teacher either, but she kept studying anyway. Mary Ellen would accept the lessons, in order to learn something she wanted to learn. Karen would say no, it's not worth putting up with this.

There was a good reason on her side, forgetting the conflict of personalities. Karen could play the piano by ear—and she didn't see much point in studying with a teacher who couldn't do what she could do. Karen could hear a song on the radio, and then sit down and play it. She would pick out the tune first, and then figure out the chords. I was always amazed at that talent, and no one could ever explain it to us. Some people have this ability, and others don't. Mary Ellen is a really fine pianist, majoring in music at college—yet she has to play by the written music, whereas Karen could see the music in her own mind.

I guess when you're born with a gift like that, study seems a waste of time. Anyway, it did to her.

Karen just sort of laughed her way through nursery school and, later, Our Lady of the Lake grammar school. She received good to average grades, in spite of doing very little homework, and she didn't worry about school. Life was just a ball to her, and the Sisters at school would call up every once in a while and tell Julie that Karen had misbehaved. Usually, that meant she had been talking in class.

Julie was more amused than worried about that, knowing how exuberant Karen is. "My little chatterbox" is what she always called her.

Still, there had to be some form of punishment. We never spanked any of the children, because we don't feel it accomplishes anything to slap someone, so when Karen misbehaved, Julie would send her up to her room for a while. Karen hated that, because she always wanted to be outdoors playing, and she'd stomp up those stairs till you thought they were going to crash into the basement, and go in her room and slam the door.

Then she'd start reading, and become so absorbed she forgot she was being punished.

When Julie would call up and tell her it was time to come down, it was as though nothing had happened. Karen was always a forgiving person. She never carried a grudge.

From the time their daughter could reason, about the age of three, Julie read to her from a story book which Catholic Charities had recommended—a picture book about a happy young adopted girl.

Julie was told that it was better for children to understand their adopted status early, so there would be no rude surprises later in life.

—And Karen adored the book. She was always asking me to read it to her. The story was intended to point out that adoptive children have been specially chosen and therefore are really, really wanted—and Karen became so proud of herself, as a result of it, that one day Mary Ellen came to me in tears.

Mary Ellen sobbed, "Why do I have only one mother? Karen says she has three—her other mother, the Blessed Mother, and you."

After I calmed down Mary Ellen, I suggested to Karen that she shouldn't boast about being adopted—at least in front of her sister. But there was no stopping her. Once she came rushing in when we were all having breakfast, and she said, "Hey, Mom, maybe someday we'll find my other mother and she'll be rich, and then we'll *all* be rich." Another time, she had a brilliant notion. "You know what? I'm going to be the first Saint Karen!"

Unfortunately, when she was thirteen and in the seventh grade, we had a setback.

One afternoon, after school, she came walking slowly into the kitchen, and I knew something disturbing had happened. Seeing Karen move slowly was a warning. I thought perhaps she'd failed a test, or something of that sort, but thank heaven, I didn't have time to ask her an insensitive question.

She said, "Mom—am I illegitimate?"

I was appalled. "What would make you ask that?"

"Sister gave us a lecture today about illegitimate children." Her face was a small thundercloud. "You've got to say. Is that what I am?"

I controlled the urge to weep, to call the school and scream "Why?" But Karen's question came before my anger. We sat down at the breakfast table, and once again I explained to her about her mother—that she was very courageous and unselfish, because you'd have to be unselfish to give up your baby.

Karen didn't want that. She always wanted a straightforward answer. "Was my mother married?"

"No."

Then I went over to the bureau and pulled out her birth certificate and showed her, as I'd done many times before, that it listed us, Joseph and Julia Quinlan, as her parents—with no mention of "adopted."

After that, I showed her the original birth certificate from St. Joseph's, listing her natural mother's name, and Karen's place of birth: Scranton, Pennsylvania.

Karen was calm. Was she resentful? Angry? There was a vacuum across that always-animated face. For a few minutes she sat silently, slowly running her fingers over the two documents, back and forth.

Finally, she said, "I want to see my other mother."

It was so touching, the way she said it; all at once I felt almost as though I had changed places with her—that I was inside her, feeling how horrible it must be, to grow up not knowing, never sure, always wondering what your natural mother looks like, how she thinks and what she is feeling. I said, "Honey, someday you'll see your other mother, and then everything will be better."

Karen nodded somberly.

She seemed to be satisfied.

But the next year was troubling for her, and there were times when she showed me she felt angry at her fate. She saw her natural father as a culprit, and she became even closer to Joe than before.

We tried to see to it that her friends were in the house a great deal, so she wouldn't feel alone or that she was different from anyone else. The Sister suggested that—the same nun who had talked about illegitimacy in class. She told me, when I called the school, that she was sorry, that she had realized while she was talking that she had made a mistake, but by then it was too late.

It was painful for a while, but Karen is a realist and she bounced back. She's that kind of person.

Karen never did locate her natural mother, although she once made a halfhearted try.

In the spring of her seventeenth year, she was visiting Scranton on a Catholic Youth Retreat with her friend, Mary Lou McCudden.

—One afternoon [Mary Lou remembers] Karen took me to a telephone booth, and had me help check out the phone directory, searching for her mother's name. We looked under all these last names that were the same as her mother's, and then Karen said, "Okay, all we have to do now is go, you know, and check, and see if this is my mother or not."

To her, it was not a big deal. It was more of a lark. And she was very curious about her parents. She wasn't dissatisfied with Mr. and Mrs. Quinlan, but she just had questions. The biggest one was, "Why did they give me up for adoption?" I guess if you're adopted, it's something you always wonder about. And she wanted to know what they were like. She wondered if her mother had a good voice, and if that was why Karen sang so well. She wondered if her father was a football player, and that's why she had broad shoulders.

She said, "Okay, let's go."

But I said, "Well, Karen, you know I think that would look very odd. You can't just walk up to a person's door and say, 'Did you have a daughter eighteen years ago that you gave up for adoption?' "

She could see the picture in her mind, and she began to realize she couldn't do it.

When it came right down to it, Karen wasn't curious enough to embarrass anybody. Especially herself.

Nor did Karen's natural mother ever try to locate Karen.

When *The New York Times* printed the natural mother's name, Julie was distraught. "I thought, if this poor woman is married and her husband may not know she had a child, then she must be living in fear. Maybe she knows it's her daughter who's in a coma, and maybe she wants to come forward and see her, but she can't. Dear God, just help her. It must be a terrible strain.

"I know every July twenty-eighth, I think of our son who was born dead. I'm sure every March twenty-ninth, she must think of Karen and long to see her."

All three Quinlan children were exposed daily to their parents' religious beliefs and personal philosophies. A framed print of Leonardo da Vinci's "The Last Supper" hangs in the dining room. The wood-paneled kitchen and breakfast room are generously decorated with plaques and samplers, reminding that "Love Isn't Love Until You Give It Away," and "Cast all your care upon Him—for He careth for you." Karen's favorite was a quatrain:

This I would be—just a little bit wiser
A little bit quicker to see
What others need most when the going is rough
And the helping out's left up to me.

Julie rarely talked about religion at home. She didn't think it was necessary.

—And there is one thing that I am absolutely sure of —you can't force religion on your children. Because Joe and I have faith, it doesn't necessarily mean that our children will, especially in these times when secularism is so popular among young people. But we did expect each of our youngsters to be thoughtful, humane human beings, and they are.

Karen was the most religious of the three, and the most sensitive. From the time she was small. She used to take Mary Ellen and John down to the lake in the summer, and the year that she was eight, there was a little boy coming to the beach every day with his mother. Apparently he was a mongoloid, because he had an enlarged head and a very small, pale body. The older children would make fun of him, and Karen couldn't bear that. One day, she gathered all those children together—some of them a lot older than she was —and told them angrily, "This boy is very brave to come down here when he is so little and so sick, and I want you to be good to him—or else."

Nobody ever made fun of that child again, because Karen was so fierce about it.

As she grew older, she sometimes carried her sensitivity to people's needs to extremes. When she was fourteen, Karen read in the newspaper about a family who was going to be evicted from their home because the father was ill and couldn't work. Karen took the allowance she had saved to buy a pair of skis—twenty-eight dollars—and put it in an envelope and mailed it to that family.

She couldn't stand suffering. She'd sit down and talk to me about things that concerned her—particularly when something troubled her. Karen had very definite ideas on many subjects, and she would express them with a maturity and an insight that was quite remarkable for her age. She would sit down and discuss abortion, for example, after a girl friend of hers became pregnant. The girl friend didn't know what to do, and she didn't want to tell her parents, so she came to Karen for support. Karen of course took this girl under her wing and brought her over to see me so that I could give her advice. Then Karen took her down to "Birthright" in Dover—an anti-abortion group that gives counseling, medical help, and financial assistance to unmarried women. Right through the birth of the baby, Karen stood by her and took care of her. She was that strong, and that protective, about her friends.

Karen was not a saint, by any means. She disliked stupidity, and injustice, and was completely intolerant of people who she decided, in her own mind, were hypo-critical. And she was totally honest, to the point of bluntness. She would never hold back her opinion. Finesse was never one of Karen's virtues.

I remember a party the children had when she was seventeen. There were perhaps fifty invited teen-agers, and another fifty or so just came over and "crashed." We didn't mind. Joe and I have always taken a "the more the merrier" attitude because—maybe we were overprotective—we preferred to have the children and their friends at our house than anywhere else in the world. So that night the family room was jammed with Karen's pals.

Mary Ellen happened to be standing by the door when she saw a girl Karen didn't like walking up the driveway toward the house. "Oh-oh," Mary Ellen said, "Look who's coming to crash."

Karen peered out the door, made a funny face at her sister, then bolted down the driveway—like our dog taking after the mailman.

The next thing we knew, Karen was back and the girl had vanished.

"What did you say?" Mary Ellen asked.

"That she wasn't welcome!" Karen said.

That was Karen. If she took a dislike to somebody, they knew it instantly. If she liked you, she would lay down her life.

Mary Ellen never could understand how Karen "got by" with her outspokenness:

—Most people can't get away with saying exactly what they think all the time, but she could. Maybe it's because she laughed everything off. She just didn't believe in wearing a mask. She thought that was hypocritical. Most people liked that.

Karen was a really outgoing person, and independent. Whatever she felt like doing, she did it. Like sometimes when all her shirts were in the laundry, she'd take one of my shirts and wear it, and it would stretch so much I couldn't wear it again, because Karen had broad shoulders, and I'm more slender. I'd yell when she did that, "You're wearing my shirt again!" and Karen would just say something like, "Yeah, it's nice, I like it."

Once when our cousin, Bobby Duane, was staying

with us for the summer, he had a pair of new white slacks and he was going to wear them on a date one night. But Karen got hold of them and wore them over to a girl friend's house. When Bobby started to dress and found his pants were missing, he was furious and he phoned Karen at her girl friend's and screamed, "Are you wearing my pants?" When she said yes, Bobby told her, "Bring them back right now!"

Well, Karen said no, and hung up on him.

About an hour later she came home, with his pants. She explained she had said no because she thought Bobby was rude, the way he talked to her.

You had to understand Karen. To her, loving meant sharing. If she loved you, she would give you anything. But to her, it worked both ways, and if she loved you she wouldn't think twice about taking something you had that she needed, either.

She would never take something from somebody she didn't love.

I didn't begin to really understand her until I was thirteen and she was fifteen. We were so completely unalike. I was quiet and liked the indoors, and she always wanted to be out swimming or skiing or something. But one night—it was about the time we were discovering boys—we got together in her room, and we started talking about how we felt on a lot of different things. That's when I began to see Karen's other side—which was quite different from the side of her that she let most people see. There are parts of you that you don't show to your friends, or even to your parents sometimes, and Karen and I shared these things with each other.

I confided to her that I was always jealous of her looks and her personality.

She was really shocked by that. "Well, that's strange," she said, "because I was always jealous of *you*. I thought you have the ability to hold friends better. You always say the right things, and I don't."

Then she admitted that she looks up to other people, more than herself. She'd say, "Boy, I'd like to be as strong as that person." Or, "I wish I had the confidence of that person."

This sounded crazy to me, because no one seemed

as confident as she is. But underneath, she had this in-
security. It was definitely a conflict inside her—that
though she looked strong to people, she didn't feel it
inside herself. Yet for some reason, she felt she had to
keep up that image to others, no matter what.

Karen always seemed to need to help people. It was
some inner urgency—something that maybe made her
feel better about herself. Always doing something for
her friends. She would give them money, and then she'd
borrow money to give them more if they needed it. She
would pick up people in the middle of the night, if their
cars broke down or something. No matter what the
trouble was, Karen would go and take care of them.

But at the same time, she never wanted to be taken
advantage of, and that was a problem because, of
course, the more you help people the more they ask for
more help and start to get dependent on you. Karen
didn't want that, the thought of people depending on
her. She talked about it a lot. About how she *looked*
dependable, but she didn't *feel* dependable.

I think that was a definite problem she had when
she started going out with Tommy Flynn. She went
with him for three years, starting when she was sixteen,
and they became very close, and they began counting
on each other. That bothered her. She fought it inside
her.

See, she didn't want him to depend on her. She
always wanted to be free.

She didn't want to feel that anyone had power over
her—or to feel so much for somebody that, you know,
if he wanted her to jump off a cliff, she would.

That's why, every once in a while, Karen would go
out with other boys—to prove to herself that she could
leave Tommy anytime she wanted to. In the summer,
the last year they dated, she got a job as counselor at a
summer camp on Long Island. Karen always spent her
summers as a lifeguard, because she was great with
people, especially kids. She could teach them to swim.

That summer, while she was away, Tommy started
going out with another girl. When Karen found out, she
was really insulted. It was okay if *she* went out with
other people, but when Tommy did it—ah! That was
different. They broke up after that, and she acted like

she didn't care. I remember one day, Grandma asked Karen, "Whatever happened to that goodlookin' fella who was so crazy about you?"

Karen said, "He's gone, Grandma. He's gone, and I just hope he *stays* gone." Grandma loved that. She always thought my sister was the greatest, because Karen would turn herself inside out to do things for my grandparents, and keep them happy and laughing.

But I think Karen probably loved Tommy, though she would never bring herself to say so.

I know he was the only one who ever made her cry. One winter night [in 1972] she and Tommy were supposed to go to a school dance, and she bought a navy velvet dress, with matching shoes. She even bought perfume. I helped her fix her hair, and she looked really great that night.

Then, just before the dance, Tommy called and said he had to be in a wrestling exhibition. Karen really cried that night, and nothing Mother or I could say did any good. I felt so sorry for her. But after a while, she went up to her room and changed into other clothes, and then went down to the corner ice skating. That was the way she would work out frustrations—with exercise.

She was all right after that. She never mentioned it. But she never wore that navy dress ever again.

It was really beautiful, and it just hangs up there in the closet.

I overheard my father saying that when the time comes—well, what he said was, "When the heavenly father calls her"—he wants her to be buried in that dress.

Chapter 6

After Karen went into a coma, Tommy Flynn felt conscience-stricken that he had let their three-year relationship end, and then refused to begin seeing her again, when Karen had wanted to start over.

—I went through a real lot of guilt when it first happened, feeling that maybe I could have done something more, maybe I could have said something more —given our relationship another chance. I know how she felt, because most of her good friends had gone away to school, and she was staying home, not wanting college but still wondering "Why am I here?" and "Why are they there?" Friendships were real important to Karen, and I thought that, in wanting us to get things together, she was just running back to something that was secure—because when things were good for us, they were really good; we could communicate really well and just enjoy one another so much. But although I still felt immensely for her, I knew we couldn't go back to coexisting that intensely. At least I couldn't, and, at the time, I didn't think she could either.

The three years we saw each other, we had a good relationship. We'd go to dances and rock concerts, go skiing and swimming. But we also talked about serious things. Many of our friends thought Karen was just a lot of fun, and she was, but there was another side of her. She had a very strong sense of self, almost of self-secrecy, and so did I, and we shared this with each other and with no one else.

We grew up together, spiritually and emotionally. Those were three years in which I burned bridges within myself and rebuilt all new values, because she could spark things inside of me, just by the vital way she lived, the way she was.

During Christmas vacation our first year [1970], she and I went to New York together. No one could believe how far we walked—down to Greenwich Village, back uptown to Sixtieth Street, back down to Fourteenth Street, and back again to the Port Authority Bus Terminal, Christmas shopping and talking constantly all the way. Karen was very small, only five-two, but she had just an incredible amount of energy. That was one of the special things about her. That and her beauty. People would turn around to look at her.

She was very determined. If Karen had an idea in her mind what she wanted to do, then she'd do it. There

was always a built-in challenge to outdo. Not to outdo
other people—she wasn't competitive at all—but to
outdo herself. Karen was always the first one to spot a
new ski trail and test it—to prove to herself she could
make it. She was always picking up something new,
whether it was action or ideas.

She read everything she could find which would stimulate her mind. Poetry, books on comparative religion,
extrasensory perception, mystical things. Sometimes
she'd talk about things out of this world, natural phe-
nomena. I'm not interested in anything it's not possible
to feel or to touch, but I wasn't surprised that she
was. She was curious about everything, and open to
anything new that would stimulate her spirit. We all
have psychic ability, but most of us don't talk about it.
She did. I don't know whether it was psychic insight or
pure fantasy, but I know Karen felt deep inside her
that she would somehow affect people in a more than
ordinary way.

She was very talented musically. She had a real pretty
voice, and I think for a while she thought about
maybe having a career in music. But she knew—we
knew that to make it you have to go through a certain
amount of tension, an intense desire mixed with a certain amount of callousness, and Karen definitely wasn't
a callous person. She was realistic about that. And
she was really shy which most people didn't realize because she'd try to cover it up. She had a fear of people
seeing a different sort of girl from the one she wanted
them to see. So what they saw was this outgoing, vital
person who didn't seem to have any inner fears or
hang-ups. But she had them. She didn't discuss them
much, even with me, but she wrote poetry—some of it
happy, some sad, some of it self-exploratory and questioning. I liked all of it, mainly because it was another
way for her to show me what she really was, and how
she was thinking.

Everybody will say how generous she was. But it
was more than just going out and doing things for people when they'd call and say, "Karen, can you come get
me?" or "Karen, can I borrow ten dollars?" She did
more. When she was really down or upset, and she
would see somebody who needed comfort or an uplift
—Karen would be there. She'd give that uplift. That's

when it's really hardest, when you need to be comforted by somebody, to go out and put on a smile and help. That was Karen.

In the end, that became a problem for us. All along I had the feeling that I—much more than she—was making our relationship go the way I thought it should go. She gave so much of her energy to all of her other friends, I couldn't tell how much I meant to her.

Maybe I was selfish. But somewhere along the way I became obsessed with the idea that in always taking her energy and passing it around to whoever needed her, Karen wasn't living up to her potential. In always doing things to make other people laugh and feel better, she was draining herself—leaving a little piece of herself behind.

I wanted her to stop and look at herself. I urged her to say, "Hey, I'm a beautiful person. I deserve to do more just for myself." I wanted her to be introspective.

Probably that was wrong. What I didn't realize then is that helping people was the way she built her strength. Her never-say-can't, never-say-die attitude—maybe she lost that, when she was alone, and not fighting other people's battles.

I don't think anything ever scared Karen. I know no person ever scared her. The only thing that frightened Karen was looking inward, at herself.

So there began to be a kind of growing apart in where we were heading, and what we wanted to do in our own lives as individuals. I became president of the student body, and an activist in a fight for curriculum reform, fighting head on for a cause. Karen didn't want to be involved in that. She would always avoid confrontation of any kind. If she didn't like the way something was, she preferred to fight it inside her.

We saw less and less of each other. Then one summer [1974] she took a camp counseling job out on Long Island. I started dating another girl a few times. When Karen came back, she phoned and wanted to get things back together the way they had been before.

I said that would be fine, but I didn't want the same total commitment. Karen said okay. But then there wouldn't be any commitment at all. It would have to be the way it always had been, or there would be nothing between us.

I was hurt. I guess she was, too. We had never hurt each other in the years of being together, and it was difficult to realize this had to be the end of it.

Talking about it—talking about her—falls so short of what we meant to each other.

In the middle of her eighteenth year, Karen Quinlan bet her friend Mary Lou McCudden that she would be married before she was nineteen.

Mary Lou remembers it as just another casual conversation:

—We were in the car—Karen was always driving us someplace, because I didn't have a car. And she said, "Well, I'll bet you ten dollars I'll be married by the time I'm nineteen."

I said, "Why do you want to get married then?"

She said, "I don't know, I just have this feeling that by then I'll be married." She was big on making predictions. One year I bought her a book on ESP, just because she always seemed to be interested in that. It intrigued her.

So that day I said, "Okay, it's a bet."

On her nineteenth birthday, I gave her a gift and a card, and she handed me a ten-dollar bill and said, "I owe you this." I gave the money back to her, and we both laughed about it.

Karen could laugh about almost anything. Even when she was in a nervous situation, she would laugh. It was a defense mechanism. Like, if we were in school, and we hadn't studied for a test, she would say, "I didn't study for this," and start giggling. Here I am, sweating it out, and she's doing that, and I would say, "How can you laugh about it?"

It was just her way. So when she broke up with Tommy, I'm sure she said to herself, "Well, I don't need him." Karen always had to feel like an independent person, especially with guys.

We'd go on trips together. We went to New York a lot, to see shows. Karen dreamed about being a singer, and I wanted to be an actress. We never thought we really would, but it was fun to fantasize about it. One time we went to see *Pippin*, the musical, and when we got home I found out that my aunt was very sick with a lung disease, and Karen said, "You go ahead over to the hospital, I'll stay with the kids." And she stayed with my two younger sisters and my younger cousin for several days, making their food and keeping them happy. They loved her because she had a big heart and was a funny person. Later, after I went away to college in Pennsylvania, I was homesick and Karen would call me on Thursday night and ask, "Do you want to come home for the weekend?" Then she'd drive up, and bring me home, and then take me back on Sunday. She had a big heart. We got serious, a lot of times I would talk and she would just listen. It was like she didn't want to commit herself. When she had something serious to say, more often she would sit down and write it, then give it to me to read. She could express her serious side in writing better than she could say it.

Of course, everybody knew about her fear of getting cancer. She could just have a bad cold, you know, and she'd say, "I told you—I'm going to die." It was always running through her mind. Once, when her girl friend Nanette's father was dying, and Karen had been to the hospital to see him, she said to me, "My God, if I'm ever that sick, I hope they let me die." I don't know if you'd call it fatalistic or what. Maybe it's because we both smoked, but I'll never forget her fear because, coming from someone as healthy as Karen, it was so extremely odd.

She was really pretty, and when she'd come over to our house, guys' heads would turn. After she'd leave, somebody would always say, "My gosh, such a beautiful girl." But nobody could compliment Karen to her face or, if they did, she was very uncomfortable. I remember the first time I heard her sing, we were on a bus coming back from a Ski Club trip, and everybody was singing, and Karen was singing along.

Well, gradually the others just dropped out, so that she was singing alone. When she finished the song—I can't remember whether it was "House of the Rising Sun," which was a favorite of hers—suddenly all the kids were saying to her, "You sing so beautifully, Karen!" and Karen just said, "No, don't say that! Just don't tell me how I sing."

It was the same when she would be dressed up, and

somebody would say, "I can't believe how terrific you look." Karen would shrink. She would get frustrated and say, "Just don't say that any more. Thank you, but don't tell me that."

Maybe that's why she usually wore jeans and a shirt —because when she wore a dress, she was always being given compliments, and she didn't know how to take them.

She would never pose for a picture, either.

I remember when Tommy's sister, Michelle Flynn, got married. Karen wore a terrific red dress, cut low in the back, with a matching fringed shawl. It was only the second time I'd ever seen her in a dress, and she looked fantastic. She was everywhere that day—the life of the party—and there was a professional photographer taking pictures all afternoon out on the Flynns' lawn where the wedding and reception took place. Later, when Mrs. Flynn got the wedding pictures, she was really upset because Karen, who was Michelle's best friend and Tommy's girl, was in only one picture—and all it showed was the back of her head during the ceremony.

Even when she began going out with Lee Swart, who was a free-lance photographer, Karen wouldn't pose for him. He got some pictures of her, but he had to take them very fast, from the side or the back, when she wasn't looking.

Lee Swart was older—twenty-two when he met Karen. She was nineteen. They made a startling couple: Karen five-two, Lee six-feet-three and usually wearing leather boots with three-inch heels which made him so tall he had to duck his head when he entered the door of the small house he was renting in Hopatcong Hills, New Jersey.

Lee was serious about Karen.

—But I never knew how serious she was about me. I couldn't tell how she really felt, because most of the time she just wanted to be going places. I had a car, she had a car, and we did some crazy things. Some of the best times of my life were with her and her parents. I thought they liked me. Mr. Quinlan made me nervous at first, because he was always so quiet, but when he got to know me better everything was fine. Mrs. Quinlan was great, always smiling and happy. Their house was usually full of Karen's friends, and John's and Mary Ellen's, and we were always laughin' and kiddin' around. They taught me how to roller-skate, I remember, and we'd go on camping trips in the mountains—twelve people in two tents, usually. Everything was laughs.

The only thing that bothered me is she could really make me jealous. I'd never felt that way before. She'd start talking to other guys, and I couldn't take it. One time I put my fist through a wall, I was so jealous. She just liked people too much, always wanting to do things for her other friends. She had to be around people and she wanted to think she was needed by other people. It got me mad, because I didn't think she cared enough about me. But all she'd have to do is start talking to me and we'd be friends again.

On her twentieth birthday, about thirty of her friends pitched in to give a surprise party at my house. They bought a big cake, we had presents, and the girls hung crepe-paper banners.

When she came in, everybody jumped out from behind chairs and doors, and Karen fell back and acted shocked. She said, "Oh no—!" But I don't think she was really surprised. One of her friends told me there was always a surprise birthday party for Karen.

I don't remember exactly how the party ended—the thing went on till three or four in the morning—but I think Karen drove some of the guests home. That's the way it usually happened. Karen would have a couple of drinks, and everybody else would get loaded, and then she'd take care of them. Make sure they got home safely. She was small, but very strong.

One day after we'd been going together for a long time, Karen and I had an argument about something and didn't see each other for a week. It was in July [1974]. During that time, I would just sit there all day by myself, wondering where she was and what she was doing.

Then one afternoon, she suddenly turned up at my house. Grinning. She said, "How ya' doin'?" as though nothing had happened. When I get mad at somebody, I'll carry a grudge, but she was the exact opposite.

So we just picked up where we left off—because that's the way she wanted it. No going over the old argument. Karen always moved ahead, without looking back.

That night we drove over to see some friends of mine who had recently been married, in a town near Landing. Coming back down Route 206, I was really feeling good. It was a pretty night, and I was just happy to be back with her. Then all of a sudden Karen started talking, and we got serious. She talked about a lot of things that were on her mind and, as we got near my house, Karen said, "I love you."

Well, that was real nice. I said, "I love *you*." I meant it, too. She was beautiful.

But then Karen said, "I think someday we'll be married."

That bothered me. Karen was too free. I don't think she could settle down. But I was flattered, and I think I said, "Yeah. That would be nice."

She then made a statement that really freaked me out. She said, "I'm going to die young. I'm going to go down in history."

I couldn't think of anything to say. I felt nervous, and I just lit up a cigarette and waited for Karen to elaborate on what she'd just said. But she didn't. Maybe she was disappointed that I didn't ask any questions, but I couldn't.

Karen never brought up the subject again, and the next month I was offered a job as road manager for a rock group. I talked to her about it, and she thought it was a good opportunity, and I took the job. I wasn't ready to get married yet, and she wasn't either.

I traveled all over for the Buzzy Linhart Band, arranging backup pieces for the group in places like Ohio, Washington, Baltimore, and Long Island. The first few weeks, Karen would drive in and see me when I was in New York, and she mentioned that she might be going to college, she didn't know. But she was thinking about it.

We never again mentioned marriage, and she didn't make any more predictions, and we finally stopped seeing each other.

The last time I saw her was about three o'clock one morning in March 1975 in a little spot called Hound and the Hare in Sussex, New Jersey. She was with a few people, and she left them and came over and sat with me and my date. It was like she didn't want anything to do with the people she was with, and I was so happy to see her, I didn't pay much attention to my date.

We talked about a lot of things. She told me she was working on cars at an auto body shop, and described where it was, and told me to be sure to drop over and see her. I said I would, and I really wanted to.

What bothers me most is I had been drinking all that night—so I didn't say anything to her I really wanted to say.

And like two weeks later, it was too late.

Nanette Foit was two years younger than Karen, and had introduced her to Lee Swart in the summer of 1973, when Nanette and Karen were lifeguards together at Hopatcong Hills, a swim resort.

She was surprised when Karen began seeing Lee steadily.

—I don't think she really had that much interest in other guys, after she broke up with Tommy Flynn. She really dug Tommy. You could tell by the expression in her eyes when she only talked about him.

Karen was a good person. When my father became ill with cancer, she'd drive me over to the hospital all the time to visit him. She really worried about him, and one night she brought my father a birthday cake. At Halloween we dressed up in glitter stuff—with green faces. My dad really liked it.

One night when Karen and I were staying at Lori Gaffney's parents' summer cottage, she told us that she was going to die before she was twenty-one. And she said she would go down in history.

Well, Karen—she could say some pretty outrageous things, just to scare people. She was always the one who kept us up all night telling spooky stories. You know, she was great at that—her imagination was so wild, and she loved to try to scare people because it was something she could do that other people couldn't. This old run-down house in the neighborhood—Karen used to love to take us younger kids down there, because she said it was haunted, and she knew we'd be impressed out of our skulls.

Anyway, that night when she said what she did about dying young, I think we said, "Oh sure, Karen, sure."

I never could figure out if she really believed it, or if it was just another one of her stories. But now I think she was serious.

In the winter of 1974, Joe and Julia Quinlan felt that Karen was almost prepared to enroll in Centenary College for Women, a small school in Hackettstown, New Jersey, known locally for the quality of its music department.

Joe remembers his feeling of relief:

—We wanted all the children to go to college, and we had told Karen she could go to any school she wanted. We'd back her up in anything she decided. Then Mary Ellen started going to Centenary, studying piano, and she was so enthusiastic that Karen became interested. Because she knew she had a unique ear for music and a beautiful voice.

The biggest factor, though, was the fact that all her friends were away, while she always had to be out looking for jobs, picking up work when it was available, and then being let go whenever things were economically hard—which happened all too frequently in our area. Her favorite jobs were working at service stations, pumping gas. It was the time when girls had just started to move into that field, and my old friend Joe Stigliano over at the Chevron station got the biggest kick out of Karen. He told me she wanted to change tires, and then she wanted to take cars apart. And he'd say go ahead. And she did.

I didn't especially like the idea of a girl as pretty as Karen working in a service station, and I went to see Joe about it. He said, "Sure, we get some young bucks coming in here trying to make a pass—but don't worry, Karen can take care of herself. Besides, I'm always here," Joe said, "and I watch over her as if she were my own daughter."

So I never objected, in front of Karen, and of course I never told her I'd talked to Joe. She was so happy, and she did the work so well. Karen could do anything well—as long as it was something she wanted to do. But whenever business was slow, it was always the newest employees, like her, who were let off first.

The last job she had [beginning in June 1974 and ending the following August] was working in a lab at Microy Plastics Company, doing experiments. I was happy that at last she had the kind of job I thought a girl should be doing. And she was proud of it, very excited about it.

But she was still Karen. She hurt herself quite seriously.

One day she was told by the foreman to use a power saw, and it didn't have a guard on it, and it slipped and her hand was cut pretty badly. She had to have stitches. It wasn't her fault. I heard afterward that the supervisor really bawled out the man who'd told her to run it, but that didn't help the situation for us.

The accident slowed her down a little bit. I guess she saw the shock on my face, and realized that it was really serious, and she could have lost her hand. She was pretty calm for a while. Then they laid her off in a seasonal cutback, and here she was collecting unemployment again.

We were always hoping Karen would start being more serious. I was praying for the day when she'd either go to college, or she'd care enough about one of her boy friends to get married and settle down. But no, Karen didn't want to get serious. And just when she'd start reconsidering college, then another job would come along and she'd forget about it. It's a shame she got these jobs.

In December of 1974—having let another college enrollment period pass without applying at Centenary—Karen asked Julia if there would be any objection to taking in a house guest for a few weeks.

Julia didn't mind:

—Karen said that her girl friend, Robin Croft, needed a place to stay, because her parents had separated and her mother was moving out of state, and Robin didn't want to leave the area because she had a job.

Of course I said it was fine with us. We often had the children's friends coming to live with us from time to time—it's sort of like a youth hotel here. If they don't mind the noise and confusion, we don't.

So shortly after Christmas, Robin moved in to Karen's bedroom with her, and she was a nice girl. Very quiet. She was Karen's age, and she would come down for meals, but spend most of her time in the room when she was at home, because she was working and also going to school.

I don't know exactly how long she was here, perhaps six weeks, before Robin decided she wanted to get her own apartment. She found a cute little apartment near here—right down on the lake, on the way to our church. But the rent was too high for Robin to handle it alone, so she asked Karen if she would move in and together they could support the place. Karen was so excited. She had never been away from home before, except to go camping on weekends, and this was something new to her.

We couldn't really object, because Karen was almost twenty-one, which is quite late these days for your chidren to strike out on their own. And, as she pointed out, "I've got to help out Robin—it's the only way she can make it with the rent." Even though she was often foolish in the extent of her generosity, I would never in good conscience discourage her from helping a friend.

So Joe and I went to this apartment and looked it over, and it was a really funny little house that you couldn't imagine two kids like this moving into. You had to go down maybe fifty steps, steeply cut into a hill, to get in the place. The man had painted one room red, white, and blue. The place was filthy, with an old refrigerator that hardly worked—oh, it was horrible. It was a mess.

"You've never worked as hard in your life as you're going to have to work on this place," I warned Karen. And I was amazed. They did it all. They scrubbed and painted for days. There was a tiny porch looking out on the lake, and they fixed it up, borrowing chairs and tables from friends. Karen brought over her stereo. When they moved in, it was really a darling apartment.

The ironic part of it is that we saw almost as much of Karen after she moved out of the house as when she was living at home. The place didn't have enough heat, and she was often coming back home for dinner and to her own warm bedroom at night. We loved that arrangement. It was the ideal compromise, allowing Karen to feel independent without that awful wrench of seeing her really leave home. We were very happy, and I thought she was happy, too.

To Mary Ellen, the two months that Karen and Robin shared the lakeside house were gratifying:

—I used to go over there a lot to visit, and Karen would come home and sleep over, and it just seemed to me my sister and I were closer than ever. I guess it's because we could be together alone, instead of just being thrown together in the same house. At home, everybody was always moving in on us—our friends, or our cousins Bobby or Debbie, they spent the summers with us—there was always a crowd. But we could be alone now, because Karen was hanging around the little house most of the time while Robin was away, working.

She did a lot of reading during that time—one of the books she loved was Kahlil Gibran's *The Prophet*—and she wrote poetry. Karen always wrote a lot of poetry, but this was more serious, and a lot of it was sad. I remember one she wrote was really strange, but I thought it was good. Something like, "If the walls could talk, I wonder if they'd ask me why I'm unhappy when they've sheltered kings and queens and they've been happy here, so why not me?" The idea was, "Who am I that I shouldn't be happy?"

Mary Ellen later found the poem:

> *The sun finally broke through*
> *into this gloomy place I*
> *call home.*
> *Time and time again I wonder*
> *what the hell am I*
> *doing here.*
> *Silence is my only answer—*

> *If walls could talk what*
> *would they tell me—*
> *Once I sheltered Ambassadors*
> *from different nations—*
> *they were satisfied—*
> *Why not me—???*
>
> *I am from Oz*
> *No one can follow*
> *only swallow things I have to say—*
> *Back over the rainbow I shall go*
> *till another rainy day.*
> *Who am I? Alice or the Pinball Wizard.*
>
> *Karen*

"Karen was searching," Mary Ellen thought.

—She was reflecting a lot and thinking, and I could tell
she had been crying sometimes when she was alone.
Karen loved all kinds of people, and she wasn't used to
this much of being alone.

I haven't worried about her at all. Because, although
she was having her ups and downs emotionally, she
was a lot more up than down. Soon as people would
come in, she was still as funny, funny a person as
ever.

I depended on her a lot. I think I needed Karen. I
think I felt that if Karen wasn't there to talk to, I
would just stop growing.

Chapter 7

On the weekend of April 5, Karen came home for dinner
and announced that she would be forced to move out of
the little house on the edge of the lake.

Julie remembers being "disappointed about the move":

—But there was nothing really to be done about it.

It seems that Robin's mother had come back to New Jersey after her divorce and insisted that Robin should move back in with her, to help pay *her* expenses. And of course, Karen couldn't afford the rent alone. She still hadn't been able to find a job, and unemployment checks are hardly enough to eat on, much less pay the landlord.

I was so sorry for her—all the work she'd done in that little place and now she had to give it up, after a little more than two months. We assumed, of course, that she'd be moving back home—so much for her fling at independence.

But no. That Monday, she informed us, she was planning to transfer her belongings to a rented room over at Cranberry Lake. "An adorable little house," she said, being leased by a couple of friends of hers. When she told us the friends were two young men who lived together, Joe and I were very upset, of course, and wanted to know why she would do a thing like that instead of coming home.

"Mom, I am independent now," she said quietly, as though she were trying to be very patient with a somewhat foolish parent. "Coming home would be just like moving backward."

Then, before we could say anything, she went on about these boys, explaining that they were old friends of her girl friend Marcia Evans, whom of course we knew. And she went into detail about how harmless they were, how they were not the least bit interested in her. "Just don't get your feelings hurt," she said. "I know I've got a home to come back to, and I love it. And don't worry, I'll be back after the trip to Florida—but just for these two more weeks, I want to stay on my own."

After dinner, she went back to the apartment to pack her things for the move, and I said to Joe, "Well, it'll be all right."

That was the last we ever saw of Karen really alive. Eight days later she was in the coma, and these people she'd moved in with—who'd brought her to the hospital, and later brought her clothes and other things back and dropped them off at our house—they just disappeared from our lives, and hers.

I doubt if we'll ever find out what really happened to our daughter during the last few days of her existence.

The only thing I'll probably ever know for certain—and it is a memory that I cling to—is that she was enormously happy the last time we talked on the phone. And that three nights later she was unconscious in that hospital.

In spite of all the testing, in the first few days at Newton Hospital, the doctors had no way of assessing with certainty what form of comatose condition Karen Quinlan was in. There are many types and variations of coma. Light, severe, chronic, acute, reversible, irreversible. With the cause unclear, a prognosis was impossible.

If Karen had become acutely intoxicated with drugs, time and treatment would bring recovery within days.

But early urine and blood samples, taken on the day Karen was brought to the hospital, revealed only a "normal therapeutic" level of aspirin and the tranquilizer Valium in her system. On the same day, tests were taken for so-called hard drugs: blood and urine samples were sent to Roche Clinical Laboratories in Raritan, New Jersey, for evaluation.

The tests came back negative. There was no trace of any of the drugs the girl Terry O'Neill had speculated Karen might have taken.

The only positive finding was quinine. That would be explained, the doctor said, by the fact that she had been drinking gin and tonics (quinine) the night before.

With no drugs in her system, the doctors could take no remedial steps to arouse Karen Quinlan from the coma. They stabilized her breathing, with the tracheotomy and the powerful MA-1 respirator. They cleared her lungs of pneumonia within six days, with injections of penicillin.

On the day after Karen had entered Newton Memorial Hospital, a woman in the Social Services Department approached Julia Quinlan as she sat in the waiting room:

—Her name, as I recall, was Mrs. Gugliano, and she said she would like to ask me a few questions about Karen. She wanted to know Karen's full name, and her age, and her occupation.

When I said that Karen was at the present time unemployed, the woman said she felt that, in a case like this, she would be entitled to Medicaid. She said that as an adult, with no present income or insurance, her hospital bills probably would be handled by the Social Security System, and that she would investigate the matter for us, if we wished her to.

I said, "Yes, please—."

We hadn't even considered the money. I don't think anyone would, if they had a child in a hospital, in a critical condition. It would never occur to you.

I told Mrs. Gugliano, "Thank you very much. I'm sure that will be a great help."

The doctors seemed to have no answers. They couldn't give Julie any encouragement.

—Everything was possibilities. Possibilities. But they didn't seem to know much more than we did. Gradually, after a few days, the doctors even avoided us. They would walk out of Intensive Care after examining her, and if they saw us waiting, they would turn around quickly and walk the other way. It was as if they couldn't give us any hope, so they preferred not even to talk to us.

A few days after the accident, we noticed a little lump on the back of her head, which had been hidden under her long hair, and called it to Dr. McGee's attention. An X ray was taken, but it showed no abnormality.

Then it occurred to someone at the hospital that Karen might have been working with lead when she had the job at Microy. Maybe that—lead poisoning—could have caused the coma. We were searching for clues, just anything.

And in the meantime, Karen's hands and feet kept turning inward. I could open her hand by straightening out the fingers, but she would gradually, relentlessly, close them again. It was as though she wanted to clench her fist.

When her eyes were open, and they would test her reaction, by lightly touching her eyelashes, she would blink. When you bumped against her bed, she would jump, almost rising up into a sitting position—as though she had been struck, or was terrified of something.

Nobody told us that was just a reflex action. At first, every time it happened, we had hope.

On April 17 Dr. McGee informed us that he was bringing in a neurologist to examine Karen. He said the man was a highly competent specialist on neurological dysfunctions and a consultant at several New Jersey hospitals.

It was the first encouraging news we had been given.

At 10 P.M. Friday, April 18, Dr. Robert Joseph Morse—a thirty-two-year-old immaculately dressed osteopath-neurologist, six years in practice—strode into the Intensive Care Unit to examine Karen.

Joe Quinlan was instantly optimistic:

—Dr. Morse seemed young, but he had all the self-confidence in the world. And he was very sympathetic. Friendly. He smiled a lot. Everybody had been so dead serious, and this was an encouraging change.

After he examined Karen, he led us to a conference room and talked to us for a good half hour about what he felt could be done for her. He had a daughter of his own named Karen, and although she was quite young —four or five, I think—he seemed to feel that gave us an extra bond, besides just a doctor-family relationship. Anyway, that's how he made me feel at the time.

Dr. Morse felt that there had been some brain damage and that Karen was in an altered state of consciousness which the doctors call decortication, but his attitude was quite hopeful. He recommended that we transfer Karen to St. Clare's Hospital because it was so modern and they had facilities there for better testing.

Of course, that was music to our ears. We loved St. Clare's. That's where they cured Karen when she was a baby, and where Julie had the breast surgery and the lump turned out to be nonmalignant. We trusted St. Clare's. And it was closer to home than Newton.

When we said it was fine with us to move Karen, he said he would arrange it as quickly as possible. He said he looked forward to treating Karen, and while he couldn't promise us any recovery, he seemed quite excited about the prospect.

That night, when we said good-by to Dr. Morse, he was almost like God to us.

A bed became available in the Intensive Care Unit of St. Clare's Hospital in Denville, New Jersey, on April 24. At noon that day, Karen was transferred there by the volunteer Port Morris Rescue Squad.

It was ten days after the onset of the coma.

In a Discharge Summary for the Newton records, Dr. Paul McGee noted:

—Dr. Morse, neurologist, from Denville, felt that the patient was in decorticate state and the reason for her decortication was secondary to "neuronal shock." He felt she probably would come around.

In an Admission Note for the St. Clare's records, Dr. Morse wrote:

—This 21-year-old female was transferred from Newton Memorial Hospital today, to the ICU, after having been unconscious since almost a week and a half now. The patient was initially seen in the Emergency Room there and the reason for her unconsciousness was never determined. At the initial examination I felt that she was decorticate, and no evidence of drug abuse was picked up on the urinalysis. There is a possible history here of overdose, past history of lead poisoning which we are evaluating, but the patient at this time is much more responsive than during her original admission.

But Karen's condition had deteriorated in the six days since Dr. Morse had examined her at Newton.

On the St. Clare's Nurses' Record, for 3:30 P.M. April 24, it was recorded:

—Patient arrived via stretcher from Newton Hospital accompanied by nurse and Inhalation Therapist. Unresponsive. Pupils dilated. Hands and feet flexed and turned inward. Responding to painful stimuli. Tracheostomy in place. Left sided grip weak. Right sided grip weak. All extremities somewhat rigid.

She was placed in a bed in the center of the Intensive
Care Unit. And it seemed to Julie that Karen was also
the center of action for the entire hospital:

—Everyone was brisk, and functioning and terribly at-
tentive. Joe and I were asked to sign one paper after
another, giving our permission for all kinds of new
tests: lumbar punctures, angiogram brain scan, and
many, many X rays.

But all the tests were inconclusive or negative. There
was no sign of lead poisoning. No tumors, or foul play,
or viruses, and nothing abnormal about Karen's blood
circulation. There just didn't seem to be any new answers. They still couldn't find out what caused the coma.
I don't know if we will ever find out what caused it.

Dr. Morse's assistant was a small, quiet, and very
polite young man who had been born in Pakistan. He
was Dr. Arshad Javed, a pulmonary internist. He'd
been at St. Clare's for several years, and Dr. Morse said
he was one of the greatest in his field—gave him a terrific build-up. He needn't have. Joe and I liked him
immediately.

Javed was in charge of the respirator, which was
essential to keep her alive. He told us exactly how the
machine works—how it pumps air into Karen's lungs
when she is not breathing voluntarily, but how if she
suddenly starts inhaling on her own, it adjusts to the
change and permits her to take in exactly the amount of
air her lungs are calling for. An amazing machine.
It forces air into her lungs when she needs it, and jus'
assists her when sometimes she breathes by herself.

The nurses were instructed to keep track of the times
when Karen would breathe by herself, and how much
air she would take in. Dr. Javed explained that her
breathing was quite shallow and fast, and didn't fill her
lungs all the way—didn't ventilate the lower parts of the
lungs adequately. So then, the respirator would send in a
large volume of air when it was needed, to fill up the
lungs when she couldn't. He said this was vital to prevent more problems, like pneumonia reoccurring.

Physical therapists began coming in every day to try
to straighten Karen's hands and legs, which seemed to
be trying to pull up close to her body. Her knees and

elbows were bending inward, and they were becoming rigid and harder to move. The doctors wanted to stop that kind of movement, because her muscles could atrophy.

They bound her legs and hands to wooden boards, like splints, to try to straighten them out. They would massage and exercise them, too. But Karen's inner forces seemed to be very strong. No matter what they did, her legs would keep straining to pull up again, toward her left side. Her knees were trying to bend and push toward her chest, and her elbows pushed in toward her sides while her wrists, bent in that stiff, strange way, would be up under her chin.

She just seemed relentless. When those splints were taken off temporarily, for the massage, she would try to pull back into that curled-up position.

By early May, Karen's head was pitched forward, and the nurses found it difficult to pull it up. She held it down so low that her chin was touching the tube in her throat. With her legs and arms folded upward, it seemed to Julie that she resembled a baby in that fetal position.

—Then quite suddenly, the position of her head changed entirely. It was almost as though her neck were broken. Her head moved way back so that if she wasn't lying on the bed you would think it would fall back behind her shoulders. I lifted her head up always, and put a pillow behind her, when she was asleep, to keep her head in a normal position.

But when she was awake, there was nothing anyone could do. Her head would forever be moving from side to side, and her face began to grimace. This was something we hadn't seen before, and it was terribly disturbing to watch.

Her mouth would open wide, as though she were trying to scream, but the only sound you would hear, sometimes, was a moan. This was the hardest of all to bear, because we felt Karen must be in pain. In some deep, awful pain.

Dr. Morse told us she was not feeling any pain, in the usual sense. He was very careful the way he said it: "Karen does not feel pain *as we know it.*" Meaning that her brain had deteriorated. That her suffering—if she was suffering—was perceived at some level other than consciousness.

You cannot feel pain, he said, if you cannot conceive pain in your mind. Dear God. I thought, if Karen's brain is this far gone, why are they taking all these measures to bring her back? To what purpose?

I don't care how logical and technical and medical you try to be, it is horrible to see your daughter suffering this way day after day, and stand by helpless.

Poor Karen. Knowing all the things she felt and said about things like this, I knew that of all the people in the world, she would be the first to say—if she could see herself, and if she could talk—"Don't do this. Just leave me alone."

Three shifts of nurses daily attend Karen Ann as she lay in the center bed of the Intensive Care Unit.

They monitored the respirator, recording the times when the patient was able to "assist" the MA-1 by breathing spontaneously. They regularly suctioned the cavity in her throat of mucus, to prevent a recurrence of infection. They tube-fed Karen and emptied her body wastes from the Foley catheter inserted in her bladder. They dispensed medicines as ordered, bathed her, and every four hours recorded her temperature, pulse, respiration, blood pressure. Every two hours they turned her to a new position in a vain attempt to eliminate bed sores. Gradually, the nurses became emotionally involved with their helpless comatose patient, and with her family.

At the conclusion of each eight-hour tour of duty, they wrote brief reports on her condition, on sheets headed VITAL SIGNS—KAREN ANN QUINLAN.

Some of these early April and May reports, with the routine duties and technical terms deleted, are reproduced here.

Karen is referred to as Pt., abbreviation for Patient.

APRIL 24, 1975: Pt. pupils somewhat dilated but respond equally to light. All extremities somewhat rigid and tend to adduct. Trach tube changed, suctioned for large amounts whitish secretions. Moves eyes and responds to painful stimuli. Quiet coma present.

APRIL 25: Color pale, grossly diaphoretic [sweating]. Facial and eye twitching noted. Chewing motion —very "spastic" when suctioned. Does not respond to verbal stimuli. Left pupil more dilated than R. Constrictures of hands and feet. Hyperextended neck. Foot drop noted and contracture of hand noted also. Pt. appears to give a loud "moan."

APRIL 26: Pt. unresponsive. Pupils delayed-reacting to light. Color pale. Skin warm, moist. Extremities rigid. Hands rotate inward.

APRIL 27: Turned and positioned. Pt. becomes rigid when turned. Pt. has facial grimacing and "chewing" movements, followed by increased rigidity. Seems as if she's in pain by facial expressions.

APRIL 28: Rigidity of arms and legs. Draws right leg up. Opens eyes when disturbed. Assisting respirator at times. Eyes roll back.

APRIL 29: Lies with eyes open. Stares to the right. Pupils react slowly.

APRIL 30: Hands and feet contract. Responds more readily to painful stimuli. Pulls and extends right leg. Raises left arm some [during therapy]. Opens eyes more frequently. Facial expressions vary. Slight tremors of left hand noted. Foot board in place. Making crying sounds.

MAY 2: Crib sheet applied to restrain legs from motion. Opens mouth and winces, as if in pain. Physical therapist treatment.

MAY 3: Grimacing frequently. Skin highly diaphoretic and warm. Facial expression changes—tearing. Contractions and spasms continue.

MAY 4: Foley catheter pulled out—apparently by activity of pt. Foley reinserted. Having spastic movements. Crying sounds noted. Moaning at times. Affixed long arm splints to both hands so as to keep wrist and fingers straight.

MAY 6: Twitching and roll back of eye balls noted. Positioned. Appears unchanged.

MAY 7: Opens eyes when called loudly by name. Appears to be sleeping for short periods. Noted skin rubbed from some toes and fingers. Hands taped and padded as flat as possible. Appears to be responding. Will blink her eyes when asked to. Appears somewhat

responsive. Moves eyes when talked to. Small lacera-
tion noted on lower lip, appears to have bitten lip.
Appears agitated, moving extremities. Exciting day.

MAY 8: Found N.G. tube on floor. Head nurse notified. Dr. also notified. Appears very restless now. Tube
feeding held until house physician comes in. Called resident—not in house as yet. Turned pt. on back and
positioned. Resident inserted no. 16 levine tube. Feed-
ings given as ordered.

MAY 9: Much more rigid. Slight tremors noted now.
Light red rash noted on buttocks. Pupils reacting slug-
gishly. Facial grimacing persists. Wincing as if in pain.

MAY 12: Temp 103.6. Moaning loudly at intervals
this night.

MAY 13: Hands in splints. Becomes rigid when
moved.

MAY 14: Pt. crying with tears when mother is speaking to her. Crying appears appropriate.

MAY 15: No specific signs of emotion. No visual
recognition. Lower arms wrapped in ace bandages.

MAY 20: Pt. moaning and crying loudly.

MAY 23: Hair washed. Family called by Dr. Morse.

MAY 24: Contractions of extremities severe. Color poor.

MAY 25: Drs. Morse and Bender in. Examine pt. and
spoke to family.

MAY 26: Extremities severely contracted.

MAY 28: Contractions of extremities severe. Rash
over body. Hands wrapped in gauze. Fingers appear to
be breaking down. Both arms and legs rigid. Has restless
periods and quiet periods.

MAY 30: Morse, Javed and family visit. Both upper
and lower extremities remain very rigid. Sleeping and
waking periods.

MAY 31: Pupils dilate and constrict. Flashlight seems
to have no influence. Yet turns head when light shone
in eyes. Arms and legs contracted over body.

On May 25, Dr. Morse advised Joe Quinlan that his
daughter had entered a different phase.

—Morse told me that she was no longer in the kind of
coma she was in at the beginning. He said that at first
she was trying to come out of the coma, but she just

couldn't make it. Now she was in deeper, having sleep-wake cycles, and that this is a different condition altogether. He said she was comatose now on a different plateau.

Dr. Morse tried to be as sympathetic as possible, in order not to shock still further the patient's father, who, unlike the mother, seemed unable to grasp the severity of Karen's brain deterioration.

Joe had enveloped himself in a defensive blanket which muffled the voices of negative people saying words he couldn't bear to hear. He didn't fully understand what Morse was saying, and he didn't ask questions.

Morse was no longer God. "Only God is God," Joe Quinlan thought. "And God will bring back Karen."

Although Dr. Robert Morse never specifically informed the Quinlans that he anticipated a possible prolonged comatose illness for their daughter, he envisioned it as early as May 6, 1975.

On that day—twelve days after Karen's transfer to St. Clare's—Morse contacted the hospital's social worker, Mrs. I. Cors.

Her notations follow:

MAY 6: Physician referred patient to this department for referral to agency for financial help, and to look into possible placement in a long term care facility if needed.

Called Newton Memorial Hospital and was advised referral was made on 4/15 to Medicaid.

MAY 7: Called Sussex Co. Welfare Board to obtain information on their nursing facility, the Homestead, and find out if they can care for pt. Will keep in touch with both agencies, so arrangements can be made in advance so when and if they are needed there will be no delay.

MAY 13: Advised that patient is on respirator continuously now. A nursing home facility cannot care for her.

MAY 16: Conference with physician. Because it is possible patient could go on like this for some time, it was decided information should be obtained re a facility that can care for her on a long term basis.

St. Clare's Hospital needed the Intensive Care bed being occupied by Karen Ann Quinlan; its value in dollars was estimated at $465 a day.

Monetary considerations aside, no hospital willingly devotes its man and woman power and lifesaving emergency machines for the prolonged care of a patient with negligible chances to recover.

Chapter 8

Julie had been the first to face reality, to realize that Karen could linger on in the coma for weeks, even months, and that ultimately she would die.

Then she had wavered. First, when Karen began to fall into sleeping-waking cycles, and again when Dr. Morse had come on the case with his initial optimism.

—But by late in May, I knew there was no chance that Karen would come back to us, and I felt that Dr. Morse and Dr. Javed had given up hope, too—certainly they had no hope she would ever be a thinking human being.

Her weight had dropped from 115 pounds, when she was brought in, to 90 pounds. They kept feeding her high-vitamin mixtures and still her weight kept going down. And she was so rigid that there was no way of circulating the food intravenously, so they had put a feeding tube through her nostrils, into her stomach.

As her head kept turning and twisting, her hair was becoming tangled, and the nurses asked if I would mind if they cut it. If I had thought Karen would ever come back, I could never have said what I did—"Go ahead." Karen loved her long hair, and only last winter a girl friend had cut it a little, just for a lark. It had turned out uneven, and Karen had to go to a salon and have it cut professionally, and the only way the stylist could do that was to make it quite short.

Oh, she hated it. Mary Ellen and I, and several of her girl friends, told her it looked pretty, and attractive and different. "Different—it looks different all right!" she cried and then, to my amazement, she was weeping real tears about it. She didn't cry for long. She bounced back, as she always did, and her hair grew out again very quickly.

When the nurses asked if they could cut her hair, I just couldn't dwell on that. "It makes sense," I said. So then they had trimmed it, a bit at a time, until it was finally quite short, curling in little damp wisps around her face. It turned darker, too. Karen had been so long away from the sun, which always streaked it and made her hair tawny.

I brought the nurses a bottle of Herbal Essence, the shampoo she used, and told them that the most important thing to her would be that her hair is kept clean. So they washed it often, and patted it dry with towels. They were wonderful about it, and I was grateful, and I knew Karen would be grateful, and I also knew it was just for nothing.

I wondered how long all this would go on—Karen lying there getting smaller and smaller, looking so miserable with all the tubes and bottles and that gray console called the respirator, with its lights blinking on and off like some giant electronic computer, making hissing and gurgling noises as it endlessly pumped air down into a hole in Karen's throat.

Sometimes I thought that sound would drive me out of my mind. While I'd watch Karen, pulling her head back and making those agonized faces—that sound was always there.

All along I had been praying that God would bring Karen back.

I had been telling Him we wanted her back any way we could have her—brain damaged, it didn't matter. If He would only bring her out of the coma, we'd make her well somehow.

I said the Lord's Prayer so many times. "Thy kingdome come, thy will be done." Then all at once I began to realize that maybe I was not really praying for His will to be done at all. I was praying for *my* will to be done. Maybe God had other plans, I thought.

At first this was hard to accept—the concept that His

will might be other than mine. Would He really want
to take Karen, someone that young and full of life?
Then I'd look at her, the way she was, and I'd remember the things she said about not wanting to be kept
alive, the way Bill Birch was and Nanette's father. I
remembered she had asked me to be sure to donate
her eyes to an eye bank if she died. It's unusual for
young people to think of things like that, but Karen did.
I thought perhaps she had an insight. Maybe she knew
more about God's will than I.

I tried to submerge these thoughts, but they wouldn't
go away. Do mothers have some intuition that lets them
perceive what others can't? I don't know. All I know is
that I had to confide in someone, and it couldn't be
Joe or the children because they were so tense I felt
one more negative idea would be more than they could
stand. Joe and Mary Ellen hadn't faced the fact that
Karen is dying, and John—nobody could even talk to
John. One night at dinner when the subject of Karen
came up, as it always did, he banged his fist on the
table and slammed out of the house shouting, "I'm going to lie in the grass and ask God why he's doing this
to Karen!" John was so bitter.

The only person I knew I could discuss my feelings
with was Father Tom. He's my boss, as well as my
friend. He knows me so well. I felt he would understand.

It would have been quite easy, Father Thomas Trapasso
thought, to mistake Julia Quinlan for a small, lost child.
When she came into his rectory office one morning in
May, she appeared so forlorn and vulnerable that Father
Tom put his arm around her shoulders and led her into
the office where they had discussed church business almost every day during the four years since he had been
assigned to Our Lady of the Lake.

He remembered Julia Quinlan more clearly than perhaps any other person in the parish from those first spring
days of 1971 when he arrived. Not only was she his first
secretary, she was president of the Rosary Society; more
important than that, she had an inherent gaiety and humor
that he admired. There are bright women in church work,
and deeply devout women, but Father Tom had found it

rare to see these characteristics, and a sense of humor, too:

—But since Karen's coma, Julie naturally was changed. She was reasonably calm. She was never hysterical, or out of control, but she was deeply worried and tearful. Julie was worried on two very basic levels.

She was afraid that Joe didn't really grasp the magnitude of Karen's illness, and that if Karen died, he would fall apart. And she said again that "Karen would not want this." She could foresee that Karen might survive indefinitely on machines like the respirator, and this was simply inconceivable to Julie. She was just very, very sensitive to Karen's wishes and Karen's fears, and she kept repeating, "Karen would never want this."

Father Tom had at first been shocked by those words, because he had not then conceived of Karen's comatose state as being a possibly ongoing condition.

—But by the end of May, I had had plenty of time to grasp the significance of what was taking place. I had begun to put it in the perspective of a moral issue. I encouraged her to tell me everything that was on her mind, and she told me how painful it was to visit the hospital with Joe, because he would stand and talk to Karen as though she could hear him, as though she would wake up at any time. The doctors had made it clear that this was no longer a reasonable possibility, because Karen had no thinking brain left. "It is irreversible, irreparable," she said. But Joe didn't understand, emotionally or intellectually.

I told Julie that once I had accepted the hopelessness of Karen's condition, I began to see her tragedy in theological terms.

In terms of what I had been taught in my training, from a moral, theological point of view, this was a classic case of a hopeless life being prolonged unnecessarily through the use of extraordinary means. I explained this to Julie, and she just quietly listened.

In the Catholic faith, there is no moral obligation to use extraordinary means to prolong life. I was taught this concept thirty years ago, in the 1940s in the seminary. As part of my training for the priesthood, we discussed the whole treatise about life issues and medical ethics. And one of the least controversial areas of my moral training involved this concept.

In the Catholic Church there is a tradition that goes far back, all the way to the sixteenth century, to the beginning of medicine as a science. It began before the discovery of anesthesia, in the days when questions of medical morality arose. For example, if a person had a diseased arm or leg which should be amputated, let us say, the moral question became: Was the patient obligated to submit to this drastic surgery which would cause all but unendurable pain? A person in those times might prefer to die than undergo such anguish which, in fact, might itself cause death. The Church took the humane position that such surgery was an extraordinary measure to preserve life, and that the amputation could be refused. Even if death was an almost certain result.

So this was the sort of primitive decision that caused the concept of "extraordinary means" to become a policy of the Church. The first principle was that one is obligated to use all ordinary means to support and sustain life, because life is sacred. But if the burden of maintaining life is unbearable, a human being may be allowed to die.

Julie had not heard of this concept before. Few laymen have.

She kept asking if the respirator, which was assisting Karen to breathe, would be considered "extraordinary" in the context of this Catholic moral law.

I said there was no doubt in my mind that the respirator is extraordinary in Karen's circumstance. And that, if Karen is hopeless, the kind of care she is getting is extraordinary and futile.

The priest based his certainty on an address by Pope Pius XII, in which the late pontiff officially updated the Church's ancient stand. Speaking before a Society of Anesthesiologists, in 1957, Pius had stated that in cases where patients have no hope of recovery, there is no moral obligation to prolong life by using technological medical devices. In this context, the Pope referred specifically to respirators.

 —Julie, I'd use this analogy [Father Tom said]. Often a terminally ill patient, in pain or blessedly unconscious, has a disease that is being held back by a technology-designed dam. Nature is demanding death, and the dam is preventing it from happening. If you make the decision that there is no need to keep the dam in place and it is taken away, then the process of nature just takes place.

 Now, this decision is not without its moral implications. You have to ask if, by keeping the dam in place, you are allowing this person to continue to live a human life. Or is the dam retained simply because of some kind of obligation to keep the purely biological organism functioning? If that is the case, then there is no longer respect for life, for the dignity of human life.

By the end of May, six weeks after Karen had been rushed to the hospital, she was still in critical condition. Her weight had now dropped to eighty pounds. She remained in the center of the big Intensive Care section of St. Clare's Hospital, attached to a respirator, a heart-monitoring console, and tubes and bottles of foods and antibiotics.

And her mother, with the help of her priest, had made the decision that the humane act would be to remove her from the machines, rather than to let her go on this way.

It was a decision they shared in privacy, because Joe Quinlan was not ready to face philosophical or moral arguments. He was not yet prepared to listen to any hints that Karen might not recover.

Julie became harshly aware of that one day when she tried, tentatively, to make him face reality:

 —We were standing by Karen's bed, and I said, very quietly, "You know, Joe, if Karen should die . . ." and Joe erupted.

 He said, "Don't you ever say that again." His voice was low and strange. I'd never heard that sound from him before. He said, "I don't ever want to hear that. Karen is not going to die."

Julie felt certain that Mary Ellen would understand:

—Mary Ellen knew exactly how Karen felt about not wanting to be kept alive on machines. We had often discussed it—how Karen, of all people, would hate to be in that bed, helpless, with all those people tending her. So one day I sat down with Mary Ellen, and we shared a pot of tea, and I quietly told her all about my conversations with Father Tom.

I said, "Father and I feel perhaps it would be best if we told Dr. Morse that he could remove the respirator and let Karen die in peace."

Mary Ellen became terribly upset.

"How could you do that, Mom?" she said, and she backed away. She seemed to think I was almost horrible even to consider anything like that.

I wasn't at all prepared for her reaction, and I tried to explain to her that it was because Karen wouldn't want this, and because there was no hope she would come back. "She is dying very slowly," I said, "and I wonder if that is fair to her."

But Mary Ellen hadn't yet accepted that her sister was really dying. She just shook her head, and was holding back tears, and she stood up and stalked out of the kitchen.

That day I felt very, very alone. There was no one I could talk to.

Mary Ellen went into her room, and lay face down on her bed and wept:

—I thought, it doesn't matter what Karen has in her throat, or if her hands are tied or her feet are crooked —she's going to come out of it.

Why would they go to all this trouble trying to straighten her out, if she isn't going to live? It didn't make sense.

But later I realized that I couldn't have totally accepted that. Because there were times when they were trying to straighten her feet, and I would just say to myself, "Well, what about when she comes out of it? Her feet will stay like that. She'll have to keep those splints on, and she'll be deformed."

Still, I wouldn't let myself think she would die.

It's completely different to think that your sister is going to be crippled than to think she is going to die. To accept that, and just stop hoping.

When Mom talked to me, I couldn't think about what Karen would want—the way Mother did. I thought about myself. If Karen should die, I thought, I'll be nothing.

Shortly afterward, the nurses at St. Clare's removed the restraints that held Karen's body to the bed.

When they did that, on instructions from the doctors, Mary Ellen saw the truth:

—It was like they were saying it's all over—she's not ever going to come out of it. I think that was the worst time. I think then I knew she was going to die.

It was also the way she looked by then that convinced me she wasn't going to come out. She was so little. Her body, curled up, was only about three feet long.

She would cry sometimes, and the nurse said it was from blinking so much, but seeing those tears running down the side of her face was so sad, and sometimes the area around her eyes was purple. They'd have to put pads over her eyes when she was sleeping. And she kept sweating. She'd be soaking wet and look as though she was in so much pain.

They said she doesn't feel pain, but I wondered if they really knew.

John was angry at Karen's fate, and his own. Because he couldn't hold back his feelings without becoming physically ill, he would challenge Julie about her religion.

"How can you still believe in God?" he shouted one night, after visiting the hospital. "How can you still love God when he's done this to Karen?"

Then he stormed out of the house, because he didn't want to listen to any answers.

Fortunately John had a good friend, a young priest

named Father Joe Fortuna. The priest would drop in at
the Quinlan house in the evenings and sit with John.
They'd have a couple of beers, and then they'd talk. Sometimes Julie could hear them laughing.

They never discussed religion. John refused to talk
about it.

By mid-June, life at home was scarcely bearable for Julie:

—Everyone was terribly touchy. As a family, I suppose
we'd never been closer, but it was sometimes an abra-
sive closeness. Almost the kind of relationship prisoners
must have, sharing the same cell.

We had stopped going anywhere, except to our jobs
and the hospital. Mary Ellen and John were out of
school on summer vacation, and they mostly just hung
around the house, not wanting to talk to "outsiders."
Friends would invite us to dinner, but after a few tries,
it became too much of an ordeal.

We even stopped going to mass at Our Lady of the
Lake because our dear friends would come up and of
course they would hug and kiss us and ask about Karen,
and my eyes would fill up. Joe wouldn't cry, but he
would withdraw even more. It was too draining, to face
the people we love and not know what to say, because
there really was nothing to say. We went to mass at
the little chapel at the hospital, where almost nobody
knew us.

Father Tom went away for a short vacation, and I
knew Joe needed to talk to other people, to keep him
from withdrawing even further. So I called our very
dear friend Father Fred Lawrence from Sterling, and I
asked him to visit Karen and then go to dinner with us.
He was a comfort to Joe. And later, when Father Tom
came back, he and some of the men at the church got
together and they would drive down to the hospital
some evenings as a group, so they could sit and talk
with Joe. Then they'd talk him into going out for a cup
of coffee on the way home. He desperately needed com-
panionship. We all did. Nothing was the same any
more. We couldn't go out, and nobody came in.

Even my mother and father didn't come to see us.
Karen was their favorite. They're both in their eighties,
and she used to drive them anywhere—anywhere they

wanted to go. She'd bring her friends over to their little apartment, and even have teen-age parties there. My mother said, "I don't want to go into your house any more. It's so quiet. I don't like it, without Karen."

One day my mother said something else which I found terribly sad. My brother's daughter, Debbie, is fifteen years old, and Karen always took *her* places, too. Karen bought Debbie clothes, and gave her advice, and was like an older sister. Debbie idolized Karen.

When Debbie was about six, Karen had taught her how to whistle, and Debbie became a real little expert at it. She could whistle perhaps better now than Karen could.

I cried when Mama phoned me one day and said, "Debbie just told me that she is never going to whistle again."

First Mary Ellen, and then John, came to the gradual realization that their sister's coma was irreversible.

Drs. Morse and Javed had both made it clear—without using the cruel word "hopeless"—that Karen's chances of returning to a state of cognizance were nonexistent.

When their young minds absorbed the futility of medicine's effort to restore and revive Karen, and as they watched her body growing daily more misshapen and rigid, Mary Ellen and John agreed with their mother and Father Tom. That she should be allowed to die in peace.

Julie warned the children to be careful. "We must never talk about how we feel, in front of Dad," she said. "He still hasn't accepted this. He is in another world."

Chapter 9

Melancholia imposes itself in different forms upon the living who are forced to watch the slow dying of a loved one.

For fifty-year-old Joseph Quinlan, it took the shape of visions—Karen awakening, her arms, her legs straight and firm as always, looking about astonished, rising, racing out of the hospital. Then, transformed into a child by his daydream, Karen would plunge into the lake and swim—free. Karen free again, that was his vision. St. Clare's Hospital had become a prison and he knew that one day she would leave it.

Four times each day, he would visit the animated shell of his daughter, and then the rest of the day was a vacuum. Places, too, the job, the house, they all seemed empty and quiet.

—I believed in miracles. I could hear people all around me saying that Karen might never recover, and I knew they were wrong. I thought what they were saying was obscene. I couldn't bear talking to them, and I tried not to listen to them.

I really thought that God loved me so much that He wouldn't let anything happen to her. And I knew Karen. She was always so strong and so determined, if anybody could come out of this, it was her.

Every day I'd walk into the kitchen and see those stairs going up to her room, and I could visualize her leaping off that fourth step and swinging herself down into the kitchen with that loud whoop of hers. I could hear Julie yell, "Karen, you're going to break your neck!" And now it was so quiet in the house. I wanted to hear some laughter again. But if anybody laughed, I resented it. I know that was illogical, but I couldn't help it.

I honestly felt she'd come back okay. We had so many things happen over the years—the time Mary Ellen went into coma after the appendectomy, and the time Julie had the lumps on her breast—and all I had to do was pray to God, and everything came out just beautiful. I was sure this would happen again, because Karen is so strong, and God is so good.

When I visited the hospital, I kept looking for hopeful signs. I was going to St. Clare's four times a day—in the morning on the way to work, at lunch hour, after work at five, and then again with Julie after supper. But Dr. Morse became cross with me one day. He said, "Well listen, Joe, how do you think it makes us feel when you come here all the time. The nurses see you coming from the window upstairs every single morning, at lunchtime, and then again at night and then back with your wife. It makes us feel terrible," Morse says. "Everybody feels bad that they can't do anything—but seeing you, it makes it even worse."

After he told me that a couple of times, I could see he was getting nervous about it. And I knew the visiting hours in Intensive Care are short, maybe five minutes every odd hour. So if they ever wanted to really enforce the rules, they could cut my visits way back. After that, I figured I'd better forget about the twelve noon visit, which was no good for my stomach anyway —grabbing a quick sandwich and eating it in the car on the way over from the office. So I cut out that visit from the schedule. But it didn't help my stomach. I felt worse when I didn't see her.

It's hard to explain but—maybe she's unconscious and doesn't recognize anybody, maybe it's even irreversible, as they say. But she's still our daughter, and as long as she's breathing I'll always want to see her as much as I can.

Julie tried to cling to stability by concentrating fiercely on the task of keeping her family, particularly her husband, from becoming so emotionally and physically ill that they could no longer function.

—I felt I was walking on eggs. Or walking a tightrope without a balance pole. I didn't dare make a false step or we'd all fall apart. By the end of June, each of us had lost weight. I'd lost only five pounds, but Mary Ellen had dropped fifteen. And John could never sit through a whole meal because something about Karen would inevitably come into the conversation, as hard as we tried to think of other things to talk about. Just the mention of her, and John would have to leave the table.

But the worst was poor Joe. He had built up his wall of fantasy, where he was absolutely certain Karen would come out of the coma and be all right. I was so afraid that if I said the wrong thing—I really didn't know what would happen. He was withdrawn and irritable. It was as though he was fighting me and the children, and didn't care about anyone except Karen.

Joe has always been a very good father. His whole life revolves around his family and his church. He has never had "a night out with the boys." Whatever he did, it's always been with the children and me in mind.

When Karen was young, he bought some property in the Poconos because Joe wanted her to be able to run free in that wonderful mountain air, and he felt one day the children could build a home on it. Now it seemed all he cared about was Karen, and this was not healthy because he was cutting the rest of us out of his life, almost as though we didn't exist. This left him alone with just one child. One child who couldn't talk to him, because she was dying. I know him so well. Joe is very quiet, a loving and gentle man. And I was terribly afraid that if Karen died, and she could at any time, then that would be the end of Joe, too.

But none of us dared talk to him about it. He was absolutely single-minded.

Even though he was seeing Karen four times a day, he would meet me at the door after I had visited the hospital without him, and he'd always ask the same questions: "How is she? Did you talk to her? Did she recognize you?"

It was unreal. I thought if he asked me those questions one more time, I would go out of my mind.

Yet I always answered. "Yes, I talked to her, Joe. No, there was no recognition. There's no change."

We had to play his game. We were afraid of what would happen to him if we didn't.

The nurses were concerned about him, too. One of them is an old friend from our neighborhood who had known Karen and, of course, us, for many years. One night she stopped by the house to talk to Joe—not as a nurse, but as a friend.

She came in and we all sat having tea, as though it were purely a social call. Then she described Karen's condition, and tried to convey to Joe how hopeless it was—how it wasn't just an ordinary coma. She said, "You must realize, Joe, that Karen's brain is gone. The thinking part of her brain is dead. Those movements she makes are just primitive reflexes." She said the most humane thing we could do would be to take the respirator away—because she had known patients who had lived for more than a year on machines like that, and it was a terrible thing to watch.

Joe was completely shocked. He tried not to show it. He was cool, but polite to her.

But after she left, he was angry. He thought she was a hard, cruel woman, to come in and talk to a patient's father that way.

Later, he grew to understand that it was Christian friendship that caused her visit, and that she had the family's interest at heart in talking so frankly.

But that night, he was furious, indignant. And he didn't want any part of what she was telling him.

I depended a great deal for friendship and advice on Father Quinlan, who would often drop by to see me. I asked him, as I had asked Father Tom, about the concept of "extraordinary means"—about removing Karen from the respirator. He helped to reassure me. But my greater strength, to the extent that I still had it, came from Father Tom. Sometimes, I told him, I really felt I should pay his dry-cleaning bills—for all those tears that rumpled the shoulders of his black jackets.

One day, I had a new idea and I asked Father Tom what he thought of it.

"You know," I said, "we have never bought a family plot in a cemetery. I was wondering if I should approach Joe and suggest—without mentioning Karen—

that maybe we should go to the Gate of Heaven Cemetery and buy a family plot. Do you think that might turn his mind a little bit toward reality? Or will it just make him angry?"

Father Tom thought the suggestion was about as transparent as a windowpane, but he believed I should try it anyway. Joe was so distracted that whatever I said to him seemed to go right over his head anyway, and Father Tom felt that maybe, since this involved a benefit for the whole family, he might consider it.

So that night I put my suggestion to Joe, and he said, "Yes, I think a family plot might be a good idea."

I was really quite surprised, and extremely relieved. I really couldn't imagine that he would go to the cemetery, if he wasn't facing up to at least a little part of the truth.

Joe said we would go to the cemetery the following Saturday.

But when Saturday morning came, he changed his mind and refused to go after all. He didn't try to give me any explanation. All he said was, "We'll go another day. It can wait."

Karen's eyes were moving very rapidly now when she was in her "wake cycle," and one day Joe became excited because he thought her eyes had focused on him.

At approximately the same time, one of the nurses spread open her hand in front of Karen's face, and then moved her hand to one side. Karen's eyes followed the motion.

Joe seized upon this as a sign that she was coming out of the coma. He began experimenting. He held his hand in the direction of Karen's vision, about four feet in front of her eyes. Then slowly, he moved his hand forward, right down to her nose.

"Her eyes didn't change at all," he said, in the weariest voice I have ever heard. "When I moved my hand, her eyes just stared right through it. She really can't see."

That was a bad night for Joe, but the next day he was right back where he had been before, searching desperately for clues that would give him hope.

When Karen would open her mouth in one of those grimaces, Joe would try to interpret it as an effort to speak to him. Dr. Morse continuously told him, "Just don't get your hopes up. These are all instinctive movements, just a pattern of stereotyped reflexes." But Joe still refused to accept that.

One morning in mid-June, Joe Quinlan confronted Dr. Morse about another change he thought he perceived in Karen, and Dr. Morse stopped abruptly, turned to Joe, and said, "What can I tell you?" He appeared impatient. "You're looking for a miracle, Joe. Even if God did make a miracle, and Karen came out of this coma, her brain damage is so extensive that she would spend the rest of her life in an institution."

Joe stood staring at the doctor, frozen. It was obvious that the statement had cut deeply into his dream.

He didn't speak. Slowly he turned away from the physician and walked down the corridor, seeing nothing, hearing nothing but his own thoughts:

—All the way home in the car, I kept thinking about what Dr. Morse said to me, regarding my wanting a miracle.

And I remember crying aloud, "O Lord, is this Your will? If it is, I'll take Karen any way You give her to me. I don't care if she's blind, deformed, retarded, or even if she must spend the rest of her life in an institution. If only she's alive, and it is Your will."

I had difficulty breathing, and I realized that I was shaking. And suddenly I couldn't see out of my eyeglasses. I slowed down on Route 80 and removed my glasses and wiped my eyes dry. Then I was more composed, and I continued to pray—"I'm sorry, Lord, if my prayers have been selfish and I sought only my will, but it's only because I love her so much. I know that You love Karen far more than I do, and that whatever You do will be best for her, and for all of us. I trust in Your love and mercy."

There were tears streaming down my face as I turned into our driveway and I cried out, "Lord, let Your will be done. In this as in all things."

I sat for a few minutes in the car then, waiting until I felt calm enough to walk into the house.

I didn't want the family to see I had been crying.

Joe Quinlan's certainty of Karen's recovery had begun to falter that night. Still he was not yet ready to give up. He had an idea:

—I thought if we could only get Karen off the respirator so that she could breathe on her own, then maybe I could find a physiotherapy facility which would treat her, and perhaps her arms and legs would be strengthened enough that maybe they would even straighten out, in time.

And if that happened, then I could rent a motor home and the whole family could drive out to Arizona. Julie and I had been in Arizona two years before, and the air is so unbelievably beautiful and clean out there. I was sure it could revive her. Out in Arizona, I thought, Karen will be all right again, and the family will be together and happy.

My imagination ran wild. If she could get special therapy, maybe she could even walk, with leg braces.

I could fix a bed for her in the motor home, right behind the driver's seat, and when we got to Arizona, maybe with a special saddle, Karen could even ride a horse. She would love that. We could ride through the hills together all day—or as long as she felt up to it.

I had spoken with Dr. Javed for some time about trying to wean Karen from the machine—taking her off it for a few minutes at a time to see if she could build up the strength to breathe by herself. I decided to set up a meeting for Julie and me with Javed, because now that seemed like the best thing to do. Instead of listening to all this negative talk, it felt good to be taking some positive action.

I went to a Trailer Sales place I had passed by a few times in Mount Arlington and asked about the price of renting a motor home. Then I figured out how much gas the trip would take, and all that. It would be five hundred dollars for the rental, and I calculated another five hundred for gas, to get out West and back. It was a pretty hefty price, but I could swing it.

I told Julie, and she said she'd call right away and make an appointment with Dr. Javed.

"Arizona," Julie thought. "Fresh air, blue sky. Just one more dream":

—I knew it was only another escape into unreality for Joe. But at least it seemed to be our best opportunity yet to make him face the truth. If he was going to talk to Dr. Javed about weaning Karen, then at last he would have to *listen* to Javed, too. Maybe Javed could make him realize what was really happening to Karen.

I phoned and made an appointment for us to meet the doctor on Friday at the hospital. Then I asked Father Tom if he could arrange to be there at the same time. This might be an opportunity for Father to tell Joe what was on our minds.

When Friday night came, I made an excuse for not going. Said I wasn't up to it. I wanted Joe to be alone with Javed and Father Tom. I thought he'd comprehend the situation more easily without my being there.

Joe looked on this as the big chance. He was convinced Karen could be weaned, and then she'd be free of the hospital and we could take her away from there. He went to that meeting so hopeful.

Later, Father told me what happened at that session.

First, Dr. Javed told Joe that he could attempt to wean Karen off the respirator, but it would involve a slight risk. He said Karen would have to be monitored with great caution and even then there were inherent dangers.

"Are you willing to take the risk?" Javed asked and, without hesitation, Joe said that he was. Then he turned to Father Tom for counsel—wanting to make sure he had said the right thing—and Father reassured him that "sometimes when we love someone we have to take a risk."

So it was arranged that night. Dr. Javed said he would get started with the weaning procedure as soon as possible.

After the meeting, Father Tom and Joe drove to a little place called Paul's Diner to have coffee. While they sat there at the counter, Father Tom saw his opportunity to tell Joe about the Church's approach to our problem. He said, "As a matter of fact, Joe, if this weaning experiment shouldn't work out—if they should take away the respirator and Karen doesn't make it on her own—perhaps that would be a liberating thing. She's really trapped in a body that will no longer function, and if she were liberated, then whatever happened would be in the hands of God. That's the way the Church would feel about it. There would be nothing morally wrong. It might be kinder."

Joe didn't say anything to Father Tom.

If he understood the message, Father told me, he wasn't ready to discuss it.

Early on the morning of May 1975, Dr. Arshad Javed removed the respirator tube from Karen's throat, for several thirty-minute intervals throughout the day—keeping the machine close by, ready for reinsertion the moment the patient experienced difficulty breathing. Two ICU nurses, a respiratory therapist, and two student nurses clustered around Karen's bed, all closely monitoring her breathing pressure with a gauge. Joe and Julie stood in the background, observing.

That day Karen was able to breathe on her own during her "wake cycles." But when she fell asleep, the respirator had to be hurried back into position to assist her.

Her respiratory reflexes seemed to disintegrate.

After visiting Karen and watching the first weaning attempt Julie spent the day with her husband, pursuing the improbable:

—Joe wanted to find a physical therapy institution which would straighten out Karen's body. Preparatory to the trip to Arizona. He thought perhaps we could put her into a different kind of hospital and that with extensive therapy, her muscles could be relaxed, and then re-formed into normal position. We drove to East Orange to see a friend of Joe's, Walt Pavachek. Walt has been repairing Joe's artificial arm for the last thirty years, because he is co-owner of a company that makes these appliances, and he also knew the doctors who are in charge of Kessler and Kim Institutes for physical rehabilitation. Joe thought maybe Walt could help him get Karen admitted to those places—and Walt really tried. He spoke to the directors of both facilities that day, but they had to say no. They couldn't take Karen. They had very few inpatients to begin with, and they certainly didn't have any way of accepting patients who needed a respirator. There was just no way. Joe was terribly discouraged, and there was nothing I could do to help. When we drove back to the hospital, the nurses told us that Karen was off the respirator that day for periods of one-half hour off, then one-half hour back on, for a total period of approximately eight hours.

That was encouraging.

But the next day, Karen was exhausted, apparently as a result of the weaning attempts. They tried to take her off again, for a short time, but she didn't respond well enough, so they attached the respirator again and she slept most of the day.

That meant that there was no chance ever that Kim or Kessler Institutes could take Karen in, if she couldn't be weaned.

My husband was hurt. He was disappointed. It was hard to accept the fact that his own daughter was lying in that bed helpless when, in his mind, she could be treated. And nobody wanted to take her in.

He called Mrs. Cors, the social worker at St. Clare's, and asked—almost begged her—to find another physical therapy facility, anywhere in New Jersey, that would take Karen. He wanted her out of St. Clare's.

Following the second day's attempt to remove the respirator from Karen, she went through a day in which the "wake cycles," which typically occurred every three hours, were absent. She lay in a deep sleep for most of the next twenty-four hours.

The hospital "medical notes" for June 1, 1975, record Dr. Javed's scrawled assessment of the patient:

—No change in general condition.
Does not tolerate periods of spontaneous breathing well.
There is no hope of weaning her off the MA-1.

J—

On June 2, the day following the vain attempt to remove respiratory sustenance from Karen Quinlan, the patient was transferred from the center bed in the Intensive Care Unit to another location. She was placed in a bed at the far edge of the large room, apart from the hub of emergency activity. Her small cubicle was curtained off.

To Joe, the sight of Karen suddenly shunted aside, into the corner, was emotionally disquieting.

—It was just as though they were saying, "We cannot do anything more for her now, except merely sustain her."

I demanded to see Dr. Morse, and I asked him why they had moved her.

He said it was because she didn't need the heart monitor any longer. They'd had her in the center of the room because of that machine, and now she didn't need it because her heart was strong.

I said, "Can't we move her to a private room then?" But Morse said no, that was impossible, as long as she was on the respirator. That seemed to be the big thing. She couldn't be alone, on the respirator.

I thought I was in shock. But I was hurt more than anything else. Maybe she can't see or hear what's going on. Maybe there's nothing they can do for her any more, but she's still our daughter. I was hurt, for Karen.

St. Clare's social worker, Mrs. Cors, made the following notations in her records for this period of time in the matter of Karen Ann Quinlan:

MAY 28: Called local Medicaid office to ask them for information on N.J. facility for long term care of pt.

MAY 30: Medicaid called. Their only suggestions were Greystone [State Hospital] or Neuro-Psychiatric Institute.

JUNE 2: Advised physicians of Medicaid recommendation. Called Greystone to discuss pt. They would care for her in the clinic building.

JUNE 4: Spoke to pt.'s mother about possible transfer of pt. Would like to speak to Mr. Quinlan.

JUNE 5: Mr. Quinlan in office—long talk about

Medicaid recommendation for pt.'s condition. Does not want to consider Greystone.

Joe Quinlan not only did not want to consider a transfer to Greystone, he was outraged that the hospital would suggest such a move.

—That was the most disturbing development that Julie and I could imagine. There were constant front-page stories in all the local papers about the treatment of patients, alleging physical abuse! And this was a state mental institution.

The thought of Karen being in there was more than we could tolerate.

I told Mrs. Cors that a move to Greystone was inconceivable to me. I think she understood.

Mrs. Cors did understand. Her notes continued.

JUNE 9: After conference with physician, Kim and Kessler will be contacted for their opinion on admitting pt. If denied, the Greystone commitment form will be completed. Called Kim Institute—they do have a respirator, but have not had a patient admitted in that condition. [Also] Do not accept assignment of Medicaid.

JUNE 11: Conference with Assistant Administrator [Mrs. Rovinski] to appraise her of situation.

JUNE 12: Dr. Morse spoke to Dr. Sullivan at Kessler Institute. They cannot take pt.

JUNE 13: Called State Dept. of Health. Spoke to a Dr. Erganian who checked available State or other facilities. Her only suggestion was the new large ICU at Englewood Hospital. Called NPI [Neurological and Psychiatric Institute] in Princeton. Dr. Morse spoke to Dr. Carnecchia there. Explained pt.'s condition and asked if the Institute could care for her. They will review the case and call us Monday.

Called the local Medicaid office to advise them of the improper lead they had given concerning Greystone. They requested a summary of this case and the lack of a facility in the state of New Jersey, so they can refer it to their central office in Trenton.

JUNE 18: Again spoke to physician at NPI. They do

not have the proper equipment or skilled personnel to care for pt. Hopefully when they complete the change-over to a neurological facility they will be able to provide this service.

Conference with pt.'s father. Brought him up to date on efforts made to find a proper facility for pt. to be transferred to.

JULY 8: Called Morris View, the Morris County Nursing Home. They do not have a respirator, and do not plan to get one.

They feel patient belongs in an acute hospital. Also questions how much longer these efforts should continue.

How long these efforts should continue . . . Julie Quinlan had made the postulation nearly two months earlier.

Now it was being confronted by others involved in the lingering on of Karen.

It was even being questioned by the pulmonary internist in charge of the patient's respiration.

Dr. Arshad Javed wrote, in his hospital notes for July 10, 1975:

—Will discuss the case with family on 7/11. Respiratory status is stable, however neurologically situation is hopeless.

One must question the wisdom of continuing intensive respiratory care in this situation.

J—

The Quinlans never saw Dr. Javed's hospital notes.

However, true to his recorded word, he called the family together for an informal conference at St. Clare's on July 11.

Mary Ellen asked if she could attend the meeting with her parents:

—I wanted to be along because Mother and I were so worried about my father—about his still having too much hope. And that's what Mother and I thought the meeting was going to be about. Another chance to more or less convince my father to face the truth.

When we got to the hospital, we found that Dr.

Morse had an emergency in Dover, so he would be very late. But Dr. Javed was there and a nurse from ICU, and we sat around and talked. Dr. Javed said that the only thing to do was to take Karen off the respirator. He repeated this quite a few times for my father's benefit. But Dad still didn't seem to believe what he was hearing. He still wasn't listening to this.

Finally, Dr. Morse came in. He didn't seem to know what the purpose of the meeting was, and he thought it had been called because Dad was so upset about the hospital attempting to transfer Karen to Greystone. So right at the beginning, Morse became angry. He started saying, "Now, you're being extremely selfish, Mr. Quinlan. Do you think it's really fair that we keep your daughter here in Intensive Care under the circumstances, when we need those beds for emergency care and not for chronic cases like Karen's?"

All the other times we'd seen him, Morse always called Dad "Joe," and was very friendly. But this night he seemed very irritable, until, a little later, when the nurse and Mom told him—in no uncertain terms—that what we were discussing was not where to put Karen, but what condition she was in.

When he realized that, then Dr. Morse calmed down and listened. And finally he looked right at my father and said he didn't think we should do anything yet— like removing the respirator.

"We won't do anything until you agree, Joe," he said.

The meeting ended up, with Morse saying, "I will do whatever you decide as a family."

He was looking right at Dad, and he said, "But we won't do anything until you make the decision yourself, Joe."

The accumulated evidence of hopelessness had become too much to resist any longer. That night as he lay in bed, staring at the ceiling dimly outlined by a night light, Joseph Quinlan discarded his illusions, one by one:

—Karen was never going to be alive again, as I had known her. I had to accept that.

Even if she woke up, she would not be able to swim or drive her car or do anything she loves.

Arizona is impossible because they won't take her off the machine.

She has permanent brain damage, and she is going to die.

I didn't know why this could happen, but I thought again—it is God's will. He has a plan for everything, so there had to be a reason. You can fight doctors, and you can fight nature and even fate, and you can say all of them, every one of them, is dead wrong. But you can't fight God's will, and as I tried to sleep, I knew what I was meant to do.

Maybe it sounds strange to feel that relief and comfort can come of realizing that—that she could never recover—then the right thing to do became as clear as day. I felt almost at peace for the first time in all those weeks, and I was able to sleep.

The following morning, Saturday, July 12, Joe said to his wife, "We can go to the cemetery today and pick out that plot."

Julie didn't know how to react. Did it mean that he finally understood the truth; or was he just remembering that Saturday when he had backed down—just fulfilling a commitment to her?

"That's good, honey," Julie said tentatively. "I think it's something we really should do."

"Yes," Joe said. "And I've made an appointment this afternoon to talk to Father Tom."

That was the clue Julie needed. She walked over to her husband and reached her arms around his waist—causing him almost to spill the cup of coffee he now carefully slid onto the breakfast table behind him—and she put her head on his shoulder and began to cry.

Looking back, Joe remembers a growing feeling of wonder—"not that Julie was crying, because Julie can cry when she's happy or when she's sad."

—But this time, something about her made me know that this was different. I said, "I'm sorry, honey, I finally figured out what you and Father Tom were telling me," and then I sat her down at the table and we talked it all out.

That's when I found out that Julie was about at the

end of her rope, from worrying about me. Not just
Karen, she had to worry about me, too. And Mary
Ellen and John came in, and we all talked it over, and
that's the first time I learned that the children had
agreed, too—that they had decided a long time before
that Karen would never want to be kept alive the way
she was. But they were afraid to talk to me because I
might be hurt, or take it the wrong way.

It all came clear to me that morning, what they'd
been through, and what we should do now.

The only thing that bothered me, and it bothered me
terribly, was the knowledge that everybody else had
come to this decision long before me, and I was the
holdout.

That meant that now I had the final say. And that,
to me, was an awful responsibility. Being the final judge.
I knew I really needed to talk to Father Tom.

They drove to the hospital to see Karen, before going on
to the cemetery. Karen was restless that morning, perspiring profusely, her temperature elevated to 100°. The
nurses had positioned a foam rubber pad under her left
hip upon which was an angry red rash. Her eyes stared
at the white curtain beside her bed.

Joe felt a sudden impetus to leave.

—It became a very strong necessity for me, at that
particular moment, to do something positive. For such
a long time I had done nothing except cause everyone
a lot of worry, and now I needed to take some positive
action.

I pulled Julie away, and we drove to the Gates of
Heaven Cemetery and bought a plot. Then we came
home, had a quick lunch, and I took off again for the
rectory to see Father Tom.

He could see the shape I was in, and he led me out
on the porch, and as we sat there, I told him how I
felt—that everybody had made this decision quite long
before me, and I'm the last holdout.

"All of a sudden," I said, "I have the final say and
this decision bothers me something terrible. Am I playing God?"

Father Tom made it easier.

"Don't worry that you're making a decision in Karen's death," he said. "God has made the decision that she's going to die. You're just agreeing with God's decision, that's all."

That made everything clear. I drove home and, for the first time in all those weeks, Julie and Mary Ellen and John and I sat down at dinner and talked together, as a family. The resentments that had built up were all broken down, and we could be honest with each other. We talked about how Karen didn't want to be kept alive on machines and how this would be her wish. We were all so relieved, to have reached a decision.

We thought the doctors would be relieved, too.

Julie said that Morse and Javed had been really very worried about me. They were afraid I was losing touch with reality. That night I felt very warm toward those two men. I had been so annoyed with them, because they wouldn't offer me any hope, but now I could see that they were just trying to make me face the facts.

I told Julie, "I didn't realize what I was putting everybody through."

And that night, when we went back to the hospital, Karen was quieter than she had been in the morning. Her fever had gone down, and she was not thrashing about. Like us, she seemed at peace.

That night Mary Ellen said something I'll always remember. Mary Ellen hated that respirator because it looked like it was causing her sister so much pain.

"It just seems like such a cold machine," she said. "And it seems to be more alive than Karen is."

Chapter 10

Julie waited until Monday to call the hospital. And when she did, she spoke to Father Paschal Caccavalle, the chaplain of St. Clare's—known to friends as Father Pat.

—Father Pat knew what we'd been going through. He knew all about the Church's position on "extraordinary means" and had talked to me about it over the weeks, along with Father Tom and Father Quinlan. When I told him that Joe had come to feel as we all did, that the respirator should be removed, he was relieved.

I asked him if we could have a meeting with the doctors, to tell them of our family position, and he said he would try to arrange it as soon as possible. "And I want to be there," Father Pat said. I guess he was afraid Joe might still be wavering, but he needn't have worried about that. Once Joe made up his mind, he never had a moment's doubt that Karen should be returned to a natural state.

The first date Father Pat could arrange with both doctors was Wednesday, July 31. That was a very long time away. More than two weeks. But we were not impatient now. The indecision had been devastating, but now a period of relative tranquillity was almost necessary. Later, looking back on it, I thought of this period as the eye of the storm.

We finally met at 6:30 P.M. on July 31.

It was Father Pat, Dr. Morse, Joe and I, and Mary Ellen.

All of us sat around a long table in a conference room. Everybody had something to say at the meeting. And we spoke more or less in the order in which we were seated at the table. I remember it started with Father Pat.

He opened with a short statement, quoting from the 1957 speech of Pope Pius XII about their being no moral obligation to use modern devices such as respirators to maintain life, if there was no hope for recovery.

Dr. Morse was seated on Father Pat's left, and he was the next to speak. He said that, from a neurological point of view, Karen's case was hopeless. There was nothing in the world he could do for her, except to sustain her physically. Her brain damage, he said, was extensive and irreversible.

It was Joe's turn, and he stated our position.

"Since the doctors can't help Karen, and they are convinced she is going to die," he said in a low voice I could scarcely hear, "it is our decision and wish that

she be removed from the respirator and be returned
to a natural state."

Mary Ellen was next. She said that she had felt for
some time that "this would be the right thing to do."

Then I agreed, adding that "knowing Karen we all
realize that she would never want to be kept alive in
this way. She would agree with what we are deciding
tonight."

Dr. Morse stood up then, and he put his hand on
Joe's shoulder, and said sympathetically, "I think you've
made the right decision."

Father Pat asked us to wait while one of the nurses
from Intensive Care went to the hospital administrative
offices to get a paper for us to sign, which would in effect authorize the doctors and the hospital to discontinue the respirator for Karen. We waited for perhaps
twenty minutes, and she came back with this authorization. She and another nurse read it over, without showing it to us, and sent the paper back for some correc-
tions. It wasn't satisfactory—apparently the wording
was wrong, they said. A few minutes later, they
came back with another paper and handed it to us. It
read:

SAINT CLARE'S HOSPITAL
DENVILLE, NEW JERSEY 07834
We hereby authorize and direct Doctor Morse to
discontinue all extraordinary measures, including the
use of a Respirator, for our daughter Karen Quinlan.

We acknowledge that the above named physician has
thoroughly discussed the above with us and that the
consequences have been fully explained to us. Therefore, we hereby RELEASE from any and all liability
the above named physician, associates and assistants of
his choice, Saint Clare's Hospital and its agents and
employees.

We understand further that this RELEASE shall be
binding upon her heirs, executors, administrators and
assigns.

It was a very official statement, and when Joe and
I signed it there was a bit of a feeling of relief. That it
was finally done.

Two nurses, Goldea Bethune and Margaret Liskorn, signed the paper as witnesses.

When we left the hospital that night, all I could think was "Karen's ordeal is almost over. And so is ours."

But it had just begun.

At 10:30 A.M. the next day, Thursday, August 1, Dr. Morse telephoned Joe at his office.

—Morse sounded very friendly and in good spirits, and he said to me, "Joe, I have a moral problem about what we agreed on last night. I feel that I have to consult someone else and see how *he* feels about it. I think I know what he's going to say, but I'd like to consult him anyway. I think it will help me."

I hadn't thought much about Dr. Morse having any moral problem with the decision. I guess I'd been busy thinking about my own problem. But I could understand, when he mentioned it. Doctors are trained to save lives no matter what the circumstances are, and I supposed maybe it *was* a little difficult for him to look at the situation from a purely compassionate point of view.

I asked who the consultant was, and he said it was a doctor who had been his professor, a man for whom he had the highest respect. [The consultant was Dr. Morris Bender of New York's Mount Sinai Hospital.]

Morse said he wanted to see the other physician, and he would get back to me on Monday. I didn't like that.

"Can't you see the doctor on Friday, and then we'll know by Saturday?" I asked.

So Morse said, "All right. I'll call him tomorrow and see what he says, and I'll let you know."

The way he said it, I felt that our decision would be carried out now no matter what this consultant would say. I wasn't worried. Dr. Morse is a Catholic, and he had talked to Father Pat. I thought he would resolve the "moral problem" in his own heart, the same way that I had.

But the next day, that Friday, he called me again at my office. And this time, Morse's tone of voice was totally different. He didn't sound friendly, he sounded abrupt.

He said he had spoken to this Dr. Bender, and that he had decided he would not remove the respirator. He was very definite about it.

"Mr. Quinlan," he said—and that was odd, because he always called me Joe—"I find that I will not do it. And I have informed the administrators that I will not do it."

I was shocked, and I was bewildered.

"I don't understand," I told him. "What did this other doctor say? Why should you have a sudden change of heart now?"

He didn't answer that. He only said, "I am sorry but I will not do it." Then he hung up.

I was frantic. What was going on here? All along I hoped Karen would recover, and Morse kept saying, "Don't get your hopes up." He was even annoyed with me when I insisted she was going to get well. Then when I finally accepted that she would die, and we signed that paper, he told me we'd made the right decision. And now he'd just turned completely around. Even acted annoyed with me.

I called Julie and told her what had happened and that I was going to the hospital right after work and try to find out what was going on.

"I'm coming too," she said. "I'll meet you."

As soon as we arrived at St. Clare's, we asked to see Father Pat, and told him what Morse had said. He was as shocked as we were, and immediately took us over to a conference room. From there, he picked up a phone and tried to call Kenneth Courey, who is the administrator of the hospital.

Courey was in a meeting, so then he tried to contact Mrs. Josephine Rovinski. She was the assistant administrator. But she was at a meeting, too.

Apparently her secretary asked Father Pat if it was important, because we could see him getting a little excited, and he said on the phone. "Yes. I would say it's important. I'd say it's extremely important. We have a family here whose child has been on a respirator for more than one hundred days, and there was an agreement between them and the doctors and the hospital for the removal of the respirator. And now, all of a sudden, the hospital and the doctors refuse to honor that agreement."

Then Father said firmly, "The family wants to meet with the administrators here. Tonight. And they have every right to."

That brought action. Not the meeting we wanted, but at least it brought the immediate attention of Mrs. Rovinski.

She apparently got out of her meeting and came to the conference room and took Julie and me to the employee's cafeteria for a cup of coffee. She was very nice, very sympathetic, and she said, "You'll have to have patience with us, Mr. Quinlan, because at St. Clare's we've never done this before."

Julie and I looked at each other, and for the first time it began to dawn on us that we might be getting involved in a matter of hospital policy. We started to realize, just a little bit, that this was not just a decision between us and Dr. Morse, but something bigger and more complicated.

"Well," I said to Mrs. Rovinski, "we signed an authorization. It was made out by this hospital. It was very official."

"I know," she said, "but it was the first time that has ever been done here, at St. Clare's. We'll set up a meeting, and discuss it. But you'll have to be a little patient."

Mrs. Rovinski was able to schedule the meeting for the following morning [Saturday, August 3, 1975].

We came [early] so we could visit Karen for a while, and then about 9:45 Julie asked the nurses for directions to the administrative offices. We'd never had occasion to go into that area of the hospital before. When we got to the right corridor, Mrs. Rovinski met us and ushered us right into the office of the administrator, Mr. Courey.

I had calmed down a lot and I really felt pretty good when I got into Courey's office because everyone was very friendly—shaking hands, smiling. I thought maybe we'd just imagined that we were going to have a problem here. It was just complete cordiality all around.

There were a lot of people at that meeting. Morse was standing against a wall on one side of the office, and Mr. Courey, Mrs. Rovinski, Father Pat, and Julie and I were seated in chairs around this cozy sort of office. We'd never met Mr. Courey until that day. I thought he was a bit strait-laced—a sort of stiff and sober man—but you expect that from the head of a hospital like St. Clare's.

He introduced us to the other man in the room whom we'd never seen before. His name was Theodore Einhorn, a fellow in his early forties, I'd say. We didn't know exactly what his job was until the meeting had been under way for a couple of minutes. Then we found out—in no uncertain terms—that he was going to be an extremely important person in our lives.

It was all very casual and friendly up to this point. But as soon as the meeting started, then everything and everyone changed.

Courey started it off with a few words. He said the hospital wanted to co-operate with us, and to honor our request. "But we have run into some legal complications," he said.

Then he introduced Mr. Einhorn—as the attorney for St. Clare's Hospital. And he asked the lawyer to take over the meeting. Now, all of a sudden, Julie and I learned that the doctors and St. Clare's were going to be very legal about everything.

This Mr. Einhorn said, "Mr. and Mrs. Quinlan, I have recommended that Dr. Morse and St. Clare's Hospital not honor your wishes. There are legal reasons for this. You, Mr. Quinlan, are not Karen's legal guardian —and not even responsible for her, since she is of age: twenty-one.

"Therefore, you have no right to recommend this action, the removal of the respirator. You will have to go to court and have a judge appoint you as your daughter's legal guardian, and then come back and make your request again."

This was something that had never occurred to me. Still, it didn't sound too difficult.

"All right," I said. "If I become Karen's legal guardian, then will you honor our request?"

Einhorn stared at me. I felt coldly. He said, "I don't know."

That's when the whole bottom fell through. I heard Julie gasp. She was sitting beside me, and she suddenly leaned forward, fighting tears, and I could feel almost physically the outrage she was trying to suppress. Then, in a strained voice that didn't sound like her at all, she started crying, "How can you say that—that we're not responsible? All along, we've been signing permission slips for all the tests you took, all the surgery, every little thing you ever did for Karen. You've asked us to sign papers before you'd do it. Why is it now, all of a sudden, our permission isn't good enough?"

Einhorn said, slowly and distinctly, "The permissions you signed were for lifesaving procedures. However, now you want to go the other way—"

Julie broke down. She was sobbing now. Somehow she managed to push back her chair and stand up, and stumble out of the room. I didn't know what to do. Father Pat got up quickly and whispered to me, "Don't worry, she'll be all right. I'll be with her—you stay with it." Then he rushed after Julie.

So I stayed there, feeling like I was on the front, with the whole army against me.

I tried to compose myself. I looked over at Morse, leaning against the wall. But he was staring down at the floor.

Finally, knowing I had lost the battle but feeling I had to have one more try at making some sense out of this strange new attitude of the hospital, I said to Einhorn:

"You cannot give me any assurance that you will honor our request, if I become appointed legal guardian?"

"We may or we may not," he said. "You will have to go to court, in any event. That's the first step."

When he said that, it was like a bolt of lightning struck. I couldn't just go to court and be appointed guardian. I'd have to find a lawyer so that, once I was appointed guardian, they would have to honor our request. It wasn't a simple thing any more. It wasn't a medical issue. It wasn't a moral issue. Now it was to be all legalities.

I stood up then, feeling intensely exhausted, and I said, "All right." I may even, out of habit, out of an old built-in respect for all this medical authority in the room, have said "Thank you." I don't really remember.

All I was sure of, as we left the hospital that night, was that now I'd have to find an attorney. I'd never

needed a lawyer before, but I knew that was the only
hope we had.

What I didn't know is that once you go to court,
your legal problem becomes a matter of public record.
Once you go to court, the whole world knows about
your problem.

Dr. Robert Morse apparently sensed what it could mean if
Joe Quinlan hired his own lawyer: interference in the
traditionally private doctor-patient relationship. Doctors
feel medicine and law should be as mutually exclusive as
religion and education.

Immediately following the tense meeting at the administrator's office, Morse began a personal campaign to
discourage the intrusion of a legal mind, functioning in the
Quinlans' behalf.

He would corner Joe at the hospital.

—And he would be extremely friendly, and unusually
sympathetic, considering what had happened. He'd say,
"Joe, I don't like the idea of your hiring an attorney,"
Morse would say. "I think that would be extremely unfortunate. If you get a lawyer in on this case, everything will become very strained."

I would say that I didn't see how I had any alternative, since the hospital had their own lawyer, and since
that lawyer, Einhorn, had told me in no uncertain
terms what I had to do.

I waited a few days, and then I asked a friend,
Robert McIlwain, a manager at my plant, if he knew
of a good attorney I could hire. Right away he went
over to speak to our corporate legal department.

Their suggestion was to contact the Legal Aid Society. Maybe Legal Aid couldn't help me directly, but
they could steer me to the right sort of man to handle
a guardianship proceeding.

So on Wednesday afternoon [August 6] I took off
from work early and drove to the Legal Aid office in
Morristown.

The Morristown, New Jersey, Legal Aid office was in the
wrong district for a resident of Landing. Joe was informed

that a new branch had opened in Dover, eight miles to the west, toward home.

It was already nearly five by the time he backtracked to Dover, and Joe rushed into the office and asked the receptionist if it was too late to consult one of the attorneys.

She pulled out a form and began asking questions: name, address, place of employment. When she inquired about his salary, and Joe answered, the girl laid down her pencil and said, "Well, I'm sorry, Mr. Quinlan. You would never qualify for Legal Aid."

She began to clear the papers off her desk. Joe reached out his hand toward her. "Wait a minute—please." He couldn't lose her attention yet. "I'll need legal aid for my daughter. It's not for me, it's my daughter. She's unemployed."

The receptionist was listening again, and Joe found himself telling her that he had a daughter, Karen, and that she was unconscious.

—"And I need to be appointed her legal guardian," I said, talking very fast, because there was a clock on the wall and I could see it was about three minutes after five. I said, "All along, you see, I've served as my daughter's legal representative—for Social Security, and Medicaid, and so forth. But now I have to be made her guardian, and I wondered, isn't it possible that my daughter might qualify for Legal Aid? I mean, since she is helpless? Since she is incompetent?"

The receptionist sat there looking at me, more or less transfixed, probably trying to comprehend what I'd been talking about so fast. Probably nothing like this had ever come up in her work.

Finally she said, "I really don't know. You'll have to ask the attorney that question. If you'll wait just a minute here, I'll find out if he can see you."

That was a relief. At least I had my foot in the door.

The girl picked up the paper she'd been filling out and walked into an office behind her desk. Before she closed the door behind her, I caught a glimpse of a young man behind a desk inside.

A few seconds later, she came back and ushered me into that office and said, "Mr. Quinlan, this is Paul Armstrong. Paul—Joseph Quinlan."

He looked like about twenty, immaculate and clean-cut, with a real young, honest face. He was not like any lawyer I'd ever seen. He pulled up a chair for me, and I looked around the office. There were certificates and degrees framed all over the walls, and the one that hit my eye right away was a diploma from Notre Dame. That really made me feel good. I knew from that, and the way he looked, that everything this man would do would be clean and aboveboard.

He said, "What can I do for you, Mr. Quinlan?" and I poured out the story. When it got complicated, along the line, Paul Armstrong would nod, and ask questions very sympathetically. You could almost see his mind clicking.

Armstrong was thirty and looked like an elongated school-boy from a rich Ivy League preparatory school: wide, innocent blue eyes, a shock of brown hair neatly parted, waving over his forehead, precisely knotted and slim tie tucked inpeccably under his vest. Fresh from ten years in college and two years of private trial practice in Michigan, his immaculate and intellectual presence might have intimidated a modest man like Joe Quinlan except for his charismatic manner and the Notre Dame diploma, juris doctor, 1972.

Armstrong saw Joe staring at the framed diploma.

"Are you Catholic, Mr. Quinlan?"

"Yes."

"I guess it's obvious that I am, too."

Joe Quinlan smiled, shyly, and suddenly Paul felt "a true kindred spirit in this man. Something that went beyond our mutual religious faith. His face was ashen, and he looked as if he may have been suffering from an ulcer." Paul, too, had had an ulcer in his early twenties "while attempting to resolve academic and philosophical problems. And those who have suffered through one know another one when they see it. I knew Mr. Quinlan was suffering, not only spiritually but physically."

As Joe's story came out—about Karen's illness, his wrestling with his faith, the decision to execute her release from the respirator, and the doctors' and hospital's change of heart—Armstrong quickly became engrossed.

"What made the doctor change his mind?" he asked Joe.

"I don't know," Joe replied. "All I know is the hospital lawyer says if I'm appointed Karen's guardian, then they'll consider our request again."

Armstrong was not only emotionally moved, he was intellectually intrigued. He had been studying constitutional law at New York University graduate classes, and almost instantly he realized the gravity of the issue being raised by Joseph Quinlan.

He thought: "This father is here, motivated by love. He and his family have arrived at a courageous stance where they can no longer sit by and watch what is happening to their daughter. For him, it's as simple as that. I felt so much compassion for them, I really had a compelling desire to take the case.

"But legally—constitutionally—I could see this was extremely controversial. Through my studies, I knew that there were diverse opinions within the various state courts regarding the right of privacy—and they were opinions that had never been resolved. I realized that if Mr. Quinlan really were to bring forth a legal plea to discontinue extraordinary means for sustaining his daughter, there would be a quick and sharp reaction. Not only from legal and medical people, but from society in general."

The prospect was awesome and, as Joe kept talking, Armstrong's mind raced. "I wondered if there were sufficient arguments that could be developed, substantial enough to support a case. . . . The First Amendment to the Constitution, which guarantees the free exercise of religion. That would be the first argument. Then, how about the constitutional right of privacy—the right of people to make decisions affecting themselves, in circumstances where there is no danger to society at large? A good possibility. I kept thinking, nebulously at this point, that if this man wanted to press his case, he'd be setting precedents. Decisions like this—they'd always been swept under the rug. His case could evolve legal standards to meet the technological innovations of the age. It was overwhelming, when I thought about it."

But perhaps, the attorney considered, he was getting ahead of himself. Maybe Joe Quinlan, in spite of his compassion for his daughter, didn't want to take the full issue through the courts; maybe it isn't what he wanted at all.

Armstrong said, "Mr. Quinlan, you realize that if you want to become your daughter's guardian, there are two ways of going about it. One is to have yourself appointed guardian by a judge, and then go to the hospital and repeat your request. Another question is—"

Joe didn't let him finish.

"No," he said firmly, "I don't think that would be honest, and I don't think it would do much good. What I'd like is for everything to be open and aboveboard. Can't I ask to be made Karen's guardian for the specific purpose of doing what we think is the right thing? Can't I just tell a judge what has happened and say I need to be appointed my daughter's guardian so that I can authorize the doctors and the hospital, as I said, to remove her respirator and return her to her natural state?"

Joe added, when the lawyer was silent: "I think that would help the doctors, too. They wouldn't have to worry or to feel guilty, if a judge made it all official and legal. If a judge tells our doctor, Dr. Morse, that it's all right to take away the machine, then that is quite different from hearing a man like me tell him he can do it. It will take the doctors off the hook, so to speak."

Armstrong didn't speak for a few minutes. He knew that Quinlan had no concept of the complexities of the case. But obviously he was a man of honor, who wanted to resolve all the questions straightforwardly. He had an utter, simple faith—in the judicial and medical systems.

Finally Paul Armstrong said, "Joe, I think there are substantial constitutional arguments that can be advanced on your behalf." Realizing he had instinctively addressed Quinlan by his first name, he stopped short. "Sorry. You don't mind if I call you Joe?"

"No." For the first time, Joe smiled. "I like it. It makes me feel more comfortable. I'm not accustomed to lawyers."

"All right, Joe. I started to say—if your case does go into court, it's likely to cause some controversy. Maybe a great deal of controversy. The newspapers will report it. There will be public discussion most likely, and I really don't know what the reaction of the public will be."

Joe looked mildly surprised, but didn't speak.

"I'm just wondering," Paul went on, "how you will be able to stand up under that. Can your wife and children tolerate this—being in the public eye? You don't have to answer now, but I think that's something you ought to consider very seriously, and talk to your family about, before you decide to go into a legal action of this kind."

Before Joe could speak, Paul added, "I'm a student of constitutional law, and I know that no one has ever been forced to bring this issue out into the open. There is nothing specifically in the Constitution that deals with whether or not the patient, or the doctor, has the final decision on whether a patient may be allowed to die. That is why I say it could be very controversial."

Joe nodded.

"It will be a struggle—and you might lose. The medical profession is powerful, and they're not going to like an issue like this being taken to the courts. You may very well go through a great deal of anguish, and then lose."

Joe said quietly, "I just want to help my daughter." It was as though the challenge had stiffened his resolve. "Thank you for telling me, but the rest doesn't really matter. If you could see Karen, you would know. I'll just do anything that's necessary to do, to help her."

When Paul Armstrong and Joe Quinlan said good-by, it was 7:45 P.M. The rest of the Legal Aid staff had long ago gone home.

Paul said, "I would like very much to take on your case myself, Joe, but I doubt that it would be possible to do that and still carry on my job here. In any event, give me some time. I'll do some research into the possible arguments and talk to my wife about it, and then I'll get back to you. I'm sure we'll find somebody who can represent you. In the meantime, talk to Mrs. Quinlan and the children and tell them what kind of struggle they can expect. Make sure they're willing to go through with it."

Joe looked at the lawyer and visualized this clean-cut, handsome young fellow standing before a judge.

He thought, "With him on our side, we couldn't ever miss."

"Thanks, Paul," he said, standing up, realizing reluctantly the meeting was ended. "For the first time in three months, I feel pretty good."

Chapter 11

While Joe sped west on Interstate 80, eager to be home and inform Julie of the meeting, Paul drove slowly, thoughtfully, through the August twilight toward his three-room apartment in Morristown.

He was preoccupied with the dilemma of the man he had just met, and wondered if there was any way, as a lawyer, he could help to resolve it.

—While I could feel the tragedy so profoundly, I knew what my role should be.

When someone comes in to Legal Aid and is ineligible for our service, I should attempt to find an attorney who specializes in the problem facing the applicant—and refer him to that other attorney.

This is my function. It is clear-cut. But obviously, the usual procedures just didn't apply to this circumstance. In Quinlan's case, how could they? How are you going to find an attorney in private practice who would be qualified—and who would have the time—to take on something like this? What lawyer could fit this particular client, with this unique problem, into the context of his practice of law?

I knew it would require a total commitment. Weeks, perhaps months, of intensive work. You'd have to give up everything else. And then you could lose. You could easily lose. Any lawyer capable of handling this case would see that—and his fees would be so astronomical, they could bankrupt a man like Joe Quinlan.

Paul was so preoccupied with his analysis that he missed the Morristown exit on the throughway and had to drive twelve miles out of his way. When finally he backed into the parking lot beside his first-floor apartment, Paul could see Maria at the window, holding the big white cat, Elmo, waiting for him. He'd done it again—forgotten to call and tell her he was tied up.

Quickly he climbed out of the Volkswagen station wagon, grabbed his brief case, and ran up the five steps, past their small porch with the cherry tomato vine his wife had planted, through the door.

She wasn't angry. Maria Luken Armstrong—brown-eyed, slender, with long dark hair braided and pinned into a coiled crown around her head—was a bride of four months. The middle child in a close family of eight, her gentleness is what had attracted Paul to her when they met while she was studying the humanities at St. Mary's College across the campus from Notre Dame Law School. They had married in Holy Name Cathedral, Chicago, on April 26—eleven days after Karen Quinlan slipped into coma.

"Sorry, honey, something really important came up."

And over a somewhat overdone dinner, Paul told her about the encounter with Joe.

Maria could see that he was emotionally affected by what he had been through, even saddened by it, as he talked about "the noble cause of this man, in a unique circumstance, and really desperately in need of help."

"Is his daughter really that helpless, Paul? I mean, a father might naturally exaggerate—you know, without knowing that he is exaggerating. He might be so emotionally involved."

"Of course, that's something that would have to be investigated," Paul conceded. "He seemed to be absolutely sure there was nothing that could be done—but anybody who decided to get into this case would have to talk to the doctors first, check out the medical records very thoroughly. You're right."

Maria was silent for a few moments. She knew him so well, knew that he was seriously contemplating the possibility of representing Mr. Quinlan because it was a "noble cause"; and yet she didn't know if she would be willing to be the good attorney's wife and agree that it was the right thing to do. As a child of seven, Maria had been critically ill with a kidney disease, and she remembered that now. She had been "in and out of the hospital for two years. Nobody understood the disease, and I was supposed to die. And I knew I was dying. But everyone kept praying, and the doctor kept looking for answers, and when I was nine years old, I had gradually become well again. Nobody understood why I had recovered, any more than they understood my disease. The experience had left me with a deep compassion for anyone who is ill—and also with a great faith, not only in God, but in medicine. And this is what bothered me about Karen Quinlan. I thought maybe there would be a miracle—there should be a miracle."

Maria stood slowly, picked up the plates. "Would you like tea?" she asked.

Paul answered, "What do you think, Luke?"

"Just a minute," she said, "while I clear the dishes." She wanted time, in the kitchenette, to analyze what she should say. "We'll talk about it in just a minute."

All that evening until after midnight, and the next day, and for two weeks thereafter, the Armstrongs discussed what Paul should do about Joseph Quinlan and his problem. Maria overcame her reluctance and found she could be open with him about the reservations she felt; Paul had concerns of his own.

—There was no doubt in either of our minds [he said later, recalling the period of decision] that if I took the case, it would be a total commitment—not only a religious and legal commitment, but in matters of time. I possibly would need to give up my job, and I knew —and Maria agreed, because she is the complete idealist—that we should not accept a fee from Joseph Quinlan. It isn't the kind of assignment you could consider charging a fee for. The principles were just too noble even to discuss it.

This led to some rather serious monetary problems. But Maria made light of them. I would ask very practically, "Do you think we could make it for a few months without my salary coming in?"

Maria would laugh it off. "Nothing to it," she'd say. "With my salary we could eat rice and beans"—Maria earned $360 a month as an on-the-job trainee at the Morris County Library. "And hey," she'd say, "we always have the patio tomatoes."

But both of us faced the fact that there were other things—my college loan, the rent, the loan on the car, the insurance. You could banter about these things just so much, and then you had to face reality.

In the afternoons, between his office closing and late dinner hours, Paul would drive to the library at Rutgers Law School in Newark to research the position of the Catholic Church on the issue of extraordinary means for supporting life, as expressed in the 1957 statement by Pope Pius XII. He looked up every available legal decision that had fallen under the First Amendment right of freedom of religion. He delved into past cases that dealt with the right of privacy, trying to draw analogies to the Quinlans' right to remove the machines sustaining their daughter.

Then he'd come home to Maria, his sounding board and devil's advocate, and discuss his findings. One night, tired, he said to her flatly, "No. I guess I'd better not take the case."

Maria countered, "Wait a minute—you have a brilliant mind. Not many lawyers ever in their careers have an opportunity to use their minds as you would."

That night as they lay in bed, Paul felt that he had developed a strong case. And he knew, from what she had said, that Maria would back him up.

Maria, sensing that her husband was approaching a decision, prayed for guidance.

Because she still had inner doubts. She "still hadn't yet resolved it in my own mind" she remembered afterward. "I had been thinking a lot of my sister Sara, who is almost the same age as Karen Quinlan. Maybe Karen is hopeless. But I kept wondering—if Sara were in the same condition, what would I do?"

Paul telephoned Joe Quinlan the next morning and asked if he might review the medical records, and confer with the doctors, regarding Karen's condition.

Joe had been waiting nervously to hear from the young attorney, and he quickly agreed.

Paul drew up a document directed to St. Clare's Hospital, stating:

—You are hereby authorized to release and give to my attorney, Paul W. Armstrong, Esquire, any information he requests covering the medical history, care, condition and treatment of our daughter, Karen Ann Quinlan.

After he had signed the paper, Joe suggested to Paul, "While you're at the hospital, maybe you'd like to see Karen? Julie and I will be there at four-thirty. We could meet you. I think you should see Karen."

That day, August 25, Paul delivered the release form to the hospital. Administrator Courey, his assistant, Mrs. Josephine Rovinski, and the hospital attorney, Theodore Einhorn, were cordial. They agreed to comply by supplying the medical data as promptly as feasible. They said, "We are with you."

Paul felt their attitude was not only pleasant, but realistic. As he constructed it later, "They felt that the hospital had a problem, and they were eager to see if the courts could work it out."

The doctors, Morse and Javed, were equally receptive when they met with Paul. "They seemingly anticipated with optimism," he felt, "a legal answer to what Dr. Morse referred to that day as 'a tragic enigma.'"

His legal business transacted, Paul met with the Quinlans and was taken into the Intensive Care Unit.

It was vital, Paul realized, for Maria to see what he had just seen.

When he returned home after that visit with Karen, Maria saw that he had been crying.

"You're going to take the case," she said sympathetically.

"No—I haven't made a decision yet," he said. "I want you to meet the family first, and see Karen. It won't work unless we're all in this together. Unless you believe in this as much as I do, we won't take it on."

Two nights later Maria Armstrong, guided by her husband and Joe and Julie, was admitted to the corner cubicle of the Intensive Care Unit where Karen's body lay.

She timidly approached the comatose patient. She looked down, and "when I saw Karen, all of my preconceptions about what Joe and Julie wanted to do just vanished. I looked into her eyes and there was nothing there. Only blankness. When Joe and Julie kissed her, and when they talked to her, my heart broke for them. I thought how terrible it must be to stand by, and watch your beloved child, every day and every night, just watch her fade."

All of them drove to a restaurant for dinner. They didn't talk about the law. They only talked about Karen—as she used to be, as she is now, the latest medical reports. Maria realized "this is their whole life."

As the Armstrongs drove back to Morristown at ten o'clock that night, Maria again told Paul of how she had felt before meeting the Quinlans and visiting Karen.

"I really had many personal doubts—you know that," she said.

Paul made no comment. Just sat listening intently, hands on the wheel, staring ahead.

"But after visiting her," Maria said, "we must help them, Paul. There is no other way."

Joe was in the kitchen the next evening when Paul telephoned. He felt tense. This could be the decisive call.

—Paul said he would like to drive over, that he had an answer for us. So now we'd know—it seemed like hours while we waited.

When he got here, Paul told us that he had decided to take the case, and that Maria would do the typing for us—he said she was as sympathetic as he was.

Of course, Julie and I were ecstatic. It was music to our ears.

Then Paul said a strange thing. He said that he had to struggle hard all those years he worked for his law degree because money wasn't easy to come by. And he said that while he was struggling, he had made certain promises to himself. One of those promises was that if he could ever do something to help someone out—or to help society—he would never let money interfere.

I didn't quite understand what he was driving at, and I said, "Oh, we want to pay you for your services."

That's when Paul said, "Joe, if you and Julie wish to repose your trust in me, I would be honored to represent you—but there will be no fee." I'll never forget how he said it. "Just the privilege of helping in a noble cause," he said, "is enough."

I looked at Julie and she looked at me, and I guess both of us were on the verge of crying.

"That's wonderful of you," I said, and we shook hands, and Paul left.

I turned around to tell Julie how fortunate we were, but she had run up the stairs to our room. She was weeping.

Having made the decision to take the Quinlan case, Paul again conferred with the doctors, Morse and Javed.

—Both of the doctors said they would co-operate fully with our legal effort to resolve the problem.

They advised me that, like Joe and Julie, they would welcome the guidance of the court to answer the question of the legal propriety of discontinuing Karen's respirator.

I had drawn up affidavits—in support of the complaint of the Quinlans. When I presented them with these affidavits, both Dr. Morse and Dr. Javed examined them and agreed freely and willingly to execute them.

It appeared that they fully supported Joe and Julie's judicial request.

The physicians, in turn, put their signatures on the following statements, under oath: "ROBERT J. MORSE: Being duly sworn, says":

1. I am a permanent resident of this State and a physician licensed to practice medicine in the State of New Jersey. I am and have been in the actual practice of medicine and surgery for 6 years. I was given the degree of D.O. [Doctor of Osteopathy] from the Chicago College of Osteopathic Medicine.

2. I am not a relative either through blood or marriage of Karen Quinlan, the alleged incompetent. I am not the proprietor, director or chief executive of any institution for the care and treatment of the insane in which the said Karen Quinlan is living or in which it is proposed to place her; nor am I professionally employed by the management thereof as a resident physician; nor am I financially interested therein.

3. On 4/25, 1975, Karen Quinlan was admitted to Saint Clare's Hospital, at Denville, New Jersey.

4. In my opinion, the said Karen Quinlan is unfit and unable to govern herself and to manage her affairs.

5. My opinion is based upon the circumstances and present condition of said Karen Quinlan and a history of her condition, as set forth below:

This 21-year-old female is presently confined to the Intensive Care Unit at St. Clare's Hospital in Denville, N.J., where she manifests decorticate posturing, oculopharangeal movements, and requires an MA-1 respirator to maintain life. Because of this patient's neurological condition she is unable to communicate by verbal or auditory or written communication. I do not feel that this patient is capable of handling her own affairs.

6. I have examined the said Karen Quinlan personally from time to time over a period of 5 months, the last examination having been made on 8/28/75.

ROBERT J. MORSE

Dr. Arshad Javed's affidavit was identical to Dr. Morse's, with the exception of his identification (item 1) and his opinion of the patient (item 5). Javed declared that he had been in the actual practice of medicine and surgery for two years, and had been given the degree of M.D. from the Nishtarr Medical College, University of Punjab, Pakistan. In his diagnosis of Karen, he stated:

—Since admission to St. Clare's Hospital, patient has required assisted mechanical ventilation; has extensive cerebral damage. Patient is fed through nasogastic tube. Has been in this condition for more than four months, and there is no hope of improvement in patient's condition.

Paul was encouraged. He felt the treating physicians had now "selflessly committed themselves to the mutual sharing of medical and legal responsibilities.

"Medicine and the law appeared to have joined hands."

During the next few days, Paul and Maria Armstrong made basic decisions involving their life style for the next two or three months. Paul assumed that is the length of time it would take to file, and resolve, a suit in Civil Court to decide the fate of Karen Ann and her family.

Maria had some four hundred shares of stock which her grandparents had given her when she was a child: AT&T, Bristol-Myers, U. S. Steel, American Home Products, Gulf Oil. They would sell them, little by little, as financial need arose.

Paul tied up as many loose ends as possible, involving his current Legal Aid clients, and then gave the society notice of his resignation, effective late September.

As a final break from the relatively routine life he had led before meeting the Quinlans, he telephoned the registrar of the New York University Law School and requested that his name be withdrawn from the graduate program in constitutional law.

There would no longer be time to study constitutional law. His goal, instead, was to change it.

Chapter 12

On September, 9, 1975, the "Vital Signs" report, clamped to the foot of Karen's bed and signed by the nurse on night duty, noted:

> 8 P.M. Mother vs. [visit]. Very upset. Finding it more difficult to see Pt. so "jumpy."

Julie was more than upset.

—My nerves were so taut I was constantly on the verge of tears. It was the way Karen looked by now. They were feeding her a high caloric diet—which seemed completely unreasonable, especially since her body didn't always accept the food. Often she would vomit. We felt those calories just made her face look round and rather plump. They'd keep a sheet drawn up around her shoulders, hiding her body, and above it, the rounded face. And she was more agitated than she'd ever been. I wouldn't have thought it possible that Karen's head could writhe so much. It was as though her body was in a vise, and her head was caught in a whirlpool.

When the nurses, under the doctors' orders, would give her what they called "painful stimuli" to measure her reflex reactions, they would drip a tiny drop of ice water into her ear. Then Karen would jump convulsively, with such force the bed would shake.

Every hour or so, the nurses had to go through a process which they called "cuff deflation." The way they explained it, there is a device which is like a small balloon inside her chest, just beneath the tracheotomy. The respirator would pump oxygen into that "balloon" so that the air would not be forced directly into her lungs, Instead it would be filtered in. Every hour, they would deflate that balloon for about five minutes' time, and then the nurses would say, "Why don't you talk to Karen now? She's deflated." That was the only time when she was capable of making any sound—when the air was let out of that device—so we would talk to her then. At the beinning, there was always hope that she might be able to talk back, in case she heard us. But now, when she was deflated, the only sound that came from Karen's mouth was a series of loud groans as though she were in terrible pain. She would just roll her head back and groan.

I would always wish Morse would come in while she was groaning. I just wanted him to hear it. I wanted to see his face. I thought then he would agree with us, that this misery had to be ended.

But he didn't come in any more. Not while we were there. I felt he'd rather not see us now.

On Tuesday, September 9, Paul Armstrong drafted a brief civil action complaint, supported by the affidavits of Dr. Morse and Dr. Javed, with the New Jersey Superior Court, Chancery Division. In it, he stated the comatose condition of Karen Ann Quinlan and declared "her vital processes are artificially sustained via the extraordinary means of a mechanical MA-1 Respirator."

Naming Joe the plaintiff in the complaint, Paul posed the plea:

After consultation with his Religious, Medical and Legal counsellors, with the support of his wife, JULIA, his son, JOHN, and his daughter, MARY ELLEN, and in concert with the tenets and teachings of their shared Catholic faith and the expressed desires of his daughter, KAREN ANN QUINLAN, the Plaintiff JOSEPH THOMAS QUINLAN therefore, with awe, sets before the Court the following prayer:

Wherefore the Plaintiff, JOSEPH THOMAS QUIN-LAN, respectfully prays that this Honorable Court enter a Judgment adjudicating KAREN ANN QUIN-LAN to be mentally incompetent as a result of unsoundness of mind and granting to the plaintiff letters of guardianship with the express power of authorizing the discontinuance of all extraordinary means of sustaining the vital processes of his daughter, KAREN ANN QUINLAN.

Dated: This 10th day of September, 1975.

Paul W. Armstrong, Esquire
Attorney for the Plaintiff

Paul slept poorly that night and, about three in the morning, suddenly sat up in bed.

The abrupt action sent the family cats, who had been curled behind his knees, lurching onto Maria's stomach.

She moaned, turned on her side, and yanked the sheet over her head. When Paul turned on a lamp, Maria said in a muffled voice, "Oh-oh. He's got an idea. He wants me to take a letter."

"You're wrong. Two letters. But they're brief."

"Can't they wait? It's still dark, for heaven's sake."

"We need the letters to go out with the first mail pickup—I think it's six o'clock—to the county prosecutor and the State Attorney General, both of whom eventually are going to become involved in this case since they are charged with the responsibility of enforcing the criminal statutes of this state. It's imperative that they be advised out of professional courtesy and deference to their offices, and that they be brought in as parties to the suit, to help us resolve the questions we are posing here."

"Please, Paul," Maria groaned, "it's three in the morning. Pretend you're not in court." Slowly, she pulled herself up. "Anyway," she said, "how would this violate the criminal law?"

"The immediate reaction to our request is going to be that it constitutes homicide. That's as simple as I can put it."

"That doesn't seem fair. How could they possible say it's homicide?"

"Karen's not dead by any of the legal criteria of death, Luke. So the automatic assumption is going to be that removing the respirator is a criminal act."

"But doesn't the court have any compassion?"

"New Jersey law," said Paul, "hasn't yet recognized humanitarian motives as a valid reason for permitting the living to die. The law isn't as kind and loving and beautiful as you are, my dear. Now, please stir your beautiful, kind, and loving self, and take a letter."

At 3:30 A.M. September 10, Maria Armstrong made her debut as a volunteer, middle-of-the-night legal secretary—a career that she was to pursue for the next eighteen months. She typed two identical letters, dictated by her husband and addressed to Attorney General William F. Hyland in Trenton and to Donald G. Collester, Jr., Morris County prosecutor in Morristown.

Headed "Re: In the Matter of Karen Quinlan," they read:

It is the purpose of this letter to advise you that I represent Mr. and Mrs. Joseph Quinlan in the above captioned guardianship action.

Due to the substantial interest of the State involved in this civil action, enclosed please find a copy of the complaint, affidavit of Plaintiff, and affidavits of Physicians.

Thank you for your courtesy in this matter.

Very truly yours,
Paul W. Armstrong, Esq.

At 6:30 that same morning, Paul drove through a sultry morning mist to the post office in Morristown where he dispatched the correspondence to Attorney General Hyland, in Trenton.

The following morning, deciding to try to discuss the case personally with Prosecutor Donald Collester, he

waited for the County Law office to open, then telephoned
Collester and briefly described the nature of the contemplated legal action on behalf of Joseph Quinlan.

Collester's reaction was instantaneous. "Why don't you
drop by and see me," he said. "As soon as it's convenient,
of course."

Paul drove immediately to the prosecutor's office and
delivered his complaint, the affidavits, and the covering
letter personally. He liked Collester's direct manner.

"Have you been able to find any precedent for your
complaint, Mr. Armstrong?"

"No. In a month of research, I've found nothing," Paul
said. "It appears this will be a 'first impression' case."

As the prosecutor looked at him across the desk, Paul
felt he was being gauged—that the obviously astute and
politically shrewd county prosecutor was assessing his potential for arguing a case of this magnitude.

Then Collester said, "This is going to get press coverage. I'm sure you're aware of that."

"Yes," Paul nodded. "I have already advised my client
that he and his family may be subjected to questioning by
the media. They're good people, with very firm belief in
their stand. I'm confident they can stand up to press coverage."

Collester said, "Then as soon as you file, I think it
would be in the interest of your client, and of everyone involved, if we bring some courthouse reporters together, so
we can discuss the issues being posed here. Do you agree?"

Paul was wary of the prospect of a press conference.
But he recognized it would be a chance to put the issues
squarely before the press, and explain them, so that they
would be properly interpreted. Everything would be as Joe
wanted it: open, aboveboard.

"All right," he said. "I plan to file the complaint tomorrow afternoon."

"Fine," Collester said, "I'll have the reporters here at
my office at four-thirty, if that's agreeable. I'll make
copies of this material you've given me, so they can take
it with them."

On September 12, at 4 P.M., Paul drove to the Morris
County Courthouse and gave the complaint, and the sup-

porting affidavits of Drs. Morse and Javed, to clerk David Anderson, along with a sixty-dollar filing fee.

The complaint was delivered promptly to Justice Robert Muir, Jr., chancery judge for Morris, Warren, and Sussex counties, Superior Court of New Jersey.

Then Paul sprinted across the street to Prosecutor Collester's office, where three news reporters, two men and a woman, were assembled. They were the courthouse correspondents for the Newark *Star-Ledger*, the Morristown *Daily Record*, and the Dover *Daily Advance*.

When he confronted the press, for the first time in his career, Paul suddenly "became circumspect. I started parsing out sentences in my mind. I'd never dealt with this kind of thing, and I was perhaps more than a little cautious. But they seemed quite personable, and eager to get on with it and ask their questions."

The *Star-Ledger* reporter threw out the first query: "What is the condition of Karen Quinlan?"

PAUL'S ANSWER: She's in a coma of unknown etiology. Her coma is the kind for which the art and science of medicine offer no hope of cure or recovery. She has irreversible brain damage. It is in that context that this prayer for extraordinary relief is set forth.

RECORD: What do you mean by "prayer"?

PAUL: That term—it's not meant within the ecclesiastical context in this case, but within the common law context. A prayer is a request.

STAR-LEDGER: Are there any precedents through out the world concerning this complaint?

PAUL: A month's worth of research—nearly a month —has failed to reveal any case precedent with respect to this specific request. There are other cases where individuals have based legal actions on religious beliefs, as you know, and where medical treatment has either been withheld or forced upon a patient with religious beliefs as a result of court action—but those cases are not fully applicable here, because in each of those cases the individual had the possibility of being returned to full health. In Karen Quinlan's case, this is not possible. She can never return to health. The law has never addressed itself to this question and asked: When can we as a society legally and morally make a decision to disconnect technological machines which are sustaining a hopeless life?

COLLESTER: Well, I'm interested in this concept of what constitutes a "hopeless" life. What constitutes life itself? That question has been debated by lawyers and physicians for centuries, and it could become an important part of this case. There are two generally accepted methods for determining death: the EEG (or electroencephalograph) method, or when the brain waves cease, and the cessation of the heart. If Karen Quinlan is not brain dead, then, by law, the removal of the respirator is homicide.

RECORD: Is she brain dead?

PAUL: The medical information we have says she is not brain dead by any criteria. However, her condition could deteriorate during the course of the trial to the point where she would be. In any case, brain death is basically irrelevant to the arguments we are raising. Medical science has outstripped our laws. We are asking whether a patient has the right to die with dignity, rather than being artificially maintained by science.

STAR LEDGER: If the respirator is removed from the patient and she dies—how do you distinguish this from euthanasia, or "mercy killing"?

PAUL: The Catholic Church, to which the Quinlan family belongs, considers euthanasia immoral and unlawful because it is a direct violation of man's right to life and is contrary to what Catholics hold to be the Divine Law of God. The Church teaches—as does the medical profession—that all ordinary means must be used to preserve life, even when there is little hope of recovery. However, there is a distinction between "euthanasia," which is defined as "good death," and the concept of "extraordinary means" as recognized by the Church. Pope Pius XII made an address in 1957 before a society of anesthesiologists, in which he set forth the argument that while we must take all ordinary means to preserve life, we are not obliged to use "extraordinary means" to prolong a life where no recovery is possible. We believe that Karen Quinlan's respirator is, in the present circumstances, "extraordinary" treatment.

STAR-LEDGER: Well, isn't this a form of "passive euthanasia"?

PAUL: No. The term for it is "antidysthanasia," which means, in Latin, "against bad death." And Pope Pius might have been referring specifically to a case like Karen Quinlan's when—in that 1957 address—he asked the question, "Does the anesthesiologist have the right, or is he bound, in all cases of deep unconsciousness, even in those that are considered to be completely hopeless in the opinion of the competent doctor, to use modern artificial *respiration* apparatus—even against the will of the family?" His answer to that question was no. It is not the removal of extraordinary means that leads to death. It is the illness. This is allowing nature to take its course.

RECORD: Are the Quinlans religious zealots?

PAUL: No. They are people who have a profound respect for their religion. I don't know exactly what you mean by a religious zealot.

ADVANCE: Is Karen Quinlan in pain?

PAUL: The doctors say that all of her brain cells pertaining to feeling are dead. She is in a vegetative state, cannot communicate in any way, and her body is in a "fetal" position.

There were more questions—about the family, the doctors, Karen's condition. The reporters remained in Collester's office for twenty minutes. Tim O'Brien, the representative of the *Star-Ledger*, was the only one who would write his story immediately. It was Friday afternoon, and his paper published a Saturday edition. The *Daily Record* writer would have to wait until the Sunday edition to file a report; the *Daily Advance* till Monday.

As the reporters, led by O'Brien who was on deadline, prepared to go, Prosecutor Collester stopped them for an announcement. As chief law enforcement officer of Morris County, he said that he would probably seek to intervene. "We intend to put all the issues before the court, including the very question of who has jurisdiction over such matters," he said. "The other primary questions, obviously, are: Is this a homicide? And what constitutes death?"

Then Paul made a short statement:

"This is a painful private family tragedy," he said. "I hope that if there are any questions in the future, you will please direct all phone calls to me and honor the privacy of the Quinlan family."

Three days later, as he stood with Joe and Julia Quinlan behind the gold antique satin drapes of their living room watching the front lawn at 510 Ryerson Road crush under an army of reporters and photographers, TV camera and sound equipment, Paul remembered that statement he had made at the small press conference.

"I realized then that it was probably the most naïve plea ever set forth in the history of jurisprudence."

Joe had just arrived home from his after-work visit to Karen on Friday night. He was in the kitchen, pouring a can of beer, when the phone rang.

—It was Paul, calling from Morristown. He said that he had filed the complaint, and there had been a little press conference afterward, and that the reporters had been extremely interested in our case.

He said, "Joe, I'm a bit concerned about what might happen at your house tonight. I have a feeling you may have some reporters coming over to see you. I've told them that this is a private matter, and specifically asked them not to bother the family—but I don't know if they'll observe my request. They may come and see you anyway."

I felt my stomach start to churn a bit and I asked Paul what we should do—what we should say if they turned up.

Paul said, "Just relax, Joe. Just be polite to them and ask them to wait for a few minutes. And then call me. Call me immediately, and I'll come over right away and lay down some ground rules. While the case is pending, there are things you shouldn't talk about, but I'll be there to answer any of the questions that you and Julie can't get into. So don't worry about it. But in the meantime," he said, "I think it would be a good idea for you to call the telephone company right away and ask them to give you an unlisted number as soon as possible. Will you do that?"

As soon as Paul hung up, I phoned New Jersey Bell. While I was talking to the business office about the unlisted number, I heard a car pull up outside the door of the family room, and my first thought was, "This is it—they've found us."

I sat there at the kitchen table, waiting for the doorbell, nervous as a rabbit. A few seconds later, when Mary Ellen walked in, I really felt foolish.

Mary Ellen said, "What's the matter with *you?* You look sort of funny."

"I am, honey," I said, and all of a sudden I started laughing at myself. Maybe it was half hysteria, but never mind. It was a release. I guess it was the first time I'd laughed in maybe six months.

No one from the press appeared at the Quinlan home that evening.

The next morning, Julie was the first to rise. She put water on for tea, then picked up the morning paper on the doorstep. She opened the Newark *Star-Ledger;* across the front page was a banner headline:

FATHER SEEKS THE LEGAL RIGHT TO
LET HIS GRAVELY ILL DAUGHTER DIE

Julie was transfixed. She walked toward the stairs, holding the newspaper open, wanting to call Joe.

—But the shock of seeing my daughter's name in the paper was so very unnerving—that big, black word DIE. I just suddenly broke down. I sat on the landing of the stairs and began to sob. John heard me and came running down from his room and knelt and put his arms around me, and asked what was wrong.

I couldn't answer, but I didn't need to. The paper was wide open for him to see and he said, "Oh, Mom . . ."

I was calm again by later in the morning. Paul and Maria arrived to spend the day with us, and we were all sitting around the kitchen table when the phone rang.

Mary Ellen answered, and I watched her face as she listened. At first she looked stunned, then she said, "Oh, please—don't release any. We don't want that. Neither would Karen."

When she hung up, Mary Ellen told us it was Sister Veronica, one of her former teachers at Morris Catholic High School, and she had said the school was being besieged by called from newspapers, wanting a photo of Karen. "But they won't give any out, because Sister said she knew we probably wouldn't want it. And she told me to tell you and Dad that everybody in the school is going to pray on Monday, for Karen and us."

That afternoon, we all went to the hospital. Karen was peaceful, thank God. We could always sleep better at night, when she looked peaceful.

Then that evening, while we were watching the television news, someone knocked on the door of the family room. I opened it, and there was a pretty young woman standing on the step outside.

She said, "Hello. Are you Mrs. Quinlan?" I nodded. "I'm Heather Bernard from NBC."

I was in a state of nervous shock. My first thought was—how embarrassing. Here's a girl from NBC, and she can look right inside and see us here—watching the news on CBS.

I tried to cover up my nervousness. "How did you ever find us?"

"Oh, we just asked directions from a couple of people in town," she said.

"We?"

It turned out she had a TV cameraman with her, and he was waiting outside in the car.

I invited her in, and introduced her to Joe, and then she and I sat on the sofa and talked, while Joe—trying to be casual—went to the kitchen and telephoned Paul. I quickly overcame my nerves, because Heather Bernard was easy to talk to. She asked me a lot about Karen's adoption—she said she was very interested in that because she and her husband had no children and were thinking seriously of adopting. So the time passed very quickly, and when Paul arrived, we invited the cameraman in.

While he set up his lights, Joe and I excused ourselves and went into the kitchen with Paul.

"I've told Heather that you can't answer any questions pertaining to the legal aspects of the case," Paul said softly, "so there's nothing to worry about. Be yourself. Just relax and be yourself, and everything will be fine."

And it was. That was our first interview, and it wasn't

nearly as difficult as we'd imagined it would be. I didn't cry at all and even Joe seemed to be quite at ease.

When Heather finally left, I fixed tea, and we all sat down in the kitchen, and I said, "Isn't it a relief—to have it all over with?"

Paul got a kick out of that. He gave me a big grin, and he said, "I hate to say this, dear Jule, but it's hardly over with. I have a distinct feeling it's only beginning."

On Sunday, our local paper, the *Daily Record*, published a story by a reporter whose by-line I had seen several times before—mostly on accounts of crimes in the area. Joe picked it up and read the story first, and I could see the color drain out of his face.

In the middle of the story, this reporter quoted an anonymous, so-called friend of Karen's saying:

"Her [Karen's] story is rather sad. I don't think anyone has the right to reveal it, and hurt the family or hurt her memory. It's something just better off left unsaid."

I was numb at first, and then I was furious. What "friend" of Karen's would ever say a thing like that? Say that her story was sad? Hurt the family—hurt her memory? Nothing could be more hurtful than innuendoes like this, which don't have any foundation in fact.

Paul tried to calm us down. He said something that, I came to realize in the months that followed, is painfully true. He said, "You know, small town papers are notorious for making their local stories as sensational as possible, to feed the public appetite for gossip. I know it's hard, but try not to worry about it."

I tried, but I never quite succeeded. But thank God, as Paul kept reminding us, we never had to face this kind of hearsay scandal story from the important papers, or the radio and TV people. They were consistently fair, and even remarkably accurate.

Sometimes Joe would mention that the big papers and magazines put quotes in his mouth he had never said. He didn't mind, though, because the gist of his remarks was usually correct.

"Matter of fact," he mentioned a couple of times, "the papers said what I said a little better than I said it myself."

On Monday, September 15, Joe left for work at the usual time, 7:30 A.M.

At 8:00 the doorbell rang, and Julie answered.

"Hello," said a slender young man, "I'm Arnold Diaz from CBS."

"Oh, no—Lord help me!" Julie thought. She was still in her bathrobe. She felt like running. Instead, she invited him in, asked him to wait, and then hurried upstairs to phone Joe and Paul. Reassured that both of them would be there promptly, she began to dress.

Julie never did get to her job at the Rectory that day.

By midafternoon, the whole world had been advised of the Karen Ann Quinlan case. The Associated Press and United Press International had carried the story on their wires. The morning tabloid New York *Daily News* had it splashed across the front page and *The New York Times* displayed it somewhat more conservatively. At 2:00 P.M. the Quinlans' front lawn was being thoroughly trampled by reporters, still and film cameramen. They were talking quietly among themselves, waiting. The photographers were taking pictures and movies of the house from all angles, and seemed particularly fascinated with a pottery statue of the Holy Virgin, surrounded by a circle of geraniums, in the front yard. One by one, they would get down on their knees to film it.

Peeking through the draperies, Julie sighed, "Oh dear, those geraniums—they look so wilted in September."

That helped Joe relax. Anytime a woman started worrying about how the house looked, it meant she was getting back to normal.

Paul, who had returned to his office after the CBS interview that morning, only to be called back to Ryerson Road when the afternoon media onslaught began, came walking briskly up the front path at 2:30. He heard a voice say, "There's the lawyer"—wondered which reporter it was—but continued striding toward the house. Once inside, he gave Joe and Julia a reassuring smile and commented, "It looks like the end of our peace and quiet."

The question was how to handle this large and disparate group. Joe and Julie were willing to talk to them, but Paul felt that a large press conference was not in order. There were too many people out there. It might easily get out of control.

"What do you think of the idea of asking them in,

more or less one paper or TV station at a time," he suggested, "depending on their deadlines? You'll have to answer a lot of the same questions over and over, but I think it'll be easier on you than trying to deal with everybody at once."

When the plan was agreed upon, Paul walked out into the yard and presented the proposal. It was eagerly accepted by the reporters, each of whom preferred the idea of his/her own exclusive crack at the story. When the "order of march" was established, with little argument among the media, Paul made an announcement, "I would appreciate it," he said firmly, "if you would all please comport yourselves with the degree of dignity that this particular situation requires."

The press is unaccustomed to being lectured about their decorum. And under the circumstances, they might have become exceedingly annoyed by it. But on this particular sunny autumnal afternoon, they not only accepted the mini-lecture, they abided by it.

In retrospect, after Paul Armstrong had become more sophisticated in his preceptions of media behavior, he reflected on that first mass encounter—and marveled that no one present had taken offense. "I think it was because I was genuinely concerned that day that, if any of the press should be too aggressive, thus putting additional pressures on Joe and Julie who already were overwhelmed by their tragedy, it might have resulted in the collapse of the Quinlans. I felt this deeply, and I think the media there were sensitive enough to realize that, and to respect it.

"In any case, they behaved themselves in exemplary fashion, taking turns going into the living room to talk to Joe and Julie, being kind, being polite. Right from the first day, the media were sympathetic to this family, and to what they were trying to do. By that evening, when the last reporters had left, Joe and Julie looked on them all as human beings—with first names, not just with newspaper or network affiliations. They were no longer frightened. They thought of these people they'd been talking to as friends."

It was not precisely a case of love at first sight, between the Quinlans and the hundreds who would speak and write about them. But it certainly was a case of mutual understanding and compassion.

That Monday night, driving home, exhausted, Paul conceived an image.

"In many ways," he told Maria, "this is like a Greek play. Julia and Joe and Karen are the principal actors in this tragedy—and the media is the chorus, chanting the story to the audience. The audience, which is becoming the whole world."

Newspapers honed in on the Karen Quinlan story and expanded upon it by contacting experts and laymen in the fields of medicine, theology, and law for their opinions of the upcoming case.

Arthur Sills, former New Jersey Attorney General, was quoted: "Most courts operate on the assumption that death comes about when the heart stops beating. Thus I would assume there would be quite a controversy in the courtroom."

Dr. Arthur Winter, neurosurgeon from East Orange, New Jersey: "When the brain is dead and all that is really going on is a heart that's beating and breathing is kept going by artificial means, the person is really dead. Once the brain is dead, just prolonging a body is not really life."

Alex Capron, University of Pennsylvania law professor and author of the definitive work on the legal definitions of death: "It is a mistake to contend that the legal question involved in this case is the definition of death. That strikes me as the evasion of the real issue. The reports I have seen say the girl continues to have minimal brain activity. None of the courts or medical profession has suggested that a person in that condition is dead. The question is when to cease treatment of a person who is incurable and has no hope of ever recovering or leading a full, human life. This brings to the public attention the need for a prior social decision for legislative means of establishing the procedures which ought to be followed here. It seems inappropriate to have the major issue be: is this a homicide?"

Dr. Robert M. Veatch, expert in medical ethics at the Institute of Society, Ethics and Life Sciences in Hastings, New York: "In most situations of the sort, there is quiet agreement between parents or guardians and physicians— usually with doctors making suggestions that the family accepts. What is unusual here is that the parents are taking the initiative, and that is how it should be. In my opinion the parents, as next of kin, ought to have the option to make such a tough choice. Since Karen does not have 'brain death,' the case moves into a gray area of ethics and law, where no precedent exists."

Dr. Veatch pointed out that a competent adult can refuse lifesaving medical care; and a court can force parents to accept lifesaving care for a child who faces a long, healthy life after recovery. "But the only legal decision that bears on the Quinlan case came in Miami, Fla., in 1974: an elderly woman pleaded for removal of painful treatments keeping her alive. The court ruled her incompetent and appointed her daughter guardian—then honored the daughter's request to end the treatments."

Attorney Arnold Chait: "The issues in a case such as this could be less complicated if the person had left a 'living will' saying if she fell into a coma she didn't want medical technology to be used to prolong her life. It could be argued that doctors are the ones who are prolonging Miss Quinlan's life and are in effect, interfering with a person's dying naturally, as would be in line with Catholicism. In most cases, doctors are exercising good judgment."

New Jersey Governor Brendan Byrne maintained: "The tragic case of Karen Ann Quinlan raises complex legal and moral questions. But it may well be that the most satisfactory solution . . . involves legislative action."

Several other attorneys predicted that the final resolution to the enigma of the Karen Quinlan case would be decided "by the United States Supreme Court."

On September 15 Donald Collester announced that the state of New Jersey would intervene and seek an injunction "to prevent anyone from disconnecting the respirator" of Karen Ann Quinlan. He said the state would also ask the court to appoint a temporary guardian for her.

Later the same day, Judge Robert Muir appointed Daniel Coburn, a Morristown lawyer, to serve as Karen's temporary guardian ad litem, representing her interests during the hearings. Coburn promptly went to St. Clare's, saw Karen, and though he had intended to dine out after the visit, went directly home.

"The first thing I did," he told *The New York Times,* "was look in on my own daughter."

Father Tom Trapasso, whose quiet parish duties were interrupted dozens of times a day by reporters asking questions, repeatedly reaffirmed the Church's position: "Extraordinary means are not morally required to prolong life."

Tommy Flynn made a last visit to Karen at the hospital, before returning to college in Florida, and told himself— as he'd often said before—that this was probably the last time he'd see her.

"The way she looks," he said, "I can't distinguish any more what is comfort for her and what is anguish. One minute, her face looks tranquil, and the next minute she looks in so much pain. And always her body is contracting and going through tremors. What the Quinlans are asking—I could understand it. Inside myself, there were times when I just wanted to pull the plug of that respirator myself. Yet I could never do it. When I'd see her, I was so caught up in it, so involved. Karen is such a positive human being, a human being with so much energy and life and fullness and goodness. She couldn't be otherwise and still be here, alive."

Chapter 13

"The girl in the coma" was a celebrity.

By the third week in September, Joe and Julia began to receive mail that numbered in the dozens of letters a day at first, then mounted to the hundreds.

Much of the correspondence was addressed cryptically —some stipulating only "To Karen Quinlan's Family, U.S.A."—but to the astonishment of the local letter-carriers, it reached the Landing, New Jersey, post office branch.

Julia usually was the first to open the letters.

—It became an emotional experience which I faced every day after work. Sometimes it was painful, but it was also, in a curious way, a diversion.

People were so sympathetic, and so troubled themselves, that it made us realize that we weren't the only ones who were going through life-and-death situations and they wanted to share them with us, hoping somehow it would help us. Many, many of them had elderly parents who were either comatose, or barely alive and suffering enormous pain, and these people said they prayed every day that their mothers or fathers could just be allowed to die in peace. And now they were also praying for us, and for Karen.

Others—not nearly as commonly—had younger members of their families, or dear friends, who had suffered through comas. Once in a while we'd hear from someone with a relative who had revived, and these were the people who wrote to us and said, "Don't let your daughter go, maybe there will be a miracle." But they didn't understand that Karen's coma is not the kind from which there is any hope of surviving, because the thinking portion of her brain is gone. I wanted to write to them. I wanted to explain that. But I couldn't. There just wasn't time to answer any of this mail, even if I had the heart to do it. Not even the letters of faith and encouragement from priests, or the sweet letters from little children.

Sometimes I would feel guilty that I couldn't answer those letters—that I would read them once, and then stack them in the cartons Joe had brought home from work to hold our mail. All the time and the heart these people put into writing to us—and I haven't the time or heart to respond. Joe felt guilty, too, but Paul made us feel better. Paul said, "For the sake of Karen, and in fact for the sake of all these people who are writing in and telling you to be strong and continue with your resolve, you both have to conserve your energy. Don't do any more than you absolutely must, I really mean that." I think, in those early days, Paul was always afraid that Joe and I were going to collapse.

Later, when we all held ourselves together and he became more confident that Joe and I were going to make it through the trial and anything else that came along, Paul said, more than once, "Religion has fortified us all." He'd give us that sweet, little-boy grin of his, and say, "Just take your tea, Julie, and the Deity will take care of the rest."

We had a new challenge when the faith healers began to arrive. Most people with religious feelings would write long letters to us, but the faith healers weren't content just to write. They came in person. They came by the hundreds, and all of them very sincere but believed that they could cure Karen if they could just get in to see her. They were sure they could just raise her up.

Mostly, these people would go to the hospital, and we'd meet them there, and they would plead, "Can we just go in with you and pray over Karen, so that she can survive?" They felt that they were getting a message from God. They really believed that.

Of course, we could never let them go up. In the first place, it was against the rules of the hospital, and if we had bent the rule to permit one faith healer in, then we would have had to permit another and another. The policy at St. Clare's was to take the faith healers into the chapel and let them pray for Karen.

We had several people come to the house, and one of them was a young man who had a young girl with him. They had come up from North Carolina. We sat in the living room and we prayed with him, and then when Joe and I said it was time for us to go to the hospital and visit Karen, he begged us to let him come, and just sit in the waiting room. We agreed to that, and when we got to St. Clare's, he asked Joe to say to Karen, "Rise up, Karen, rise up."

When we came down after our visit and he didn't see Karen come down with us, he became dreadfully upset. He was crying. He was shaking. I tried to explain to him that although he believed God had chosen him to help Karen, perhaps he was trying too hard to push his own will upon God. I said, "It is wonderful that God has chosen you to help Him, but maybe in this particular case you are trying to raise Karen up and it's not God's will that she be raised." I said, "We are all born to die, and there comes a time when God wants you and wants to take you home to Him. You are a Catholic. You believe in life after death with God, and maybe this is what He really wants for Karen. Perhaps He doesn't want her to rise, except to Him."

I was trying to help, but it didn't get through to him at all. He was still shaking and crying. We couldn't leave him there in that state, the poor man.

My mother and father were with us, so Joe told me to drive them home while he stayed with the healer, to try to soothe him. This was about 3:30 in the afternoon, and when Joe hadn't come home yet by 6:30, I was really concerned.

When Joe finally arrived home about 7:30, he told me what had happened. The young man had asked Joe to go into the chapel at the hospital and pray with him. He said he felt that God wanted a nurse from the ICU to pray with them, too, so Joe had to go to ICU and fortunately the nurse on duty was our neighbor: For Joe's sake, she went to the chapel and prayed, too. "And then," Joe said, "this boy really believed that Karen was going to get out of bed and walk into the chapel. When she didn't he broke down again. When I finally left him, he was still in there, with his girl."

We have wondered many times what happened to that man, and to all the others. Whether they lost a little faith in themselves, or what they were trying to do. I do hope not. They were good people who really, really meant well.

Judge Robert Muir set the trial date for October 20, with pretrail hearings to begin September 22.

Paul Armstrong knew he faced a massive task, converting his voluminous research into legal documents. He thought of his old friend, James Crowley, from the days at Notre Dame Law School. Crowley was now a thirty-three-year-old attorney with the Wall Street law firm of Shearman & Sterling. He had studied theology and canonical law in Rome for four years—had even, at one time in the 1960s, planned to enter the priesthood.

Paul phoned him in New York City.

"Jim, have you heard of the concept of 'extraordinary means'?"

"Sure," Jim said.

"Well, hold onto your hat. I'm planning to bring that concept into the courts."

When Paul described the plight of Joseph and Julia Quinlan, and his desire to help them, Crowley said under his breath, "Holy mackerel."

"What was that?".

"Well, I think morally, canonically, theologically, or whatever, you have a good case," Jim said. "Sight unseen, I agree with what these people want to do. But listen, Paul, I've never heard of something like this being argued in a civil court."

"It hasn't been," Paul said, "but it has to be. These poor people really need help. The whole world needs help. It's a man against technology."

"I agree. It's risky, but I agree."

"Then"—Paul took a deep breath—"how about taking some time off to give me a hand?"

Crowley was intrigued. He was also practical. "You know I'd like to, but I'll have to ask the senior partners here whether it's possible. I'll have to give them a concrete proposal. Otherwise, they just might not believe this. Give me a few days."

It took only a day. The senior law partners in Jim Crowley's firm, Henry Harfield and Myles Wayland, were perceptive to the *pro bono publico* role, in which all attorneys must serve for the good of society and of the profession. They promptly offered not only Jim's services to the Quinlan cause, but they also donated secretarial assistance, clerical supplies, printing and duplicating services—and the use of Shearman & Sterling's offices as a headquarters for preparation of the briefs.

Buoyed and excited, Paul and Jim promptly bought themselves sleeping bags and concentrated their efforts inside the quiet nighttime environs of 53 Wall Street, "like a pair," as Paul put it, "of mad insomniacs."

With the New York Law Library around the corner to help their research, they survived the next several weeks on street vendor hot dogs, an occasional Chinese dinner in a nearby chow mein parlor, and cat naps on the carpeted office floor when absolutely necessary.

Across the Hudson River in Morristown, Maria Armstrong had the cats and her needlepoint for company. But she admitted musing, in lonely moments, on the wisdom of having married an idealist.

Across the East River on Staten Island, Crowley's wife,

Mary Jo, had a more absorbing kind of company—an un-born baby, due to arrive on the opening day of the pre-trial hearings. Mary Jo and Jim had been jointly taking a preparatory course in natural child birth, and he was as determined as she to be present when the infant was born.

With the hearing set for Monday, September 22, Jim came home on Saturday night the twentieth, and said, "Don't worry, honey, the baby will come this weekend. There's a full moon."

"What's that got to do with it?" Mary Jo asked.

"Statistically, more babies are born when the moon is full."

Shortly after midnight, Mary Jo woke up and said, "I feel a little funny." Jim calmly took her to the hospital and, as he described it, "We spent the next day having the baby, and he arrived about quarter to six Sunday evening. Perfect order. Accommodating providence. The next day I could go to the hearings, knowing everything was in hand. Or in crib. However you want to put it."

The stately Morris County Courthouse was packed with people and camera equipment when Paul and Jim arrived for the pretrial hearings at 10:00 A.M. that Monday.

There were no histrionics or legal fireworks; the hear-ings were conducted coolly, methodically, in the tenor of a business meeting.

Still, Paul was unnerved to see for the first time how many advocates in opposition to the Quinlans would be aligned against him at the trial. Not only were there at-torneys representing the hospital and the doctors, but also the guardian ad litem, the Attorney General, and the pros-ecutor had elected to take part in the trial.

It would be Paul Armstrong, with James Crowley at his side, for Joseph Quinlan, versus Daniel Coburn, guardian; William Hyland, New Jersey Attorney General; David S. Baime and John DeCicco, deputy Attorney Generals; Donald Collester, Morris County prosecutor; Ralph Por-zio for Drs. Morse and Javed; and Theodore Einhorn for St. Clare's. Seven lawyers altogether in opposition—and they had a battery of medical experts ready to testify on behalf of the hospital, doctors, guardian, state, and county.

But Paul was not unduly worried—"not at this stage. We had no friends, outside the press. But the size of their operation didn't necessarily make them more formidable. It wasn't as though I was fighting seven different, and resourceful adversaries. I was merely fighting one redundant voice.

"When I looked at it that way, I wasn't as apprehensive."

What he needed desperately, Paul realized, was an expert neurologist to speak up for his client in court—a sage, authoritative counterbalance for the team of physicians scheduled to testify for the opposition. Someone who could testify to the irreversibility of Karen's brain damage. One such physician, Dr. Fred Plum—president-elect of the American Neurological Society—had written a sympathetic letter to Joe Quinlan saying he would welcome the opportunity to testify on his behalf. But the letter had been addressed to the hospital, and by the time it was forwarded to the Quinlans, a fellow physician had contacted Dr. Plum to come in as an expert witness for the guardian, Daniel Coburn. (Plum stipulated that he would, however, only testify to the facts—not favoring either side in the suit.)

Paul had phoned more than one hundred doctors. He found many who were sympathetic, and who confirmed that the removal of life supports in hopeless cases was almost "routine" hospital practice. But they backed away from stating this truth "under the white light of litigation."

—Then one day a fellow attorney tipped me off to the fact that Dr. Julius Korein had just testified in a case in New York concerning brain death. Dr. Korein was Professor of Neurology at the New York University Medical Center, and chief of the EEG labs at Bellevue, and I admit a great deal of skepticism had slipped into my soul. I had been turned down by so many lesser doctors, and I didn't think a busy doctor like this would take us on.

But I called him immediately, on September 25. And, to my amazement, he agreed to meet me and discuss the case.

I drove into New York to see him. We discussed Karen and the philosophical concept of withdrawing technological life supports in hopeless cases, and he was extremely forthright. After our talk, and some thoughtful reflection, Dr. Korein said, "I believe in what you are attempting to do, Mr. Armstrong. I think it's about time the public became aware of what goes on."

Other doctors had agreed, on a philosophical basis, and then backed away from being involved—but not this man. There was no hesitation, no searching for excuses. "I'll be glad to serve as a witness on behalf of the Quinlan family," he told me.

I was deeply grateful that afternoon. I had almost given up hope of finding a doctor with this much courage.

On October 10 Dr. Korein drove to St. Clare's and examined Karen for an hour and a half, observing and testing her during both "wake" and "sleep" cycles.

In a lengthy report, dictated following the visit, the neurologist noted:

—This patient cannot be considered to be in a state of brain death, although her "coma-like" state, in my opinion, is irreversible, and I would characterize her to be in that class of patients who are described as being in a "persistent vegetative state."

A total of seven other specialists examined Karen during the weeks before the trial, preparatory to testifying on behalf of all the parties to the litigation.

In their analyses of Karen's medical condition, their letters of assessment concurred almost precisely with Dr. Korein's.

However, one letter, from Dr. Henry R. Liss, Clinical Professor of Neurosurgery at Rutgers Medical School, went far beyond the others in its evaluation of the patient, the machines that sustain her, and the issues before the court.

Dr. Liss had examined Karen on October 2—at the request of the Attorney General and the Morris County prosecutor—in company with four other specialists: Dr. Plum, whose credentials are mentioned above; Dr. Stuart Cook, Professor of Neurology, New Jersey Medical School; Dr. Eugene Loesser, Professor of Neurology, Rutgers; Dr. Andrew Bender, Clinical Neurologist, Westwood, New Jersey.

In his report, Dr. Liss stated the following conclusion:

—Without the ventilator and with no antibiotics her inevitable demise would be a kindness. The death would be of a pulmonary nature. No doubt she has small posterior abscesses of the lungs because of the long period of time she has been lying immobile in bed. She could survive on regular hospital floor care for a while but the pulmonary status would soon deteriorate and lead to her death.

The means which currently keep her alive are extraordinary. She is on a respirator, has meticulous care to the trachea and lungs and receives antibiotics periodically. Her feeding is artificial with the pure amino acid formula. If these three modalities were withdrawn, nature would be able to follow its will.

There are two considerations here. One, of course, is the legal aspect and the other the humanistic aspect. It is hoped that the courts will decide that it is not legally necessary for St. Clare's and the physicians to apply extraordinary measures. From a medical standpoint they are not warranted. It is over a 99% chance that this young lady will never again function in what we think of as a human fashion.

Medical information would dictate that no further treatments be offered.

Dr. Liss's report was strongly supportive of the Quinlans' plea.

Yet, although his examination had been conducted at the request of the Attorney General and the Morris County prosecutor, neither Hyland nor Collester elected to call this witness to testify.

Paul was outraged.

"I will never understand the failure to meet what I believe to be the fundamental responsibility of bringing this evidence before the court. Had Dr. Liss's opinion been introduced, it could have been a major influence in the ultimate trial court decision."

Chapter 14

For years, Julia Quinlan had depended on her clock-radio to waken her—with John O'Hara's eight o'clock local morning news.

—I needed that stimulant to get me up in time for work. Otherwise, I could sleep all morning. Karen used to say I could sleep right through World War II. But now, I was awakened by an entirely new kind of early morning sound—cars pulling up in front of our house, crunching the dead oak leaves out on the street.

They were the cars of reporters for the afternoon papers, and they'd usually start arriving at 7:00—sometimes 7:15. At first it was unnerving, knowing I had visitors arriving before I even had a robe on, or a cup of tea to clear the fuzz from my mind, but fortunately our stairway is located in the middle of the house where no one could see me going down, and the breakfast room and kitchen are in the back, looking out on the back yard. The reporters never walked around back. They were usually considerate. Didn't even ring the doorbell, because they knew Mary Ellen would be sleeping late. They just waited out front, till we would have to come out and leave for work.

Poor Joe was the one who suffered most in the first few days, because he would already have had breakfast and be about to leave when they would arrive. As he said, "They must have a hundred pictures of me walking out to get the morning paper, and another two hundred pictures of me climbing into the car." We understood. They had a job to do. And as time went on, we thought of many of them as our friends. We knew most of them by their first names, and whenever it was raining, of course we'd invite them to come inside and have

153

coffee. And it did seem to rain a great deal that autumn.

A curious thing happened to me during this period. Sometimes I felt almost like a spectator, standing back away from what was going on, watching all these strange happenings take place. These things were occurring to *us*, but it was easier to detach yourself sometimes and feel outside of it all. I suppose it was a defense mechanism. Psychologically, we were withdrawing into our own shells because it was safer that way. More comforting that way. Us—watching the world watching us.

When we'd go to the hospital and slip past the reporters who were a fixture there now, and take the elevator up to the third floor and go to Karen's bed, only then did the reality always come back. Looking at Karen wiped away the fantasies. Her helplessness was so very, pathetically real.

It never failed to remind me that I am a mother, a mother who is needed. Rather than just some character in this huge drama.

One day during this period, one of the nurses became very excited. She believed that Karen could see!

She showed us why she believed this. She held her hand out, a few feet from Karen's face, and she said, "Karen, Karen watch me"—and then moved her hand forward. When she stopped it, just short of Karen's face, Karen blinked her eyes.

Joe immediately tried the same experiment, feeling perhaps there was some reason for hope again. Karen blinked when his hand was almost on her face.

But then he leaned forward, so that his head was directly in her line of vision, and he slowly, slowly moved his face toward hers until their noses were almost touching and, again, Karen blinked. But she didn't see him. Her eyes were staring right through him, as though he weren't there at all.

It was only another reflex action. Karen couldn't see. There was no change at all.

But there *was* a change in Dr. Morse's attitude. He was not happy with us for hiring a lawyer, and he told us so several times. He would call Joe at work and ask if we could meet with him. He'd say, "But I only want to see you and your wife. Don't bring your lawyer."

So then we would meet Morse at the hospital, and he would remind us that we were going to court against his wishes.

We didn't understand why he should be so annoyed at us, when we had only done what the hospital lawyer had said that we had to do.

Paul was calling us at least ten times a day, usually from New York, where he was doing a lot of his work with Jim Crowley. He'd tell us how the preparations were going for the trial. He kept us as informed as he could and said that he and Jim were preparing the briefs based on constitutional issues involving the freedom of religion and the right of privacy.

Paul also asked me to try to remember specific times and places when Karen had talked to us about not wanting to be kept alive by extraordinary means if she were hopelessly ill.

He said, "If we are allowed to introduce testimony on that subject, it will help a great deal. It's our only opportunity to get Karen's personal convictions on the record. She can speak for herself, through you and whoever else heard her talk about the use of extraordinary means."

I said that would be easy, but I had to admit to Paul I was not sure that she ever used the specific words "extraordinary means." I think she put it a different way.

Paul said, "That's fine. The intent was the same. Just keep thinking about it, and remembering the circumstances."

I had no trouble with that at all. There were two tragedies that touched us, and Karen had discussed them at length with me. The first time was when her friend Nanette Foit's father was dying of cancer, and Karen would drive Nanette to the hospital every night to visit him. That was in February last year [1974] and it made a deep impression on Karen. She never saw Mr. Foit, but Nanette told her how much he was suffering, and Karen could see how painful it was for his family. That hurt her. She couldn't stand seeing people in

pain. During that time we would have long talks about
how cruel it was to be kept alive that way. Karen,
Mary Ellen, and another of her friends, Lori Gaffney,
and I—we'd discuss it. And Karen felt, even more
strongly than the rest of us, that this was inhuman.

Then in March of this year [1975], a friend of our
family, Bill Birch, was dying of cancer. Two weeks before his death, he asked to return to his home so he
could die there, instead of in Intensive Care, and the
doctors allowed it. Karen just totally agreed with that—
that Mr. Birch should have the right to die in his own
home. She said very specifically, again, that if anything
like that ever happened to her, she would not want to
be kept in the hospital, attached to machines, if she
were dying.

It sounds unusual for someone so young and healthy
to talk that way, but Karen did. Karen talked about
anything and everything, and she had strong opinions.

Mary Ellen said, "I'll bet she wrote a poem about it,
at the time Mr. Birch was dying. She liked to write
poems about things that struck her as really sad or
really important."

So that night Mary Ellen went through Karen's old
notebooks, and I rummaged through the drawers in the
kitchen and the sideboard in the dining room. Karen
left her poems in all sorts of odd places. It was as if,
once she composed them and got them off her mind,
she'd just put them away in the handiest place. I read
once that creative people are not very organized. That
was Karen.

We looked high and low that night. We found one
verse that I didn't remember reading. It was different
from any she had shown me. More haunting.

> *A song still rings within the glen.*
> *For all who shun the ways of men.*
> *For there a song of peace is heard*
> *without a single spoken word.*

I asked Mary Ellen, "Do you think she really wrote
that?" Mary Ellen said, "I suppose so. It's in her hand-
writing." But there was nothing about the illness of Bill
Birch.

—One evening late in September, I had a phone call from little Lori Gaffney. We had been in touch with her because she would visit the hospital to see Karen every week, and of course she was going to testify at the trial about the conversations with Karen on not wanting to live with extraordinary means. So Lori had our unlisted number.

She said, "I hate to bother you about this, Mrs. Quinlan, but a state policeman came to my house today and asked all kinds of questions about Karen."

"The state police?" Oh dear Lord. "What kind of questions would they be asking?"

Poor Lori, she was almost crying. She said they'd asked "all kinds of things, like who were her best friends, and whether she took drugs, and whether I knew the people she was with the night of the coma. I said I didn't know them, and I never knew her to take drugs, ever. It was like they didn't believe that, when I told them."

No sooner had I thanked Lori and hung up when Joe Stigliano at the Chevron station called Joe. He was unnerved. "Two state policemen just left my place," he told Joe. "They were here for almost an hour, asking questions about Karen. What's going on?"

Joe tried to act calm, but he was as deeply distraught as I was. Why were the New Jersey State investigators asking questions? It didn't make any sense. There already had been two investigations into the circumstances of the coma, and they'd turned up absolutely nothing.

The Sussex County prosecutor [George T. Daggett] had talked to everybody who was with Karen the night she went into the coma, because it took place in Sussex County. And he talked to the doctors at Newton Hospital, and the Lakeland Emergency Squad in Andover, and everyone involved—and he said there was no need for any further study. He said, "I am convinced there was no crime involved."

Then the Morris County prosecutor investigated and found nothing new.

So we kept asking ourselves why, after all that, the state was going around now, stirring people up. Lots of Karen's friends, and ours, were being visited, and the nature of the questions seemed to indicate that they were looking to find out something scandalous about our daughter.

I will never, ever forget how hurt we were by this investigation, which began in September and continued for nearly four months.

The reporters found out about it, of course. On Wednesday [October 1], the local papers came out with a huge black headline—STATE COPS ENTER THE QUINLAN CASE.

In the story, Attorney General Hyland admitted that he had been conducting "a special inquiry" into the coma for several days. He said that "in doing this, I have not suggested that anyone has made a mistake in the previous investigation."

Then what *was* he suggesting?

Whatever it was, they were attacking the reputation of our daughter, who was helpless. And we are helpless to defend her. That was the terrible part. They kept looking for something bad about Karen, and they made headlines while they searched, and in the end they never found anything—there was nothing ever to defend her against, except the innuendo.

Joe prayed for strength, to help him face this injustice.

And, right from the beginning, I tried to stay close to God in prayer. But I was not always successful. There were days when I told God I hated Him. Yet He never stopped loving me, never left me for a moment.

Some people might not understand how I can tell God I hate Him. But you have to be honest, that's all. When you don't agree with something your dearest friend is doing, if you can't express your real inner feelings, then I don't think you have a real closeness at all.

Sitting alone in the waiting room fifty yards down the hall from Intensive Care, Julia composed "A Poem for Karen":

> *I kiss her*
> > *on her cheek*
> *She cannot feel*
> > *my kiss*

I look into her
eyes
She cannot see
me

I call her name
She cannot hear
me

There is a grimace
on her face
She cannot feel
the pain

A red light on
the machine
Tells me she is
breathing

The machine is
keeping
her alive
There is no life . . .

In my heart
I hear my Karen
whisper

Remove
from this machine
Let my heart beat
on its own

When it grows tired
it will stop
And,
I will go to sleep

So not wake me
now
Do not place me
on that machine,
again . . .

Let me sleep
For I have waited
long

Let me sleep
Peacefully,
Eternally . . .

—*October 15, 1975*

In the week before the trial, one of the most concerned men in New Jersey was Morris County Sheriff John Fox.

Fox was young and able, but he also was sufficiently experienced in sensational court procedures to realize that his officers faced a potentially dangerous situation.

—The year before [in 1974], we'd been through a similar situation in the same courthouse, when our men had to handle the hordes of media and curious who came to the Joanne Chesimard trial. There was plenty of hysteria then, plenty of emotionally aroused people and news coverage, and it gave us problems—but we knew it wasn't as big as the Quinlan case.

Everybody involved with this event—Prosecutor Collester, Dan Coburn, the Quinlans, General Hyland—everybody was getting letters, sometimes packages, from all over the world. Judge Muir was getting a lot of mail too, and he never looked at it. Most of the letters were turned over to us. The people who wrote seemed to take two basic views. One was "Don't let Karen die, or we'll kill you." The other was, "Let her die, or we'll kill *her*." There are a lot of cranks out there.

When packages would arrive, they'd be intercepted and turned over to us. Any suspicious boxes were taken to the Picatinny Arsenal Bomb Squad. Fortunately, they all turned out to be harmless. Many of them contained vials of "holy water," or crucifixes, along with elaborate instructions on how to go about getting Karen out of the coma.

Judge Muir personally called me into his chambers just before the trial. He obviously realized the potential dangers, and asked me to see to it, personally, that each participant got safely in and out of the courthouse.

The entire operation was plotted very carefully, with specific plans for everyone involved to go in and out

all the different exits. But I don't care how many precautions you take, or how many men you allocate to a
job like this, things can get out of hand. There was so
much publicity involved in this tragic case that we
expected plenty of problems—but there was no way I
could envision the animalistic behavior of some of the
people who came. Even the media were so eager to get
stories that they completely blocked the courthouse
complex, and harassed some of our officers.

It was complete chaos!

Chapter 15

October 20, 1975. Julie wakened to the noise of wind-
driven rain scratching at the windows.

—It sounded so dreary I instinctively dug deeper under
the blankets. Then, remembering what day it was, I
jumped out of bed and ran over and slammed down
the window—in full view of at least forty people, hud-
dled down below under trees and umbrellas. I ducked
back of the curtains and, fortunately, nobody was looking up. So the papers were spared a picture of Julia
Quinlan in nightgown and shock. I don't know why I
was shocked to see all those reporters—I suppose I assumed they would all be at the courthouse. And you
never quite get accustomed to the feeling of being surrounded, in your own home.

About eight o'clock, Father Tom came in, ready to
drive us to the courthouse. Our thought had been that
everyone knew my car and Joe's, but they weren't
familiar with Father Tom's. So maybe they wouldn't
notice us when we drove over. Of course, that was a
dream. As we opened the side door, the flashbulbs began to pop like fireworks. I said a silent prayer—"God,
see me through this." We answered as many questions
as possible, and when we jumped into the car, the press

jumped into theirs, and they trailed us to Morristown. Instead of being incognito, we looked like the lead car in a parade.

I had never been inside the big, old, Georgian-style courthouse, and as we drove past it, the sight was magical. The rain had almost stopped and the sun was trying to filter through the mist, and the building, with its majestic white columns, was almost like a re-enactment of *Gone With the Wind*—Tara, the mansion, surrounded by the troops. There were giant oak trees with brilliant gold leaves all around the building, but there were more people than leaves on those trees. Someone said it looked like a lawn festival. All of them seemed to see us at the same time and began pouring toward the car.

Father Tom tried to be calm. He stepped on the gas, praying no one would run in front of us, and we spun around the corner and turned into the courthouse garage across the street. The cameramen managed to get there before we did, and we were afraid of bowling them over so we had to slow up. When we finally got inside, Father Tom said, "Do you suppose they'll really use pictures of a car going into a garage?" But of course they would. The judge had closed the courtroom to all camera and sound equipment for the duration of the trial, and the photographers had to take whatever pictures they could get.

Maria was waiting for us inside the garage, with a sheriff's deputy named Bert Rosa. Bert had been in charge of protecting the family throughout the trial, and he escorted all of us across a closed passageway, elevated above the street, and leading directly into the second floor of the courthouse. There were guards at the entrance to the courtroom, and they began inspecting my handbag. Bert stopped them, and laughed, and said, "It's okay, men, you can let Mrs. Quinlan through." The guard looked so embarrassed, I tried to put him at ease by asking questions: "What are you supposed to be looking for?" He said, "Cameras, guns, knives, tape recorders." Bert must have thought that would make me uneasy. "All routine security, Mrs. Quinlan," he said. "Nothing to worry about."

The courtroom reminded me of the interior of a small church. High ceilings and mahogany benches covered with red cushions, like pews. High up above the floor there were huge windows, through which I could see those beautiful gold leaves outlined against the sky —nature's version of stained glass—and I thought to myself that if the trial became too unsettling, I could look up at those windows. I felt that their beauty would give me strength.

We were ushered up to the front row—Father Tom, Joe, Mary Ellen, Father Quinlan, and I. My sister, Alberta, was there and so was Father Fred Lawrence. There was a space left open for John. He was going to drive over later, after his morning classes.

Directly in front of us, at a counsel table, were Paul, with Jim—and across from them, at another table, there were the five other lawyers who would be opposing us. Behind us there were twenty rows of reporters, and the rest of the benches were filled with people who (Bert told us) had been waiting outside in the rain for more than four hours to get in. And all along both sides of the courtroom there were artists, who would be making sketches for newspapers and TV stations. At first I felt I might be self-conscious, knowing they were drawing pictures of us. But I forgot all about them. I was concentrating on the judge and the lawyers.

It suddenly struck me how young most of them were. Except for Ralph Porzio, the attorney for the doctors, and William Hyland, the Attorney General, not one of those lawyers looked much more than thirty. Not that much older than Karen. Even Judge Muir, even though he was balding, had a youthful face. Suddenly it occurred to me that when I was their age, we never ever talked about death. It was something you tried never even to think about.

I wondered if these men really had lived long enough to feel what we were going through. So young, I thought, to be arguing about death.

"Gentlemen," said Judge Robert Muir, "we will start with the openings. I ask you, Mr. Armstrong, to state all the facts which you expect to prove with respect to the case. Let's proceed."

Paul, appearing more confident than he felt, and carefully referring to the notes in his hand, briefly outlined the position of the Roman Catholic Church and said he would introduce evidence to show that Karen Ann Quinlan had "expressed her wishes" with regard to the action of removing extraordinary means of life support.

"The Quinlans," he said, "believe that the earthly phase of Karen's life has drawn to a close, that the time of life striving is over, and that further treatments merely hold her back from the realization and enjoyment of a better, more perfect life.

"There will be set forth within the context of this trial complex legal, medical, theological, and ethical propositions," he promised. "But what must be borne in the minds of all who participate in this question involving the tragic plight of Karen Ann Quinlan, what must be borne in the minds of the lawyers, physicians, and theologians, what must be borne in the collective mind of every facet of our society—is that throughout our history the men to whom man has turned, for wisdom, advise that truth is found in simple forms.

"I suggest that the answer to the tragedy of Karen Ann Quinlan is to be found in the love, faith, and courage of her family, who ask only that she be allowed to return to God with grace and dignity."

Paul Armstrong was followed immediately by Daniel Coburn. The court-appointed guardian for Karen, a thickset and blunt-speaking attorney, Coburn reminded Julie of a television detective. He spoke extemporaneously:

"I think there are some things that should be said right now, so that no one has any doubts as to what my position is going to be in this case," Coburn said firmly. "People have soft-shoed; everyone in their briefs has talked about compassion for the family—sorry for Karen. I'm certainly sorry for Karen Quinlan. I wouldn't wish this on anyone. I'm sorry for the family in the sense that no family should go through what I'm sure the Quinlans have gone through. I'm also sorry for myself, as the guardian, because compassion has no bearing on this case at all . . . the doctors' testimony here will say they are ninety-nine and forty-four one-hundredths per cent sure that her condition is irreversible. That may very well be good for cleanliness. But that has nothing to do with a court of law. Where there's hope, you can't just extinguish a human life because she's an eyesore. And that's what this is."

Julie winced. Coburn continued:

"Karen Ann Quinlan is alive, and if she's going to die, and people want to talk about God's will—well, God's will will take second place to what medical science will do for her. As to the theory that she's not really leaving this earth—that she's just getting to the next world a little bit sooner—in all frankness to the court, and I'm not trying to be flippant, my attitude is that if the Quinlans want an express, I'm going to take the local.

"I've heard 'death with dignity,' 'self-determination,' 'religious freedom'—and I consider that to be a complete shell game that's being played here," Coburn concluded bluntly. "This is euthanasia."

As Daniel Coburn said "Thank you" and strode briskly to the counsel table, Paul looked over his shoulder at the Quinlan family, hoping to reassure them.

Attorney General William Hyland's opening statement seemed, by contrast to his predecessor, restrained and sensitive.

"If it please the court," said Hyland, "this case was borne in tragedy, and I think all of us have been touched by it. I'm sure we've all tried to place ourselves in the position of this unfortunate family in an effort to understand how difficult it has been for them to give up that intense hope."

But, he said, "I am here today to discharge what I perceive to be my solemn obligation as a representative of the countless others who will be affected by what we do here. I do not view criminal liability as the real issue before the court," he said. And then, dramatically lowering his voice, "To wave the fist of justice at an anguished family, or at a noble profession dedicated to the alleviation of pain and, like the state, committed to the maintenance of human life."

Nevertheless, he said, "We're dealing here not only with Karen, but with countless others as well." Saying that he was present on behalf of the state of New Jersey "to avoid a judgment of execution," the white-haired Attorney General looked across at the doctors and added, "The law and medicine need not be enemies.

"Human life, in whatever form, is the responsibility of the state."

Hyland concluded by saying that those physicians "are

morally, ethically, and legally justified. Moreover, the continuation of treatment is mandated—by the obligation of the state and its judiciary to protect human life."

The next speaker—Morris County Prosecutor Donald Collester—followed the same temperate tone as his superior, Hyland: intransigency modified with words of compassion.

"We obviously must be struck with a human element here of great sympathy for the family," Collester said, glancing at the Quinlans. "But we are in a courtroom. Therefore, we must rid ourselves of the natural compassion that we have for the family.

"What is being postulated here on their behalf, I submit to the Court, is a right to die as opposed to a right to live. What is being asked is to place a judicial stamp of approval on the taking of human life. I submit to the Court that sympathy must be outweighed by the duty to preserve life and the sanctity of life upon which that duty is based!"

As Collester stepped down, Judge Muir called on Ralph Porzio, attorney for the physicians.

Porzio was the veteran attorney for the defense—a man in his late fifties with a deceptively frail stature and the local reputation for being oratorically eloquent, with a penchant for fire-and-brimstone delivery.

He began his statement in low key, but quickly accelerated into the form of locution for which he was renowned. Calling upon Judge Muir to resist pronouncing "an execution—a death sentence" upon Karen Quinlan, Porzio said: "There are hundreds of thousands of people in the United States who might qualify for execution—for death sentence—merely on the basis of somebody's definition of the 'quality of life.' Fresh in our minds are the Nazi atrocities. Fresh in our minds are the human experimentations. Fresh in our minds are the Nuremberg Code."

Porzio went on, relentlessly—declaring that this case was "in the area of Olympian decisions," as well as "in the area of homicide. Supposing for a moment that we forget about this patient and think about a hypothetical patient. She has been examined, let's say, by a thousand of the world's most outstanding physicians and they had unanimously pronounced that this patient has sixty minutes in which to live. Now, if someone comes along and performs or commits any act that ends that life at the end of fifty-five minutes, Your Honor, that is homicide!

"I think it is utter nonsense for us to deal in all of these niceties where the net effect is the termination of a human life, whether it is pulling the plug, giving arsenic poison, an overdose of drugs, or anything else. . . . We are not here, Your Honor, to debate whether a thousand angels can dance on the head of a needle—as was a favorite subject of medieval debate. I say you are being asked to place your stamp of approval upon an act of euthanasia.

"We are not gods. We are mortals. So let us then, as in this hour of trial as we begin, so conduct ourselves that when the eyes grow dim and when our own lives shall fade, and when men and women in some distant day shall gather to warm their hands over the fires of memory, they may look back—they may look back and say to us: They searched for truth, they nurtured justice, they know compassion; but above all, above all, they walked with honor and wore the garments of understanding." Following the verbal flourishes of Ralph Porzio, the final opening statement by Theodore Einhorn seemed the essence of brevity and simplicity.

Speaking on behalf of St. Clare's Hospital, Einhorn urged that guidelines be set by the court for the future conduct of physicians, hospitals, lawyers, and citizens in general.

"I would submit," he said, "that it would certainly be a great benefit to the medical profession, to the legal profession, and to the public as a whole . . . if somehow the Court, in the decision of this case, could indicate and state to the medical profession that they can, with a certain amount of reliance, without being worried about criminal prosecution, without having to worry about civil prosecution—they can, keeping in mind the new technological and scientific advances, use more advanced criteria to determine whether or not a person is dead."

The opening opinions abruptly concluded, Theodore Einhorn returned to his seat at the counsel table, and Paul Armstrong walked quickly toward the bench and called the first witness.

"Dr. Robert Morse, please."

Dr. Morse is a thirty-seven-year-old, compact man with an assured manner and an easy smile, which he turned

toward Joe and Julie as he walked to the witness box.
He quickly became somber when Paul Armstrong began
the questioning by asking him to describe Karen Quinlan's
present condition.

She is comatose, he said. With sleep-awake cycles.
"There are two types of coma," Dr. Morse explained.

PAUL: Would you explain them?

MORSE'S ANSWER: One is described as sleeplike unresponsiveness, and the other is described as awake unresponsiveness. When Karen was originally seen at
Newton Hospital, she was more in a condition like
sleeplike unresponsiveness. When I transferred her to
St. Clare's, she was in that same condition. But as time
came on, she switched—she developed what we call
sleep-wake cycles. Now, a person can have these sleep-
wake cycles and still be in a coma. "Coma" is the lack
of consciousness. So you can be awake and still be
unresponsive to your environment.

Q: Would you explain to the court exactly what you
mean by "awake"?

A: I mean she has her eyes open. She blinks, and
things of that sort, which is the arousability factor of
the coma. But a person—if you and I and the other
attorneys were standing there, it is my impression, and
even the attending doctors', from watching her on a
daily basis and even feeding her, that a rudimentary
supportive mechanism such as getting your food—when
you go to the zoo, the animals will come over to you
by instinct. Karen doesn't even follow the act of
hanging the IV bottle up to get her food—and many
other things that we have observed, on an ongoing
basis, you know—

Q: Such as?

A: Dr. Javed and I, in examining her, decided what
the modus operandi should be, and she's totally unaware we're there.

It's interesting. We had a lot of doctors come out,
good enough to give their opinions and to try and help
us with this particular case—and I won't mention the
particular doctor—but it's interesting that he said, "You
know, with three or four of us standing here, the interesting thing is she doesn't seem to be aware that we're
here." You know, when you have a consultation in a

hospital room, your eyes follow one doctor to another to define what he's thinking. She's aware. She does fall into episodes of sleep, but she is in a state of coma.

Q: Can you define the concept of coma any further? Are there, within medical authorities, a further term that may be applicable?

A: Again, everybody has their own bailiwick, and I will only assess her based on the concepts that I follow. If you want to put—I don't think it serves any constructive value, in this particular case.

Q: What I was referring to, Doctor, is the persistent vegetative state that we talked about.

A: I think, I would say the nearest that I could categorize Karen is she is in a chronic persistent vegetative state.

Q: Doctor, in your opinion, is the nature of the damage sustained by Karen irreparable?

A: Well, my personal feeling is that no doctor ever likes to arrive at a position where—no doctor can ever say that someone is definitely irreversible. But after six months and watching the—her recovery, one has to be very, very pessimistic that she could lead some sort of a functional existence. I don't know what level she'll return to.

Q: Do you know the nature, or the regions, that have been destroyed by this insult in Karen's case?

A: No one can know. No one can know specifically but her presentation is one of what we call decortization, indicating that the cerebral hemorrhage, subcortical white matter, certain portions of the diencephalon, and certain portions of the brain stem might be involved. It's much like a case of multiple sclerosis. You can look at the person, see certain modalities, but you know there are silent regions. I would say that the major insult here is in the cranial hemispheres and subcortical white matter.

Q: Is it possible for those regions, once they sustain an insult, Doctor, to repair themselves?

A: Anything, I guess, is possible. I would personally say, from my observation of watching her on a daily basis, again, I can't talk in generalities. I have to talk about the patient I am taking care of. My personal feeling is that I haven't seen that much improvement after five and a half months.

Q: When you say you haven't seen "much improvement"—have you seen anything?

A: She has gone from sleeplike unconscious to wakelike unresponsiveness; that usually happens after three or four weeks when a patient comes in.

Q: In your opinion, Doctor, is there any course of treatment that will lead to the improvement or cure of Karen's condition?

A: I personally don't know of any. And we have tried to investigate. Remember, the history is most important and we have not been able to uncover any. I personally don't know of any, and that's why I have asked other people to come in to give Mr. and Mrs. Quinlan and their children an opportunity . . . because sometimes you are so close to the case you are so subjective. In this case here, it's been a difficult case, because it's been a hardship on the family. And I had asked another doctor to come out, and he examined the patient. And I tried not to tell him the particulars before he came out, so he has some understanding, could be objective. So I would say that I don't see how she could go back to—I don't know what plateau she'll arrive at. One can't say the plateau of existence that individual will be. I don't know what kind of a functional existence she'll ever arrive at.

Q: You mentioned "improvement," Doctor. It seems to be somewhat of a value-charged word. Has she come out of this state at all, in any sense of the word "improvement"?

A: She's in a coma. A person in a coma for six months. There's a difference. When a person is in a sleeplike unresponsiveness, you really don't have any idea. You can't really assess the person in a wakeful state . . . because there are only certain things you can assess in a patient that's in a sleeplike coma. When a patient, on a daily basis, changes to where they get to a state of wakeful unresponsiveness, you begin to see how the central nervous system is working. It's like examining a patient, you know, before delivery; you can feel the fetal parts, you can say, "Gee, this is a transverse lie," or "This is a head presentation, or breech presentation." But oftentimes the delivery, you know, it's different. There might be a shoulder, or something that you're not aware of.

I think in watching this patient over a six-month period I begin to see certain things that I don't know from my experience, and watching, talking to other doctors who are in the field. We talked to the doctors to get some idea as to what we could do with this young girl. And I just don't see how she can reverse these different principles which are hard-fast in neurology.

Q: How many patients have you seen in similar conditions of such a persistent vegetative state, or coma?

A: Well, each case is different, Paul. And I've seen a lot of patients that have been—I've never seen a patient with all the facets that Karen has, this way, and I'm sure that other doctors will say the same thing as you go along in the testimony.

Q: I see.

A: And there are many, many things that go into it. It's sort of an impression one gets. It's not that Karen is any different from whether it was my own daughter, Karen. There are definite principles that we follow in evaluating a patient; otherwise we would have no way —it would be saying that this patient is this: this patient is this. I've seen many, many patients in coma— otherwise, I would not be able to evaluate Karen.

. . . What I'm saying is I have seen all the things that Karen has, and I may never, never, ever see them again. I see other patients pass before my eyes that I've seen with a little bit of this, a little bit of this, but irrespective, it would not matter, because Karen is an entity in herself and we would examine Karen as she presents, neurologically.

Q: Doctor, what is the necessity of the respirator?

A: Well, she doesn't breathe, so it forces air in and out of her lungs. And don't forget that the air, the oxygen change, is in the lungs. So if you don't get any air in there, then you're not going to be able to breathe. Then, the brain itself is very dependent on oxygen saturation, and this is a patient who is already injured to start with, so God knows what her requirement is.

Q: Could you tell us, in your opinion, why it is that she's incapable of breathing spontaneously, or breathing by herself?

A: Well, we don't know the exact reason, Paul. As to where the lesion is, and all the different things that are involved to make her less respiratory dependent, I could

not say. I would say that she probably has some brain
stem dysfunction. This is the usual pattern.

Q: Doctor, do you have any opinion as to how long
it would be possible for Karen, her vital processes, to
be sustained with the assistance of the respirator?

A: I don't think anybody, Paul, can give an assessment of that. Each individual differs. You don't know
the extent of the insult. Some people might say one
hour; another person, two weeks. They may all be correct. Personally, I never gave it any consideration like
that, because I really don't know.

Q: Doctor, would it be fair to say that utilization of
the respirator itself, that there are inherent dangers in
so doing?

A: There are inherent dangers in anything, even IVs.
But beyond the inherent dangers of the respirator, it's
outweighed by the benefit that it gives to this particular human being, at this particular point in time.

Q: Doctor, how long do you feel that Karen could
survive without the aid of the respirator?

A: I don't know, Paul.

Q: Have you run a test to this effect?

A: I have not.

Q: Do you mean take her—or wean her—off the respirator? Is that what you mean?

A: We tried that, naturally. This was part of our
assessment in her neurological status. We tried to get
her onto a floor where they could have the privacy of
their family. But we were unable to do so.

Q: Why is that, Doctor?

A: Well, actually—I'm just going to talk out. Her
tidal volume, which is the amount of air she moves
through her lungs, would fall down at times to critical
levels where we knew that if she didn't move a certain
volume of air through her lungs that then she would
not have enough oxygen to saturate the blood, and
thereby go to the brain.

Q: Doctor, with reference to the course of treatment prescribed by you for Karen, was this initially
done with the permission of the Quinlan family?

A: Yes, it was.

Q: And how did you acquire that?

A: Well, I would talk to Mr. and Mrs. Quinlan and

try to keep them appraised of the case, and they were trying to give us all the information they could gather, and naturally that's the mother and father, and I think I met Mary Ellen once or twice. And, you know, you have to try to work with the family. After all, I mean, we would never do anything for her without the family's permission.

Q: Did there come a time, Doctor, when you were requested to suspend certain aspects of the course of treatment, by the Quinlan family?

A: Well, you see one of the problems here was that this is a patient—what we have been doing is following the patient. Our modus operandi was to try to see if we could get the patient off the respirator, to get her into a chronic care facility, which we could not do. That was futile. We couldn't find an institution. . . . I had talked to several doctors about placing her, and we couldn't get anywhere. And then the question came up about extraordinary means of care.

Q: How did this come up?

A: As I recall, first of all we showed EEGs to the family. She did not meet—she is not brain dead. And the question is that, with the medical care that we have today, there were certain perimeters that we have to stay in. But the moral issue—Mr. and Mrs. Quinlan became aware of this moral issue—and so we tried to look into the feasibility as to whether there was some medical cases that substantiated this, that would deviate from tradition as it is now.

Q: Substantiate what, Doctor?

A: Well, you know, what is the quality of life? You know, brain death are the parameters that we followed.

Q: That does not apply in this case.

A: It does not apply as far as we are concerned. . . . I showed the EEGs to Mr. and Mrs. Quinlan and explained them. The question of returning her to a state of grace and dignity—the total patient is involved here: moral fiber, legal fiber, and her medical care. So we tried to investigate the feasibility, but I couldn't find any other case to go on. You must understand the empathy involved here is tremendous. These people have gone through a lot. We have spent twenty-four hours a day, but they have, too.

Q: And, to date, you've not honored the request of the Quinlan family?

A: Well, with the guidelines that we have available . . . for brain death and chronic vegetative state, there is no case that I can refer to. Nobody seems to be able to tell me of any case that would fit the criteria.

Q: Then, Doctor, is Karen presently receiving the medical measures that you have prescribed for her?

A: Oh yes.

Q: In your opinion, Doctor, how long will she remain in this form of existence?

A: I really don't know, Paul.

Paul nodded, "Thank you, Doctor." And as he walked toward the counsel table, Judge Muir reminded the witness: "Dr. Morse, you have to be cross-examined by the other attorneys.

"Mr. Coburn?"

Daniel Coburn was speaking brusquely, even before he reached the witness stand.

"Doctor, my name is Mr. Coburn. I'm the guardian for Karen. We have never spoken before right now. Is that correct?"

Morse answered "No," and the cross-examination began.

Q: Did you have a chance to read the records at Newton Memorial Hospital concerning Karen?

A: Yes, I did.

Q: The records you reviewed were the result of tests that had been performed on urine and blood. Is that correct?

A: Yes, on urine. Of the records available to me, the only examination was urine.

Q: What were the results?

A: Quinine was present. So that day I called the State Drug Control Center—that evening, up there—to find out if there was any drug that I was unaware of that might be broken down into quinine as a metabolite. They informed me they didn't know of any. Of course, New York handles such a high volume of it, I right away called them.

Q: You mean the New York Drug Center?

A: Yes.

Q: Did you determine, at some later point, the presence of any other drugs or toxic matters?

A: Yes, but they were in the therapeutic range, you know. I think that to put it in its proper perspective, I am dealing with a patient at one point of time. All I knew is that there were a combination of drugs that were all within the therapeutic range that were present in the urine and in the serum.

Q: What were those drugs?

A: The initial ones that we found were salicylates, which was normal.

Q: What is that?

A: Aspirin. She had some barbiturates, which was normal, .6 milligrams per cent; toxic is 2 milligrams per cent, and the fatal dose is about 5 milligrams per cent. So it was well within normal limits. There were traces of Valium. No hard drugs, or anything like that.

Q: Is there anything significant to the quinine?

A: Well, the quinine—again, quinine, from what they told me—I asked them, I said, listen, what is the usual circumstances in which you will find quinine? And they said, mixing in drinks as soda water. People who are at parties, and things like that. So, personally, it would not have made any difference three days later, in seeing the patient. I felt that that was a plausible explanation, and followed suit in the absence of other hard drugs. I know what you are intimating.

Q: Now, coma can be induced by the consumption of drugs. Is that correct?

A: Right. That is correct.

Q: In that situation where a person is in a drug-induced coma, is there some sort of paralysis of brain functions?

A: Well, if a person has a toxic insult to the blood, such as the present drugs, and in combination with alcohol, what it does is it decreases the vital structures of the brain so much so that it leaves the patient defenseless. If it is in certain quantities, it can cause irreparable damage by, for instance, let's say it suppresses the drive to breathe. Well, if the person doesn't breathe, then as a follow-through the patient sustains dysfunction to higher portions of the brain. But it is not a one-to-one relationship, because people are drinking all the time. It is a combination of the patient's state of health at the time it happened, what the episodes were, what was taken and in what combination, whether there were any other things that we didn't know about such as a head injury and things of that sort; it is the sum total of everything.

Q: Karen's condition, as it exists today, had its origin in anoxia. Is that correct?

A: We feel that is the most probable diagnosis.

Q: Lack of oxygen, for one reason or another.

A: Yes.

Q: You say there were no physical signs of violence?

A: I didn't see any. We always look for this. I examined for battle signs, head injuries, and if I had thought there were any I would have transferred her from Newton, for an angiogram, right away. If you notice, through this case, I never asked for a neurosurgeon to come in because there was no need—because there was nothing to evaluate. If I felt there was a problem such as a subdural hematoma, something like that, I would have asked a neurosurgeon to come in and evaluate it.

Q: Do you know of any case, similar to Karen's, of people who have lived six months?

A: Well, in a chronic vegetative state, yes, they can.

Q: How similar to hers—because hers is not exactly the same?

A: That's the point. She could live eight months, nine months, she could die tonight. I would not be able to give you any definite answer on that, in all truthfulness.

Q: You also couldn't give a definite answer as to what plateau she will reach?

A: Absolutely not. It is an ongoing feeling. I would never say what plateau she could be at, except that my personal feelings as the attending doctor and most intimately involved with her, I don't see how she could; and from my understanding of neurology, except for an act of God, I don't see how she could lead a functional cognitive life. She might "exist" in a ward.

Q: You say "functional cognitive life"?

A: If she can't communicate, then she can't learn.

Q: How about down to questions of "severely retarded"?

A: I really don't know. At this stage, now?

Q: Yes.

A: After six months, my personal feeling is I can't see it. I am not absolutely sure. I can't see it.

Q: Would you say that her condition, whatever it may be in the future—her "living," as it may be—that the chances of that occurring are greater on the respirator; or off the respirator?

A: I couldn't answer that. I know what you are saying; I can't answer. I don't know what will happen if she goes off. As with the other doctors, they are in the same boat we are in: One doesn't know.

Q: Is there any chance her condition would improve, off the respirator?

A: Your guess is as good as mine.

Q: We are in a guessing game.

A: The whole point is, if I can make myself clear, she doesn't need the respirator, except she can get infections. The measured air that is going through is also preventing her lungs from collapsing. She is breathing, but what quality of breathing, God only knows.

Maybe she will only use two third of the lungs. The only parts may have increased dead space and she can get an infection.

Donald Collester, cross-examining, asked Dr. Morse to describe, quickly, the parts of the brain.

"Fine," said Morse. "Well, the brain is divided into the cerebral hemispheres which are responsible for most of the conceivabilities of an individual; prima receptive areas of, like pain, touch, place your left leg certain ways."

COLLESTER: And those senses are located—where?

MORSE: They're in the cerebral hemispheres, usually. To interpret vision, for instance, if a person puts a light into your eyes, you recognize light. It's usually a conceivability/speech communication. Then you get into the earlier development of the brain, which is the diencephalon, which is the thalamus and relay stations of the brain—

Q: Slow down. Explain that for me, please?

A: —then you get into the relay stations. One touches your foot with a pin. The impulse goes up. It goes to many parts of the brain. And it's like a computer, where you get input from one section to the other, tells you this is a sharp pin prick. Such as a relay station.

You get to the brain stem, which has three primary areas: the mid-brain, the pons, and the medulla.

Q: What is the brain stem? What sort of sensations—what sort of activity—does the brain stem control?

A: The brain stem is usually for the vital functions. It has to do with the—there are different tracks, like the verticular activating system, tracks like that, and the cranial nerves that have their end point, basically, in the brain stem itself—respiration.

Q: Respiration being one; am I correct?

A: Yes.

Q: Now, based upon your examination of Karen Quinlan and based upon your treatment of her over these many months, it's your opinion, is it not, that she has some brain stem function which can control respiration?

A: That's right.

Q: Because she does have spontaneous respiration, correct?

A: Yes.

Q: She also has other senses that we're aware of which we normally associate with being alive. Isn't that so?

Q: How about the sense of pain?

A: Well, I can say this for you: The sensation of pain is a subjective thing. In other words, if you stick someone with a pin, I might feel the pain one way; another person might feel it another way. I can tell you this, that when you do stimulate this individual, there is a reflex. Where it goes, I don't know. Whether it stops at a certain level, goes out, I don't know.

Q: In other words, let's say you pinched her—touched her in a certain area—she would react? Would she withdraw from it?

A: She moves, all right. Whether she withdraws from me—I know what you're asking, and I'm trying to be honest. Yes, she does move. She does feel. What quality she feels these impulses at, God only knows. I don't.

The cross-examination of Dr. Morse continued into mid-afternoon. The neurologist repeated several times his belief that Karen Quinlan's brain damage was irreversible; but since she was not *"brain dead,"* by any medical criteria, he would not discontinue the respirator that was supporting her breathing.

He testified that he, like the Quinlans, was a member of the Roman Catholic Church—but that he had not heard of the concept of "extraordinary means" until informed of it by Joe and Julia Quinlan, the hospital chaplain, Father Pat Caccavalle, and the Quinlan family priest, Father Thomas Trapasso.

"When this moral issue was raised," Dr. Morse testified, he had thought that "perhaps the Church had some medical support to make their decision on. That is what we were trying to find out. It was on that basis that I would have considered it—if there was some medical tradition that would support that case, other than brain death.

"The issue was: In a long, vegetative-state coma, was there some medical support for the moral support that I could go on—and [still] stay within medical tradition?"

Finding no medical precedent to support the Church's extraordinary means concept, the doctor concluded, he had telephoned the Quinlans—"and I said that I personally empathized with them. I knew what they were going through. But I said 'I cannot break medical tradition.' "

As Paul had predicted, there were no surprises in Dr. Morse's testimony.

But later that afternoon, shortly after Dr. Arshad Javed had been called to the witness stand, the Quinlan family were startled by a sudden interchange between the pulmonary specialist and Paul Armstrong.

Q: As far as your treatment is concerned, with the maintenance of the respirator, Doctor, was that done with the permission of the Quinlan family?

A: As you realize, I am consultant on the case, not yet a physician. So my responsibility probably is more to attending physician than to the family. I am not saying that I have no responsibility to the family, but I was asked by the attending physician to manage the patient.

Q: Did there ever come a time when you were asked by the Quinlan family, is what I'm asking.

A: I don't know if I was asked a direct question by them, or they asked me—yes, I have been talking and discussing the patient with them, and they are aware of the fact that I am on the case.

Q: Did there come a time, Doctor, when you were requested to suspend the course of treatment—and by that "course of treatment," I mean the utilization of the respirator on Karen?

A: Again, those discussions—if there were any discussions—they took place between the attending physician and the family; and at a point, I knew about them eventually.

Q: Were you present at any of these discussions, Doctor?

A: I was present in the meeting in Mr. Courey's office—administrator of the hospital.

Q: Were you present at any other meeting with the Quinlan family, with either Joseph Quinlan or Mary Ellen Quinlan?

A: I have met them. But we never discussed taking her off the respirator.

It was all Julie Quinlan could do to keep from gasping aloud.

The family looked at one another in disbelief.

Chapter 16

At eight o'clock on the night of October 20, following the opening trial session, Father Tom had scheduled a "Prayer Vigil" at Our Lady of the Lake, to ask God to give courage to the Quinlans and wisdom to Judge Muir.

Simultaneous prayer services were being conducted in three other Catholic churches—in Morristown, in a Nebraska city, and in Quebec, Canada.

In spite of the late hours, more than 350 parishioners appeared, filling every seat in the chapel. A musical program of singing and guitar playing preceded the priest's mass.

While the music was playing, Father Tom was called to the telephone in his office.

He will always remember that phone call although, in his dismay over its import, Father Tom forgets the name of the caller.

—It was a reporter, perhaps from one of the wire services. He said, "I thought you ought to know, Father, that the Vatican has made a statement. It just came over the wires. It's *against* the Quinlans."

If you had taken my heart and drained it out of my body, I couldn't have been in more pain.

Then the reporter read me a brief section of the statement—something about there being no "right to die," but only the "right to live."

I was really in a state. I've been in the Church long enough to know that not everything that comes out of the Vatican is official. Like the government, they sometimes send out trial balloons, to see the lay of the land and get reaction on how the laymen think.

But this was a very strange statement. And maybe it was official. I couldn't know.

All I knew at that moment is that I was very disturbed and very unhappy.

I tried to hide it. I didn't want to spoil this night for Joe and Julie.

But when I went out a few minutes later to say the mass, I made a few extemporaneous changes.

I remember I accentuated the positive. I laid more emphasis than I had intended to on "life."

I was frightened.

Julie wept as Father Tom prayed with his parishioners—unaware of his personal crisis, thinking only of Karen.

—"We are dealing with a life that, whatever course the future will take, is a life out of which much good has already come and from which much good is yet to come," he said. "The question of life, the question of death, have plagued the human mind and heart in the very beginning of time. Death had always been the ultimate question that every man must face and every man must endure.

"Science has progressed a great deal. We have progressed to the point where, through technology, we are able to sustain life to an almost unbelievable degree. That is precisely the problem that we are dealing with now. How do we deal with technology? How can we use it in a way that enriches man's life? Is technology to be used to a point where somehow we no longer need God?

"With gifts of bread and wine we will place the life of Karen, and we will offer it as a beautiful and loving gift to God to choose and take when He wills. We will pray that in our world and in our society, men will love and respect life. We will pray that all the arguments that will be used in this case concerning the sanctity of life and reverence for life will be remembered. Let us pray for that."

Following the taking of Communion, Julia meditated silently:

—I just prayed, not only for Karen, but that somehow God would give me the courage to stand up and thank all of these beautiful people, let them know what's in my heart. That night was such an exemplification of charity and of love—they were really reaching out to Joe and me, they really loved us, and it was truly lovely. So God did give me the courage to stand up in front of those hundreds of people and thank them all. And the whole congregation rose, right afterward, and sang "Let Charity and Love Prevail."

That night, when we went to bed, I said to Joe that this was a miracle.

The faith healers are always talking about "miracles," about how they're going to go in and just raise Karen up. If God wanted her to be raised up, He could have done it Himself. If He wanted to take her, He could have done that. So I don't believe that He makes miracles like that, with all the drama and fanfare. Miracles are done very quietly and very privately, and I believe this night was one. To see all those people come in, and fill the church and just pour out their love in prayer—that is a miracle.

We went to bed almost happy that night.

At the Rectory, Father Thomas Trapasso retired "in an extremely emotional frame of mind."

—After the Vigil, a reporter had handed me a copy of the complete wire service story out of the Vatican. It quoted Gino Concetti, a "Roman theologian writing for the Vatican newspaper," as saying that the doctors should not give up on Karen and that "a right to death does not exist. Love for life, even a life reduced to a ruin," he said, "drives one to protect life with every possible care."

When I went to bed, I was thinking very seriously about what the Church would do—and what I would do. I had no fear about the moral principle of "extraordinary means." That is an established concept of the Church, and I knew they couldn't condemn me for my spiritual guidance on that. But I thought what the Vatican might be against was the taking of the case to the courtroom. Maybe they felt that was the wrong forum.

Of course, I hadn't given any spiritual guidance to the Quinlans to go to court, but that was the only grounds I could think of that might make them say, "Trapasso, pull out. This matter has gotten beyond you and beyond the Church. We don't want to get involved with what has now become a legal political issue."

I realized if that were to happen—if they wanted me to bug out and leave the Quinlan case alone—then I'd have a serious decision to make: follow my own conscience or my Church duty.

And I decided that night that my higher duty was to Joe and Julie. There was no way I could abandon the Quinlans and leave them hanging on their own. It was a Church issue, and I couldn't say I'll withdraw without saying the Catholic Church is withdrawing.

I decided that, if it should become necessary, I would

disagree with the hierarchy. If it meant resigning the Parish, that is what I would do.

I fell asleep praying I wouldn't be forced into making that choice.

The morning newspapers printed excerpts from Vatican theologian Concetti's editorial. But in most publications his religious opinion was buried on the back page.

The front-page stories proclaimed the second trial session as "the day Joseph Quinlan takes the stand to plead for his daughter's right to die."

The crowds were larger and more insistent on Tuesday, October 21. More than two hundred media engulfed the courthouse grounds, matting yesterday's rain into the grass until it sponged beneath their feet like marshland. When the doors opened and the accredited press and first-in-line spectators had pushed their way in, there was still a large overflow crowd who declined to disperse. They sprawled on the courthouse steps, or reluctantly retreated to their cars, prepared to wait all day if necessary to learn, first-hand, what Karen Ann Quinlan's father had to say.

Inside Courtroom Number One, the spectators also had to wait for Joe's testimony. Paul Armstrong called, as the first witness, Dr. Julius Korein, the lean, graying chief neurologist from Bellevue Hospital, New York, the only medical witness for the Quinlans.

Paul guided him through a series of questions which he felt would emphasize Korein's brilliance and vast experience in treating coma patients.

PAUL: Is there a general term with which you could describe Karen's condition?

KOREIN: Well, the umbrella used for this is "persistent or chronic vegetative state." This covers such syndromes as apallic syndrome.

Q: Will you explain that, Doctor?

A: That's the bilateral cortex completely wiped out —the cortex. Also, syndromes such as akinetic mutism, coma vigil.

Q: Are these all altered states of consciousness and awareness, then, Doctor, that you're referring to?

A: They all refer to an altered state of consciousness, where you cannot communicate with the patient. There is no ability for the patient to have purposeful activity—higher cerebral activity. But they lie there. Their eyes are open. The eyes—and I'll paraphrase— the eyes hold the promise of speech, but there's no speech. You may think, and if you look at the patient, you may think they're following you, but they never directly follow a target.

Q: Are you referring to what's commonly known as the "locked-in" syndrome?

A: No. The locked-in syndrome is something else.

Q: Will you explain what that is?

A: The locked-in syndrome is lower down the brain stem, bilaterally, where the motor outflow is affected bilaterally without impairing consciousness or involving the reticular formation, which is the common feature of the persistent vegetative state. These patients may, in fact, look like they're in coma, but they have at least upward movements of the eyes and you can communicate with them by saying, "Look up, for yes. Look down, for no," and they will do so. They have normal sleep-awake cycles and carry on very complex conversations using their eyes. So you can establish communication with these people.

Q: Is that the circumstance here, Doctor?

A: No.

Q: Doctor, can the art of medicine repair the cerebral damage that was sustained by Karen?

A: In my opinion, no.

Q: Doctor, in your opinion is there any course of treatment that will lead to the improvement of Karen's condition?

A: No.

Q: Doctor, how many patients have you seen, in similar conditions of persistent vegetative states?

A: Exactly like Miss Quinlan, none. In terms of "persistent vegetative state," I would say upwards of fifty. Now I should qualify this, if I may? The patients that I've seen are "better"—are "better" than Miss Quinlan. In fact they did not have a respiratory problem. They breathed.

Q: Is the condition that distinguishes Karen's from these other patients, then, Doctor, the fact that she is incapable of breathing herself?

A: That she has this difficulty in breathing, associated with stimuli and with the sleeplike state.

Q: Doctor, in your opinion, is Karen dependent upon the respirator? Or is it merely performing an assistive function?

A: That's very difficult to answer. I'll try and answer it. If they take her off the respirator, and she starts showing respiratory difficulty as I have gathered occurred on several occasions—I mean, how long are you going to wait, in terms of "respiratory difficulty," to decide whether she's "dependent" or not? Because once you get low enough oxygen, I mean you're going to cause more and more damage.

Q: Okay.

A: So, in that sense, I think she's dependent. But this is not to mean that she won't breathe on her own without the respirator for minutes, hours, days, even years. I don't know.

Q: Doctor, is there any significance within the medical context of your area of specialty, of the words "extraordinary" and "ordinary" care?

A: They have meaning. But the meaning is not precise, not well defined. I could give you examples—

Dr. Korein then recounted certain procedures which might be considered "extraordinary"—such as an iced saline solution for a period of time, then replaced with fresh, whole blood from donors.

Now this is a tremendous procedure," Korein said. "It requires a huge number of personnel, tremendous technology, and I would consider it 'extraordinary' in terms of, you know, effort." However, he added, such procedures should be used "in acute situations where there is a possible outcome that's successful. I think in the past six cases that I know of that received such procedure, there were two survivals with recovery. Now that may sound poor, but these people seemed doomed, and they had some potential for survival—meaningful survival—and it worked on them.

"I would say that the 'extraordinary' procedures have to do with the utilization of medical personnel, medical technology, and time. And they should be used in all situations where the outcome has a reasonable possibility of being successful. . . . They are to be used in acute situations that will save life."

Q: What type of "life," Doctor?

A: There is a value judgment that is implicit in this: You are not interested—excuse me—I, and many of my colleagues are not interested in saving a life that will lie as a vegetable for ten years.

Q: Doctor, in your medical opinion, is the medical care and treatment presently being administered to Karen "ordinary" or "extraordinary"?

A: It is extraordinary.

Under further questioning, Dr. Korein testified that it was his belief that every physician must use "value judgments" in the practice of medicine.

Q: Is it not a fact, sir, that these value judgments are made within the confines of certain accepted medical standards?

A: Yes.

Q: And are there any accepted medical standards to be used to determine what is or is not an extraordinary procedure?

A: There may be. It varies.

Q: It varies from doctor to doctor?

A: Or facility to facility. But there are standards, yes.

Q: Are these standards which are commonly accepted throughout the medical profession, sir?

A: I believe the standards are accepted, but not spoken of.

Q: Are you saying something in terms of an unwritten law or unwritten code, sir?

A: That's right, exactly. And I think—may I?—I think one of the purposes of this trial is to make this written.

The cross-examination of Dr. Korein by the defense attorneys was stern, and both the witness and the lawyers occasionally became testy. As the defense attempted to break down Dr. Korein's testimony of Karen Quinlan's hopeless state, the doctor became increasingly explicit in his descriptions of her condition. Julia Quinlan, sitting only ten feet away from him, concentrating on every word, became disturbed. . . .

Q: Anything is medically possible, Doctor—is that correct?

A: If you wish.

Q: You are the expert. You answer it.

A: I will say that anything is possible, with the proviso that: If I am holding a pencil and you ask me, "Can this pencil go up when I open my fingers?" the answer is "Yes, possible. By quantum mechanics, it has been shown—but the probability is so small that it is infinitesimal," and you would bet your life on it, that it would fall down.

Q: I wouldn't bet my life, after this.

A: I would bet mine.

Q: Let me ask you this. Correct me if I am wrong in my assumption. Is it accurate to say that, when a person is at a level of brain death, their human function—their cognitive function—is zero?

A: Yes.

Q: We will take yourself, as a skilled physician. We use those two examples, as the outside limits of cognitive function. Do you think you can work it within that framework?

A: What is the question?

Q: The question is: Karen is at some level obviously above brain death. Is that correct?

A: I see. You want a scale—between normal cognitive function, and zero?

Q: Right . . . Is it possible for you to give a mental age—when I talk about "mental age," I'm talking of the cognitive age of Karen's condition. Can you characterize her reflex, everything you've seen as far as Karen's cognitive function, in a stage much as a two-week-old infant, a five-week-old infant, seven-year-old child, or something like that?

A: It would be inaccurate, but I would make an attempt. Do you wish me to make an attempt?

Q: Yes.

A: The best way I can describe this would be to take the situation of an anencephalic monster. An anencephalic monster is an infant who's born with no cerebral hemisphere. Only the thalamus is left. Okay? [Pause. Then, answering his own question:] All right. Now, these babies may give the appearance of normalcy. They suck. They do all sorts of things. They could look perfectly normal. They [adults, parents] usually start to pick up, behaviorally, after six weeks.

Q: Pick up what?

A: Pick up some sort of behavioral aberration—maybe earlier, I'm not sure exactly—before and after six weeks. Now, the way they usually pick this up is that they hold up the child—and they see the light bulb shining through the kid's head. Then they know something is wrong.

Q: That's how they determine if it's in this condition?

A: If you take a child like this, in the dark, and you put a flashlight in back of the head—the light comes out the pupils. They have no brain. . . .

Julia Quinlan was not in the courtroom to hear the end of Dr. Korein's graphic testimony. A few minutes before, she had left the courtroom:

—The way he described Karen's condition, in every detail, down to the last twisted toe—I couldn't take it. I tried to leave very graciously, unobtrusively. I didn't break down until I got outside.

Bert brought me a cup of tea and took me to a private room until I settled down.

I was so sorry and so embarrassed, that it happened when Dr. Korein was testifying—the one doctor who was courageous enough to speak for us. Later that day, when Paul introduced me to him, I thanked him and apologized. "I'm sorry, Doctor, but your description was so accurate that I couldn't bear it."

He kindly assured me that he understood.

Joe was concerned about his wife when she fled the courtroom without a word to him, and he contemplated following her. But that would only have compounded the significance of the incident. And anyway, he was the next

to be called to the witness stand, and Paul was motioning
with his head: Joe interpreted it as a "stay calm sort of
nod." Joe didn't feel nervous.

—But I was apprehensive a little bit. Knowing how
important this was, and knowing that when Paul got
through with me, I was going to have to face cross-
examination by those five other attorneys. I'd asked
Paul in the morning, "What do you think they're going
to get into, when they ask me questions?" He had said,
"Don't worry. They won't be asking you any technical
questions. They know you're not a doctor. Just tell the
truth, just speak your heart. You'll be fine."

There was one thing that was really bothering me,
and I told Paul about it. That was what Dr. Javed had
testified yesterday. When he said that he had never
recommended that we take away the respirator. I just
didn't think that was right, and I wanted Paul to ask
me about it, so we could get our side on the record.

It was one of Paul Armstrong's first questions to his
client, after Joe was sworn in.

PAUL: Mr. Quinlan, how did Drs. Morse and Javed
advise you as to Karen's condition?

A: As to her condition, they were both telling me
that it was hopeless, and that she couldn't survive.

Q: Did the physicians suggest to you that you remove the respirator from Karen?

EINHORN: That is a leading question. Objection.

THE COURT: Sustain the objection.

PAUL (resuming): What advice did you receive
from the physicians concerning this condition?

A: One of them advised—the advice of one of the
physicians was that we terminate it, that we turn the
machine off.

Q: Who was that?

A: Dr. Javed. Dr. Morse was the doctor in charge
of the case, and Dr. Morse, at that time, didn't advise
any way, one way or the other. He simply stated the
facts and more or less left the decision up to us; but he
didn't advise us as to the machine at that time.

[Joe felt more relaxed now. He had said it.]

Daniel Coburn was the first to cross-examine Joe Quinlan.

"Now, Mr. Quinlan," Coburn said, "are you paying any of the bills in this case, the medical bills?"

A: I'm not personally. Medicaid is going to pay it.

Q: Has that been determined?

A: Yes, sir. I have a claim number, and all the doctors and all the hospitals have been notified by letter weeks ago.

Q: And that is because she's an emancipated child?

A: The fact that she was of age and she wasn't living at home and she had no income. She hasn't had any income, naturally, all this time. So, naturally, she would be entitled to Supplemental Security Income and the Medicaid that the state supplied along with it.

Q: She's receiving that now?

A: All the bills previous to May 1st, when I applied for Medicaid, had to be put through on a retroactive form. These bills have been taken care of. They may even have been paid by this time, I don't know. The ones from May 1st on, they're current bills, they're running bills. I won't receive a bill until they're final, I guess—except Dr. Sod, the one who gave her the angiogram, he sent a bill, and I signed the Medicaid form and sent it right back to him. I don't think the hospital has sent me a bill. The two doctors are attending her now until their part in this case is finished. Until their bill is complete, I asked them to send a bill to the State Department of Health, when it's convenient or when their bill is complete. It's up to them.

A short recess. Then Ralph Porzio, representing the doctors, quickly attempted to challenge Joseph Quinlan on his earlier testimony that Dr. Javed had advised turning off the respirator.

"Now, Mr. Quinlan," said Porzio confidently. "Dr. Javed was the man who was in charge of the respirator, was he not?"

A: Yes.

Q: In your mind, all during these months, he was not the attending physician, the chief physician, was he?

A: No. From what I understand, Dr. Morse, as the neurologist, was the doctor in charge.

Q: And you know, did you not, at that time during those months, and even right down to today, that Dr. Morse is the man who makes the decisions, from the medical standpoint. Isn't that true?

A: Yes, sir.

Q: So I want you to think back a minute, please, and think about Dr. Javed and what you had mentioned before. Isn't it a fact, Mr. Quinlan, that Dr. Javed never said to you, "I'll turn off the machine," did he? I mean, permanently.

A: When it came near the end . . . Dr. Javed advised us to turn the machine off.

Q: Well, now, Mr. Quinlan—

A: I hate this. I hate to give this bad reflection on these two men. I told you before—I love them both. I really feel in my heart that they've done everything possible for my daughter, and I hate putting them on the spot, if I am. I'm just being honest, and I hope they understand.

Mary Ellen looked at her mother, surprised. But Julie understood Joe's quiet emotional outburst. "The children felt impatient with the doctors, and knew that we were, so they couldn't understand how their father could love them and be furious with them at the same time. But I didn't see it as a contradiction. We could be angry with them, and still love them, for taking care of Karen with devotion in their hearts."

PORZIO (continuing): Your recollections could be mistaken, Mr. Quinlan, could they not?

A: They could very well be.

Q: Now, Mr. Quinlan, just let me remind you of a statement that you made on direct examination. You said that there was a period of time when there was an effort made to get Karen off the respirator. Do you remember that?

A: Yes, sir, right.

Q: And you also said that Dr. Javed told you that that was rather risky. Do you remember that?

A: Before he did it? No. He said he would try it,

but he would watch it closely, and it would have to be with supervision, and things to that effect, but he was willing to do it. And that was enough for me, to convince me that it wouldn't be risky, under the circumstances that he had mentioned. Afterward, he had mentioned that it would be risky to try it again, you know, after the first day. The second day he said it would be so risky that he just wouldn't do it again.

Q: Is it correct that they used the term, "trying to wean her off the machine"?

A: They had a machine at first. Well, they took her off the big machine, and they put her on this other machine that was intended to wean a person off—in that, when it didn't have that thing like an accordion that goes up and down and pumps the air. If she should breathe, the machine would just stop, and it would just wait for her to breathe again for, I guess, so many seconds. And if she didn't, then the machine would have to breathe for her. But it allowed her every benefit to breathe for herself.

Dr. Javed felt that this machine would be risky to put her on again—because it didn't have the alarms and all these other things that the big machine had.

Q: And, Mr. Quinlan, he assured you that he would watch it closely, is that right?

A: Yes, sir.

Q: One more thing, Mr. Quinlan, before closing. Didn't Dr. Javed report to you that Karen couldn't come off the the respirator? Didn't he report back to you?

A: That she couldn't come off?

Q: She couldn't come off the respirator. Didn't he report that to you?

A: No. He said that she would probably die.

Q: And that was a part of the decision, was it not, the ultimate decision, Mr. Quinlan, made by you that, after much prayer, that you wanted this to happen, and then that ultimately brought you to Father Trapasso, isn't that right?

A: I didn't want what I just said. [Pause.] I didn't want her to die. I just wanted to put her back in a natural state and leave it up to the Lord to decide.

Q: And there is one more thing that I want to clarify—and I think I'm trying to clarify it for your benefit. I notice some hesitancy on your part during the examination, and during the cross-examination, to use the words "terminate the life," or to use the word "death."

A: Not "death," no. "Terminate" is a word that I don't particularly like. . . .

Q: So that it is consistent with your belief, Mr. Quinlan, and consistent with the belief in the Roman Catholic Church, that you really don't die. Isn't that true—that what we in this world call death is really not death. Isn't that so?

A: That it's just death to this world as we know it. There's a better world.

Q: Moving into another world; it's just a phase that we're in now?

A: Right.

Q: And then let's say, to use a kind word, it comes to an end, and we move into another world. Isn't that right?

A: We go back to our permanent home.

Q: And what you, Mr. Quinlan, wanted for Karen was to get her back into a natural state. Isn't that right?

A: Yes, sir.

Q: So that then, if it was the Lord's wish, she would then go into a better and more everlasting life—isn't that true?

A: Yes, sir. If it was the Lord's will.

PORZIO: That's all.

As Joe stepped off the witness stand and walked toward her, Julie couldn't remember ever feeling more tenderness toward the man she had married twenty-nine years before, than she felt now.

—Paul was always talking to us of nobility—of the noble ideals we represented—and all at once, everything noble seemed to me to be in my husband. I don't suppose other people realized, even though they sympathized with him and admired him, how difficult it was for this very sensitive, quiet man to pull his heart out in front of everyone.

His love for Karen, his love for Christ, they all just came through clearly. I was so proud of him.

The next morning—day three—Father Tom Trapasso and Father Paschal Caccavalle, consecutively, were called upon to relate their roles in informing Joseph Quinlan of the "extraordinary means" concept of the Catholic Church, and in reassuring the father that this concept was applicable to the circumstances of Karen's illness.

The thrust of the cross-examination of the two priests appeared to be an attempt to clarify the voluntary nature of the concept:

Q: Father Trapasso, you told him [Quinlan] this is an *optional* tenet of the Catholic Church?
A: Yes.
Q: Certainly nothing required on his part.
A: Right.
Q: It also had to be a personal decision on his part in the sense, you might say, that it's morally acceptable; if he felt it was immoral, he should not do it.
A: Yes. He would ultimately have to follow some conscience, yes, sir.
Q: The Catholic Church does not require termination of extraordinary means?
A: That is correct.
Q: You say it does?
A: No, no. The Catholic Church does not require the termination of extraordinary means. . . .

After a fifteen-minute recess, Julie heard Paul's voice announcing distinctly: "I would like to call Mrs. Julia Quinlan, please." She hadn't anticipated being nervous.

—I was absolutely composed the moment before I heard my name and now, Lord help me, I thought I was going to collapse. It was only about twenty feet up to the front of the courtroom where Paul waited for me, but it felt like ten miles.

As I began to answer questions, though, my nervousness gradually vanished.

Most of my testimony related to the various times when Karen had seen friends or relatives very ill, terminally ill, and had told me that she would never want to be kept alive on machines. All of that was so clear in my mind, and most of the lawyers acted very sympathetic and kind. There was just one man, Mr. [David S.] Baime, the deputy for Attorney General Hyland, who appeared skeptical. He tried unsuccessfully at one point to get Judge Muir to dismiss what I was saying as "hearsay." So when I saw him coming forward to cross-examine, I felt just a bit uneasy. Because I didn't know what to expect.

BAIME: Mrs. Quinlan, I think the first instance you mentioned with regard to a patient who was dying occurred in January of 1972. Is that correct?

A: I would say approximately three years ago, yes.

Q: What was the relationship between Karen and that patient?

A: That was her Aunt Eleanor.

Q: What was her aunt suffering from?

A: Cancer.

Q: What type of cancer?

A: It was cancer of the breast.

Q: Had she been suffering from this illness for a substantial period of time?

A: No, she had not been.

Q: So this was a sudden development?

A: Yes, it was.

Q: Was she in pain?

A: Yes, she was.

Q: Was she in great pain?

A: Yes.

Q: So then Karen's statement to you with respect to this patient, her aunt, related, did it not, to a patient suffering great pain, and knowing full well that she would die. Isn't that true?

A: I would say yes.

Q: You mentioned a second instance. When was that?

A: The second instance was in this year—January of this year, or February.

Q: This statement was also made with respect to a patient at a hospital. Is that correct?

A: Yes.

Q: Who is that patient?

A: This was her girl friend's father.

Q: What was her girl friend's father suffering from?

A: From cancer.

Q: Do you remember what type of cancer that was?

A: No. I am sorry.

Q: Are you familiar with this man?

A: I am sorry, Mr. Baime, the second one did not occur—I was thinking of Mr. Birch when you asked me the date. The second one was in February 1974.

Q: Let's go to the last one.

A: Yes.

Q: Who was the patient?

A: The third person was Mr. Birch, B-i-r-c-h.

Q: He was suffering?

A: Yes, he was.

Q: Do you know what kind of cancer?

A: Yes. It was a brain tumor.

Q: And did Karen visit him at the hospital?

A: Only his family was permitted to visit.

Q: And how familiar was Karen with this girl's father?

A: They have been our very dear friends for, I would say, about twenty years.

Q: Do you know whether this patient was in pain?

A: I would say yes; but I don't know if it was extensive pain. He was in pain, yes.

Q: He was in great pain, wasn't he?

A: Perhaps he was.

Q: He was conscious?

A: I wasn't able to visit him, so I really can't state, you know, just to what extent his pain was.

Q: Again, you would agree, would you not, that Karen't statement related to a patient suffering great pains, in the throes of a terminal illness, knowing that that person certainly would die?

A: I would say that Karen's statements were related to her own way of living, to the way that she accepted life.

Q: I understand that. But again, the context in which that statement was made, again, was with respect to, or instigated by, an incident involving a patient suffering from cancer, terminal illness, knowing full well that patient was going to die, and suffering great pain?

A: In reference to that question, I would have to say

yes. But this was not the only occasions that Karen and I had discussed this.

Q: You say there was an occasion before this?

A: No. I mean, just general conversation. We had discussed the fact of being kept alive by extraordinary means, not referring—not making references to any individual.

Q: But again, the incidents which she was concerned with related to these events. Isn't that true?

A: No. I couldn't say that, because it wasn't only those three instances. It wasn't only on those occasions that she had made this reference. It was on many other occasions that she had made the reference that she would not want to be kept alive that way.

Q: She said she did not want to be kept alive if, in quotes, "extraordinary means" were necessary?

A: Yes.

Q: Did she use the term "extraordinary means"?

A: Yes. I'm sure that she did—by any "extraordinary means," or as I said before, that to in any way that she could not live her life to the fullest.

Q: What you are saying, then, is that Karen expressed a wish to deny medical care if she did not live life to its fullest?

A: No. I'm not saying that at all.

Q: I'm sorry, then.

A: I'm not saying that at all.

Q: Will you tell me what—

A: There are—Karen would not refuse medical help. I'm saying that if she had to be kept alive by extraordinary means, that she would not want to do this. This was not her will.

Q: You don't know what she meant by "extraordinary means," do you? In other words, she never expressed it, "If I have to live by virtue of a respirator, that I would rather pass away." She never said that, did she?

A: No, because I was—or she was not familiar with the machine—respirator—before this occurred.

Q: So she really wasn't familiar with medical terminology, medical technology?

A: No, she was not. She was just saying it in her own simple way.

BAIME: Thank you.
PORZIO: No questions.
EINHORN: No questions.
THE COURT: Step down.

As she walked back to rejoin her family in row number one, Julie felt "totally frustrated—for Karen. Because she did say those things. She did feel that way. I wondered—well, I only hoped I had conveyed her beliefs and desires to Judge Muir."

Paul called Mary Ellen Quinlan to the stand.
He was permitted to ask her only six brief questions —establishing her identity, religious faith, and understanding of the canons of the Catholic Church—before Daniel Coburn, the guardian, interrupted impatiently.

> COBURN: Excuse me. We have gone through the father, the plaintiff, and the mother, who could be a comparable guardian. We are to the sister, and I'm sure we are going to have the brother. I would object on the grounds that whatever her beliefs are, now we are getting beyond the question of relevance, much less admissibility.
>
> THE COURT: Mr. Armstrong, isn't her position, insofar as your legal arguments, only in concurrence of the familial approach to the constitutional right of privacy—
>
> PAUL: Yes. In addition to that, Your Honor, I think what I'm trying to demonstrate to the Court is the fact that all the Quinlan children were educated in the same fashion, as far as the religious teachings and canons are concerned.
>
> COBURN: It's stipulated.
>
> THE COURT: All right. It's stipulated solves the problem.
>
> PAUL (resuming): Mary Ellen, do you support the decision of your mother and father?
>
> COBURN: I'll object to this. Once again we have had testimony here from other witnesses who indicated this is a family decision. I have no reason to dispute that. It's stipulated.

THE COURT: Rather than spending a great deal of time, allow her to answer the question. Go ahead. Do you support—

MARY ELLEN: Yes, yes.

She was nervous now. And as the questioning proceeded, under frequent objections from Coburn and Deputy Baime, Mary Ellen's testimony was at times almost inaudible. Twice, she was reminded, "You are going to have to keep your voice up." And "You'll have to speak into the microphone."

She was permitted only one substantial and uninterrupted reply to a question by Paul Armstrong. He asked her what Karen had said to her about not wanting her life prolonged.

"Well, she said," Mary Ellen spoke quietly, "I guess about the same thing that my mother said. But I would like to point out that in the circumstances my mother is referring to, Karen was talking about Mr. Birch dying, and her girl friend's father dying. But when she talked to me, she was saying, in so many words, that she wouldn't want to be kept alive because she watched part of the family die, too. Not just the person who died legally. And she was saying that, like she was very good friends with this girl, and she watched what this girl went through— and that was what she was referring to, to me, when she said she wouldn't want to be kept alive."

There were no questions. No cross-examination of Mary Ellen.

Karen's friend through school, Lori Gaffney, was called to give similar testimony on Karen's thinking. There were no questions for her, either.

When Paul announced, "I would like to call John Quinlan, Your Honor," Judge Robert Muir himself interceded.

His testimony would be "cumulative only, I take it, Mr. Armstrong?" Muir inquired.

"That's correct," Paul answered.

"I don't think it is necessary for him to take the stand," the judge ruled flatly.

Young John was already seated in the witness chair when the justice declared, in effect, that what the boy had to contribute was an unnecessary and unwanted echo of his mother's and older sister's testimony.

John stood up, frowning, appearing bewildered, and as he began the slow saunter back toward the family, Julie wanted to rush over and wrap her arms around him.

"My heart broke for him," she said later. "Here at last, John had this one chance to tell how he felt, to finally do something that might help his big sister whom he mourned and loved—and they were saying to him no. Go away. We don't want you, we won't listen to you. I felt, this will be the last straw for John. He will be more bitter than ever. I felt angry and sorry, for him and for myself, because, I thought, 'Now I will never know what John is really feeling.' "

Paul approached the judge's bench.

"Your Honor, that completes the plaintiff's case.

"But I would like to reiterate the motion that petitioner had made at the outset, in that the plaintiff is asking the Court, as supreme guardian, to decide whether a certain course of action will foster Karen Quinlan's best interest.

"In order for the Court to exercise this judgment, we feel it should consider not only the legal arguments and the medical testimony presented in this courtroom, but should personally witness and appreciate Karen's present condition. Accordingly, we reiterate the motion that the Court, at its earliest convenience, repair to the Intensive Care Unit at St. Clare's Hospital where Karen Ann Quinlan is presently confined."

(Paul felt that if Judge Muir would visit her, then he, like himself, might gain a keener awareness and a deeper understanding of Karen's plight.) Judge Muir appeared to deliberate the motion, did not answer for a few moments. Then he said, in a tone which Paul interpreted as that of a man wrestling with the correctness of his decision, "Mr. Armstrong, this is a matter that is directed to my discretion.

"As we all recognize, I'm an ordinary human being, with ordinary thoughts, ordinary emotions. My position in this case is to decide it on the basis of the evidence presented.

"I have the right to go and see Karen, if I think it is appropriate. However, given all of the considerations and recognizing that emotion is an aspect that I cannot decide a case on, I do not think it's appropriate for me to go see her.

"So I'll deny the motion."

The following day, Tommy Flynn would read in the newspapers an account of the justice's refusal to see Karen, and wonder: "How could he really say that an issue like this can be decided without emotion? There is no life without emotion, no death without emotion. It's the heart of everything. It's what this case is all about."

The case for the defense was relatively brief.

Four doctors, all neurologists, testified as expert witnesses in behalf of Drs. Morse and Javed, St. Clare's Hospital, the state of New Jersey, Morris County, and the guardian ad litem.

Each physician confirmed, in his own distinctive manner, his opinion that Karen Ann Quinlan lay in what is known medically as a "persistent vegetative state."

Dr. Fred Plum, neurologist in chief at New York Hospital—an expert on comas—explained what the term meant: "a subject who remains with the capacity to maintain the vegetative parts of neurological function but who, as best as can be determined in every possible way by examination, no longer has any cognitive function."

Dr. Sidney Diamond of Mount Sinai Hospital, New York City, was asked to describe his impression of Karen, and appeared reticent:

"I'm sorry if the description causes any anguish to the family," Dr. Diamond began. "She was lying in bed, emaciated, curled up in what is known as flexion contracture. Every joint was bent in a flexion position and making one tight sort of fetal position. It's too grotesque, really, to describe in human terms like fetal."

Dr. Diamond expressed the opinion that Drs. Morse and Javed "have no choice but to continue the MA-1, if the patient cannot be 'weaned' from it. When respirators are disconnected in cases of cerebral death—and I have attended many such decision-making things—the plug is being pulled, or the respirator is being turned off, a dead person. A person without life. The life is over, and then the physician is ethically, and so far legally, permitted to terminate those supportive measures. I do not think, based on my examination and experience, that anybody would interrupt the use of this device now, on this patient."

Dr. Eugene Loesser, a neurologist from Chatham, New Jersey, was asked if he foresaw any improvement in Karen's condition.

"My opinion," he said, "is that the chances of improvement are—nil. I see no hope of improvement at this point."

Still, hopeless or not, Karen Ann Quinlan was not brain dead.

The final defense witness, Dr. Stuart Cook, Professor and Chairman of Neurosciences at the New Jersey Medical School, described briefly the legal criteria for brain death:

"The Harvard criteria," he said, "refer to a patient who is in a comatose state, unresponsive and unreceptive, who has no evidence of motor or reflex activity, has absence of spontaneous respiration, has a flat or iso-electric electronencephalogram—repeated over a twenty-four-hour period.

Q: Can you tell us, in your medical opinion, whether Karen is brain dead?

A: In my opinion, Karen Quinlan is clearly not brain dead.

That was the crux of the legal issue, as dealt with by the Civil Court. It permeated the closing arguments on Monday, October 27, 1975:

Karen was legally and medically alive and, therefore, the defense contended that to remove her respirator would be homicide.

In an impassioned closing statement, the attorney for the doctors, Ralph Porzio, invoked memories of Nazi atrocities and warned that a decision in favor of Joseph Quinlan would be a "God-like" one. It "would swing open the gates to the potential deaths of hundreds of thousands of people in the United States," he cried, "who are doomed to die because of a low quality of life under somebody's definition. . . . I implore you not to open the door to a culture or to a society that can go mad. . . . And, Your Honor, dare we deny the divine command, 'Thou shalt not kill'?"

William F. Hyland, the Attorney General of New Jersey, softened and concretized the issue: "This law has been well briefed, and I think very eloquently argued.

"I don't want to be repetitious, so I'll simply state that, while there is a homicide statute as a background against which this case has been tried, I think the far more important thing at the moment is for us to consider what changes in the law are being requested—with respect to the quality of life, the right to practice religious beliefs, and so on. I have read in the paper," Hyland said, "that I have equated the pulling of the plug—and I hate that term, but I have to use it—with murder; which simply is not the case.

"I have said that there is a grave risk of criminality presented, if conduct of this kind is engaged in, and of course we're talking about homicide, not necessarily murder.

"All of us would agree that the discontinuance of the respirator would be humane, but with the first critical step taken toward the development of a society which, as Mr. Porzio said, might well go mad, I think that we have produced the possibility of stepping into a darkness instead of into light. Because, for the first time, a court in this country, in a civil matter, would have issued a judgment of execution.

"I don't think this Court has a right to do that . . . and I ask that the complaint be dismissed," said Hyland.

Paul Armstrong, in his closing argument, asked the Court to "take into account that complex of values and attitudes which recognize and give meaning to them, 'dignity of man.'" Describing Karen Quinlan's condition—"a poor and tragic creature whose life is no more than a patterned series of the most primitive nervous reflexes, her now disunified and unperceiving body constrained to function against all natural impulses," he posed the question:

"Could anything be more degrading to a human being— a human being who has come on this earth full of love and promise, who has known peace and joy? Can anything be more degrading than to be offered up as a living sacrifice to the materialistic and misguided belief that death can somehow be cheated, if only we find the right combination of wires and gauges, transistors and tubes?"

Asking the Court to respect Karen's own prior expressions, her constitutional right of privacy, her parents' and the Catholic Church's moral views, Armstrong said, "Thus it is, Your Honor, that we conclude our review of the sad and weighty issues that have brought us here before you in rare unanimity of spirit.

"The plea of all of us through this trial has been: Help us resolve these issues.

"The Quinlans' request, which initiated these proceedings, is clear: We love Karen, but we know that hope is gone. Let her return to her God, but let none who suffer by her illness suffer yet the more by her departure.

"This Court, moved not by compassion but by thirst for justice, can grant this request to the full. It can say not only: Karen, pass on in peace; it can say as well: Mr. Hyland, Mr. Collester, there is no murder here. Mr. Einhorn, your clients may accede to the request. Dr. Morse and Dr. Javed, you have come to us for guidance. We give it to you now. Six long months of vigils over Karen's bed, six long months of loving conversation with Joe and Julia in their anguish, six long months of searching and doubt, these will not be counted nothing by us. Take counsel, once again among yourselves, far from crowded courtrooms. We have seen enough to know that your decision will be true. Take your sister Karen, and if in your heart of hearts, counseled by your brother physicians and unfettered by fears that uncomprehending law will stay your hand, you determine that further ministrations would be no more than useless punishment, return her with our blessing to that state where her own body can heed, if it will, the gentle call that beckons her to lasting peace."

The Civil Court trial in the matter of Karen Quinlan was ended.

Judge Muir rose. "All right, gentlemen," he said, "I would like to express my appreciation. Now it is my intention to render an opinion within ten to fourteen days. You may contact Mr. Anderson, my court administrator, and he will advise you when I am ready to make the decision.

"I thank you. Court is recessed."

Julia Quinlan could hear the rustling in the courtroom, building into a hubbub; could see Joe rising; Paul stacking his books and papers and nodding his head solemnly in response to something Jim Crowley had said. She saw Judge Muir, in his long black robes, disappearing into his chambers.

—And I knew it was over at last. I wasn't sure whether it had gone well or badly, but at that moment it didn't seem to matter. All I could feel was the deep, numbing relief of having it over. Knowing that this was the last time I would ever have to walk out of this courthouse, with my heart beating so fast that it frightened me, and my head held high as if I were the strongest woman in the world.

Chapter 17

Judge Robert Muir had promised a decision within two weeks—and Julie promised herself that she would make an effort to return the family to some kind of normalcy.

—We desperately needed this time to gather ourselves together.

I thought, if we can just return to a normal routine, even for only a week, it will restore our strength.

But I quickly found that the old routines of our household were hopelessly behind us now. There was no such thing as "normal" procedure any more and—this was the thought that haunted me most—perhaps there never would be again.

Mary Ellen and John returned to school, of course,

but Mary Ellen found she couldn't practice her piano as she always had, late in the afternoon or following supper. Now she couldn't sleep, and she would be downstairs playing at midnight. Joe and I didn't mind. Actually, we found the music soothing. But John would become very annoyed and yell down, "Would you *please* go to bed!" Then Mary Ellen would play louder. And John would yell louder. At least they were getting rid of their frustrations.

The house was cluttered, and that bothered me, but the job of keeping it clean was so enormous I couldn't keep up with it. There were letters piled on all the tables, newspapers stacked on sofas and chairs, and the dishes—always wet dishes, draining on the rack. Everything seemed such an effort, and I tried to get my mind off it by writing poetry. Poetry is therapy for me.

"Besides," Mary Ellen would kid me, "I don't think Queen Elizabeth is going to drop in on us for tea, so don't worry so much about the dishes."

Mary Ellen has a nice, dry sense of humor. She's not wildly funny, as Karen often was, but she has a lovely feeling for the absurd. And during this strained period, she would say anything idiotic that came to her mind, if she thought it would make me or her father smile.

Every day's newspapers and magazines seemed to be filled with stories about Karen and about the trial. Paul would pick up the latest editions and bring them over for us to read.

So we lived and relived it constantly, even though it was all over except for Judge Muir's decision.

Whenever one of the stories would use the phrase "pull the plug," we would wince. It was such a crude, terrible way of putting it. It makes it sound like an execution. And of course, it's not realistic at all. No one would ever "pull the plug," because if they ever pulled the plug of the respirator and left all the stale air in the machine, Karen would be breathing that stale air— she would choke on it. We would never allow that to happen.

The first thing that they would do if it was decided to take away the respirator, is to disconnect the tube from the tracheotomy. Then she would be taking room air into her lungs.

Probably the *last* thing they would do is to take the plug out of the machine.

Paul hated the term even more than we did. When he'd see it used in a story, he'd groan out loud. He had rented a Xerox machine, to make copies of some of the legal documents, and late one night when he was finished running off the sheets he called over to Maria and said, "Okay, that's it, you can pull the plug now."

Maria told us Paul was so embarrassed when he realized what he'd said. "He apologized to me," Maria said, "to *me* of all people. He was really shaken up. That he could have said anything so insensitive."

We were all touchy during this period. Little things that wouldn't normally bother us would put us on edge.

For instance, I heard that Karen had run a fever one day during the trial, and they hadn't told us about it. It was explained that the nurses were trying to protect us, knowing we were worried enough about all that was happening, but I couldn't accept that. Perhaps it wasn't logical, but I became terribly angry.

And when *Newsweek* magazine came out [on November 3] with a new sketch of Karen, showing her lying on the bed, looking like a ghost—that shattered us all. It was bizarre. More like a ghost than our daughter. We couldn't object. We had to hold it in, because if we said that doesn't look like Karen at all, then they would ask what she really looks like. And we didn't want them to know how she looks.

Karen would have hated that.

Most of the artists drew beautiful sketches, because the public wanted to think of her as a "sleeping beauty." They always painted her with long hair. They didn't know her hair was cut short. And they made her face very thin, drawn. They couldn't know that it was more full and round than it had ever been when she was healthy. One thing always puzzled me; the sketches invariably located the respirator on the exact wrong side of the bed. I suppose one artist had drawn it that way, and the rest had just picked it up. Thinking perhaps the first artist had been permitted to see her.

We were told that some of them did claim that they had seen her, but that was impossible.

Karen had been guarded, even before the trial, by a rotating guard of Interstate men. There was one man outside of that Intensive Care Unit, at all times, twenty-four hours a day. No one ever got past them without our permission. Even Karen's friends—Mary Lou and Tommy, for instance—even though they knew the nurses, and had been there often, they weren't just allowed to come and go any longer. The hospital was really protecting her. Because of all the publicity, the circus atmosphere that had somehow taken over.

One day when we came to visit, the guard told us he'd just gotten rid of two "priests" who'd come up to Intensive Care and claimed they were friends of Father Tom's. The guard was a big, burly man and he said, "You'll have to have Father Tom bring you in himself. Nobody gets by without authorization."

Thank heaven. It turned out those two men were a reporter and a cameraman, dressed as clergymen.

One day I was contacted at home by a reporter who offered me $10,000 for a photograph of Karen in her bed.

I was shocked by that, of course, but what came later was even worse.

Another day when I was at the Rectory, someone telephoned and claimed to represent a worldwide news-photo agency. Then he said, "Mrs. Quinlan, I am authorized to offer you $100,000 for a photograph of your daughter."

For a moment or two I couldn't speak. When my voice came back, I said, as calmly as I could, "I'm sorry, but Karen would never want anyone to see her like this."

The man didn't miss a beat. He said, "Actually, $100,000 is only a starting figure. We could go higher."

I slammed the phone down.

Many of the Quinlans' friends had been saving newspaper and magazine clippings about Karen and the trial.

Finally, Joe realized he should get some kind of scrap-book to mount them in.

—I asked Julie to look around in the stationery stores when she had time. She did, but said that even the biggest ones were too small to hold very many clippings. And the prices were fantastic: eight to ten dollars at the least.

One day during this waiting period, a woman at my plant suggested that I go over to the Delta Paints store in Ledgewood Circle, which is a shopping center near us. She said they gave away wallpaper sample books toward the end of the year, when their new lines are coming in. "They're really huge things. You could take all your articles and mount them, and it won't cost you a cent."

So one day after work I dropped over at Delta Paints, and they gave me one of their books—big, heavy thing, 19 × 20 inches—and after that, I spent a lot of evenings putting my clippings in it, in chronological order, beginning with the first story back in September. Being a wallpaper book, half of the pages were colorful patterns, and the other half had printed instructions on them. Such as "pre-pasted, fully trimmed," "scrubbable vinyl —stain resistant, strippable." Of course, I would try to cover up the printing whenever I could, and it became almost like working on a complex jigsaw puzzle.

Julie said, "I'd go out of my mind working on a job like that."

But I enjoyed it. I get a lot of satisfaction out of doing things with my hands. Maybe it's like—they say the blind are more "aware" of what's going on around them than people who have their sight. Whatever it is, I've always liked to work with my hands, and I'm very meticulous about it.

I covered the wallpaper book in a plastic-coated contact paper with a simulated wood-grain pattern, and across the top of it—in adhesive-backed gold letters purchased at the hardware store—I spelled out IN THE MATTER OF KAREN ANN QUINLAN.

Every night, after visiting Karen, I'd sit down at the dining room table and work on "the book," sometimes till three or four in the morning. I couldn't sleep anyway, and I couldn't concentrate on television or distractions like that. I'd read over the clippings, and sort out which ones to include and which to leave out—because, of course, there was a great deal of repetition, so I couldn't put *everything* in. And the more I read and relived what had been happening, the more I became aware of what our daughter—our daughter's tragedy— was doing to people's thinking, all over the world.

You know, when we started all of this, it seemed

such a simple thing. Just wanting to do the right thing
for Karen, that's all. You might say it was almost just a
selfish decision, wanting Karen to stop suffering and
pass into the loving hands of the Lord. But now, looking at what people were saying in the papers, we realized
that people had needed something like this to happen—
so they could talk about dying. Face it, instead of
sweeping it under the rug.

Some of the stories told about people who were
really critical of us hated what we were doing, and I
guess the natural inclination in my mind was, "Well,
maybe I could just leave this story out of the book
because it hurt me to read it."

But I found that I couldn't leave out the critical
stories because, somewhere along the line, it really
struck me: All these people who were against us—they
were suffering, too. They were fighting for what they
thought was right, just as honestly as we were. And
they had laid their emotions on the line, just as we had.

It was an enlightening experience, those long nights,
reading what other people thought about us. Sometimes
it was painful, as I said, but it opened my eyes. And my
heart, too.

In the end, I was no longer angry or shocked by
what our opponents would say. And I put everything
in. The pros and cons.

Everything that made any sense at all went into "the
book."

Among the most disheartening of the clippings Joe taped
into his book was an opinion from Dr. Corraao Manni, a
specialist in resuscitation procedures at Rome's Catholic
University, who had given an interview on Vatican radio.
Following up on the negative viewpoint posed earlier by
the Franciscan priest, Gino Concetti, in the Vatican newspaper *L'Osservatore Romano,* Dr. Manni said that removal
of Karen's respirator "would be an extremely dangerous
move by her doctors, and represent an indirect form of
Euthanasia."

Father Tom had felt "very much alone" since the night of
October 20. The critical reports from Rome had been
hardly less devastating than the silence at local levels.

Then on October 31, an official Vatican spokesman, Frederico Alessandrini, announced that the Vatican would take no official stand on the morality of disconnecting a respirator from Karen Ann Quinlan. "The Vatican cannot make pronouncements on individual cases of this nature," he said.

However, the morality of the case, he told reporters, could be decided by the local ecclesiastical jurisdiction—which, in this case, would be the Bishop of Paterson, New Jersey, the home diocese of the Quinlans.

Father Tom had no direct communication from the Vatican. He heard of the statement, typically, from a newspaper reporter.

Before the priest had time to savor his emotion of cautious relief, his telephone rang. It was his old friend, Monsignor Frank Rodimer, with whom Father Tom had grown up in Rockaway, New Jersey.

—Frank said that somebody downtown—"downtown" is what we call the Chancery—somebody there was going to prepare a document. It would support our stand. He said they would call me in soon to look it over and comment, if I wanted to, and then the Bishop would release it.

I didn't need to tell my old friend how happy I was. This whole crescendo of events, started in Vatican City, had caused so much confusion.

And now, bang, everything was coming back in perspective.

The Most Reverend Lawrence B. Casey, Bishop of the Diocese of Paterson, New Jersey, was severely weakened from two surgical operations intended to slow the progress of cancer.

Despite his condition, the seventy-year-old Bishop drafted, on November 1, a lengthy and eloquent statement affirming the moral correctness of the Quinlans' request to discontinue use of the respirator "as an extraordinary means of sustaining the life of Karen Ann Quinlan."

The request, wrote the Bishop, does not represent euthanasia.

—Since many are concerned that the decision in the case of Karen Ann will establish a precedent it is necessary to look beyond the immediate decision regarding this young woman.

What may be the overriding issue in this case is whether society is prepared to distinguish in law and in practice between the non-obligation to use extraordinary means of treatment in cases that are determined by competent medical authority to be hopeless—and euthanasia, so-called mercy killing. Can society understand and accept the distinction between the right to die a natural death peacefully, and the call for a right to take another's life or the life of oneself even for reasons of compassion?

It is both possible and necessary for society to have laws and ethical standards which provide freedom for decisions, in accord with the expressed or implied intentions of the patient, to terminate or withhold extraordinary treatment in cases which are judged to be hopeless by competent medical authorities—without at the same time leaving an opening for euthanasia.

Competent medical testimony has established that Karen Ann Quinlan has no reasonable hope of recovery from her comatose state by the use of any available medical procedures. The continuance of mechanical supportive measures to sustain continuation of her body functions and her life constitute extraordinary means of treatment.

In bold, capitalized print, the statement concluded:

THEREFORE, THE DECISION OF JOSEPH AND JULIA QUINLAN TO REQUEST THE DISCONTINUANCE OF THIS TREATMENT IS, ACCORDING TO THE TEACHINGS OF THE CATHOLIC CHURCH, A MORALLY CORRECT DECISION.

To emphasize even further his support, the terminally ill Bishop insisted—against medical advice—upon leaving his bed in St. Joseph's Hospital, dressing in full clerical raiment, and issuing the statement personally and publicly.

He wanted, he announced at a press conference in the hospital, to make it abundantly clear that the Diocese of Paterson "firmly supports our beloved brother and sister in

Christ, Joseph and Julia Quinlan, faithful members of the Parish of Our Lady of the Lake. . . ."

His statement was considered, by clergy of all faiths, to be a particularly bold, courageous act in the face of what had become a world-wide religious controversy.

And ultimately, the Bishop's decisive move succeeded in reversing the opinion of the Roman theologian, Father Concetti.

Backing off from his earlier critical view of the Quinlans' plea, the priest wrote that although it is the obligation of physicians to make decisions based on "right consciences" in cases involving the incurably ill, "Christian solidarity and charity demand that each one be helped to make the transition to death with serenity, and in the light of faith."

For weeks, Paul Armstrong had been accepting telephone calls at his apartment—calls at all hours of the day and throughout the night. From the media, facing deadlines.

—We were getting up to 150 calls a day. The doctors and St. Clare's Hospital didn't have that problem. They had immediately hired their own public relations man— a fellow named Larry Stern, with an organization called Media Methods, Inc. He was dealing with the press, and the TV and radio people, on behalf of St. Clare's and Drs. Morse and Javed.

Joe and Julie, having no budget, of course, for a "media relations expert," had to count on me.

I didn't mind all the calls, because I had a genuine admiration for the members of the press we dealt with on a daily basis. But the problem is that Maria and I were never able to get a night's sleep.

One day Joan Kron of *New York* magazine asked me if I dreamed about the case—if I ran through the trial in my dreams. "Afraid not," I had to admit. "You can't dream if you can't sleep."

Another morning at about 3:00 A.M., when a reporter from the London *Times* phoned, Maria moaned, "Oh, if I could only get a good three hours' night's sleep!" After that, we turned off the phone between 2:00 and 5:00 A.M.

At 10:00 A.M. on November 7, 1975, Paul picked up his insistent phone, speculating that it was probably Bruce Hallett of the New York *Daily News* or Joseph Sullivan of *The New York Times*—both of whom usually gave him a call about this time of day. Again, he would have to report, "No news from the courthouse."

"Good morning," Paul said brightly, using the salutory he preferred—he felt it concealed his weariness more effectively than a drab "Hello."

"Paul, this is Dave Anderson," said the voice on the phone. "Judge Muir has reached a decision. Can you and the Quinlans be in the Chancery Courtroom Monday at two o'clock?"

It was raining again on Monday, November 10—an icier, steadier rain than the downpours during the trial—and Joe felt a foreboding that seemed, to him, logical.

—During this whole time, the weather seemed to match our mood. It was a strange thing. The good days for us were fair. The bad days it rained. Sometimes it makes you wonder.

I woke up at the usual time, 5:30, and drove slowly through a very soupy mist to St. Clare's. Karen had had a very restless night, and it always hurts me to look at her after a bad time like that. Her hair was wet with perspiration, and she was sighing and when I kissed her, I thought dear Lord, please help her. I couldn't get much past that. It had been a rough night. I hardly slept at all. But the nurses were wonderful. As always. They kind of got together as I was coming in, and later, as I was leaving. They said, "Good luck, Mr. Quinlan." And "Have a good day." It helped me go out in the rain and face it.

Julie and I had lunch at the Rectory with Father Tom about 11:30, and he looked exhausted, too. He'd offered an eight o'clock mass—for Karen, for us. A lot of reporters were outside the Rectory, in the rain, so Father Tom invited them in to keep dry. So when we sat down to eat, they were all around us, and Father Tom described my feelings exactly. "It's like eating in a store front window," he said. They kept asking questions, of course, which didn't make it any easier. I'm

proud I didn't spill any of the chicken soup on my tie.
But in a way, it was better having all the excitement. It
lifts you out of yourself a bit. I don't think I'd have
done myself any good right then, being alone with my
apprehensions.

Paul had told me that morning, as he had in the past,
that I shouldn't get my hopes up too high. So it didn't
look good. One of the reporters asked Julie how she
felt and she said, "I can accept whatever ruling the
judge makes. I can live with it. I've often thought
about what he'll do," she said. "But I can't venture a
guess."

I realized then that I was guessing too much.

Just before we left, Father Tom said—in answer to
a question I didn't hear—"No matter what happens, I
just want to make sure that no one ever condones
euthanasia."

When we pulled up to the courthouse, all we could
see were sheets of rain pounding down on what looked
like a sea of umbrellas. Most of the umbrellas were
black, and that made it a dark and depressing scene.

We met Paul and Jim in the courtroom, and Mary
Ellen joined us there. John was still in school, but he
was going to come as soon as his classes were over.

The other lawyers were all there, too, including General Hyland with his wife. We all said hello, but that
was about all the conversation there was. I think everybody was a bit apprehensive. I know we were. I kept
thinking about what Paul had told us that morning—
not to get our hopes up too high. Paul is usually more
optimistic than that, so it didn't look good.

We waited about ten minutes, in almost complete
quiet, and then the judge's clerk came in carrying a stack
of papers. He handed them out to each of the lawyers,
but there was nothing for us. Julie reached over and
took my hand. Hers was ice cold. And there was nothing
we could do but look around, studying the faces of all
the lawyers, trying to figure out what the verdict was.
They were all leafing through their papers, and they
didn't show anything. At one point, one of the lawyers
raised up his arms partway and gave like a little surprised shrug—what did that mean?

We went through this suspense for about another ten
minutes. Then Paul and Jim, who had been sitting in

the back row, had a little whispered conversation between themselves, and stood up and walked toward us. I could tell then that we'd lost, because neither of them could smile, and Paul leaned down and confirmed it.

He said, "Joe, it's what we might have expected. The decision went against us."

The attorneys arranged for the family and Father Tom to adjourn to a small office near the courtroom, where they all could go over the forty-four-page decision together.

Judge Muir's opinion was even more devastating than they had anticipated.

One by one, he had rejected each of the constitutional and religious arguments set forth by Paul Armstrong.

The constitutional protection against cruel and unusual punishment did not apply in the Karen Quinlan case because (Judge Muir contended) "medical treatment—where its goal is the sustenance of life—is not something degrading, arbitrarily inflicted, unacceptable to contemporary society, or unnecessary."

On the Catholic issue of "extraordinary means," Muir declared that since Karen was both medically and legally alive, the court should not authorize termination of the respirator. "To do so," he wrote, "would be homicide and an act of euthanasia."

Karen's past statements that she would not want her life artificially prolonged did not convince the Court that she would elect her own removal from the respirator, if she were presently competent. Muir contended: "The conversations with her mother and friends were theoretical ones. She was not personally involved. It was not under the solemn and sobering fact that death is a distinct choice."

Referring to legal precedents, in the few rare cases where other courts have allowed patients to die (when that right was sought, knowingly, by the patient), the decision stated:

"There is no constitutional right to die that can be asserted by a parent for his incompetent adult child. The life and death decisions must be made by physicians—not by Courts of Law.

"The morality and conscience of our society places this responsibility in the hands of the physician.

"The single most important temporal quality Karen

Ann Quinlan has is life," declared Justice Muir. "This court will not authorize that life to be taken from her now."

Up to this point—the last page in the decision—there were no real surprises for Paul Armstrong and Jim Crowley.

Paul had known from the beginning that "historically it is rare in a first impression case for a trial court to recognize and vindicate important constitutional rights. This is a task that, quite properly, has fallen upon the highest courts of the states and the nation. What I had striven to do was to put the issues on the record, for review by the New Jersey Supreme Court if Joe and Julie decided to appeal."

To Joe and Julie, the most distressing portion of the court decision came at the conclusion: Judge Muir decreed that Daniel Coburn, rather than Joe Quinlan, be appointed guardian of Karen's person.

"Mr. Quinlan," Muir wrote, "impresses me as a very sincere, moral, ethical and religious person. He very obviously anguished over his decision to terminate what he considers the extraordinary care of his daughter. That anguish would be continued and magnified," Judge Muir contended, "by the inner conflicts he would have if he were required to concur in the day by day decisions of the future care of his daughter. I, therefore, find it more appropriate and in Karen's interests if another is appointed."

Justice Muir had appointed Joe guardian over Karen's property. But he named Coburn the guardian of her person.

Julie was not only "deeply disappointed for Joe," she feared Coburn. He had made too many blunt statements, both in the courtroom and to the media, which the family felt were insensitive, not only to them but to Karen.

"I'm afraid of him," Julie said. "Of what he could do to Karen."

Paul responded immediately by moving in open court, on behalf of the Quinlan family, for a stay of the appointment of a guardian, or for the appointment of someone other than Daniel Coburn. Judge Muir declined to honor either request.

Then Paul asked the judge if he would meet with the family, and he agreed.

In Muir's chambers that afternoon, Joe and Julie, with Mary Ellen and John, told the justice of their disappointment that the father had not been appointed guardian of his daughter, and of their distress and concern over the selection of Coburn.

Judge Muir's position was unmovable. "I think Mr. Coburn is a capable man," he said.

"We are afraid of him," said Julie.

The meeting ended in an impasse.

Chapter 18

Outside the courthouse, the sky was darkening. It was still raining steadily, and the grounds swarmed with damp, irritable human beings who had waited nearly two hours for the opportunity to capture the feelings and emotions of Joseph and Julia Quinlan. Traffic had been stopped, and the street filled with spectators, craning for a view of the famous family. Even infants were hoisted onto the shoulders of fathers.

At least two hundred members of the media had jostled for position below the courthouse, amid cables stretched and curled over the grass. A six-foot tower had been erected atop the courthouse that morning because all three major TV networks were scheduled to interrupt their programming to carry the Quinlans' reaction live.

When Joe and Julie appeared at the door, the crowd surged forward, and Julie instinctively shrank back and looked up at Joe. "I don't believe this," she murmured.

But the crowd almost instantly quieted down when Joe and Julie approached the microphones and cameras. "As always happened," Paul recalled later, "a normally unwieldy professional throng became respectful and even reverent when Joe and Julie arrived. Their collective sympathy was always apparent."

Two separate press conferences had been arranged. The first, for the live television crews and for news reporters on early deadlines, was held in the Morris County Hall of Records, across the street from the courthouse.

After seeing the Quinlans, the media sprinted to the scene
ahead of Joe and Julie. By the time Joe and Julie had been
escorted across the avenue by sheriff's guards, and stepped
into the 12×15-foot room, overheated to 110° by the TV
lights, it was so crammed with people that they had to
sidle in.

Because of the intense heat and the pressure of deadlines (it already was late afternoon), the session was mer-
cifully brief.

In response to shouted questions, both Joe and Julie
expressed relief that the ordeal was over. They tried to
conceal their disappointment.

"We were under a lot of pressure," Julie said, "but it has
brought the whole family closer together. And it has
brought me closer to God."

"What are you going to do now?" a reporter called
out.

Joe squinted into the camera lights and said, so softly
that the outstretched microphones barely picked up the
words, "We don't know what we're going to do now. We
had prayed we would be able to accept what the judgment
would be."

"Well—will you accept it?"

Joe shook his head, rather than answering. He didn't
really know.

By the time of the second press conference, a more lei-
surely and less crowded session conducted in the basement
of St. Margaret's Catholic Church in Morristown, Joe
and Julie were fatigued, but markedly less nervous.

In answer to a question, Joe admitted his disappointment with the decision but expressed appreciation for Justice Muir's efforts. "He [Muir] showed courage in saying
that the matter belonged with the physicians," Joe said.
"But we had been praying for him to show even more
courage—and grant our request."

Asked if they would go through this again, in another
court, Julie responded wearily, "Oh yes. We would go
through this again. We've done everything physically and
spiritually possible for Karen. The courts were our last
resort."

"Then you intend to appeal?" someone asked.

Joe replied, "We still have our two other children to
consider. Life has to go on for them. We'll need a while

for all of us to rest, and talk about it, before we make any further decisions."

He added, "But we still hope other Karens will be helped. The issue must be decided someday."

It was a family matter, whether or not to appeal their case to a higher court. For several days, they discussed it quietly, alone. Then it was time for questions.

"How can we expect to win the case when Judge Muir went against us?" Mary Ellen asked Paul.

"Well," he said, "you see, it would have been very unusual for a trial court judge like Judge Muir to recognize constitutional rights such as the ones we were arguing. Historically, it's the highest courts of the state that uphold constitutional rights."

"Do you think we really have a chance, then?"

"I surely do," Paul said. "It's pretty well recognized that the Supreme Courts of two states have the finest judicial minds in the country—and the states are California and New Jersey."

"Who said?"—from John.

"I said." Paul grinned. "We have a legal avenue here, and personally, I think it looks to be a good one. On the other hand, do you think you can subject yourself to doing this again?"

"Does it mean testifying again?" Mary Ellen wanted to know.

"No," Paul said. "You wouldn't have to testify because the appeal would be based on the testimony which is already recorded. It would be based on the evidence of the trial. All it would involve is filing the briefs, and giving an oral argument before the Supreme Court."

"Oh well." Mary Ellen was satisfied. "Then why not?"

"All right with you, John?"

"Yeah, I guess so. Sure."

Paul didn't need to ask Joe and Julie. He knew they had wanted from the beginning to appeal.

"If you know much about St. Paul," Joe had said, "then you know that he viewed life as a race. You prepare yourself for it like an athlete, struggling to win. We've only gone one lap."

"Besides, we have no choice, have we? If we're to help Karen?"

On November 17, 1975, Armstrong drove to Trenton and filed an appeal with the Appellate Division of the Supreme Court.

He told the press he would contend that Judge Robert Muir, Jr., "erred in setting forth the maxim that there is no constitutional right to die. Judge Muir's opinion," he said, "merely catalogues or sets forth the status quo—posing questions without resolving them. It certainly doesn't resolve the questions as far as the Quinlan family is concerned; nor does it set forth guidelines for physicians and attorneys who turn to it for such.

"Therefore, we have no recourse but to appeal."

On the same day, the Supreme Court reacted promptly by announcing it would hear the case (thereby bypassing the intermediate Appellate Division), due to the "important issues presented by the tragic plight of Karen and her family."

Hearing on the appeal was set for January 26, 1976.

Reporters immediately hurried to the Quinlans' home for a reaction, and Julie told them, "We are very, pleased, of course. We've received so many letters from people in similar circumstances from all over the country. Some agreed with us, and some said the respirator shouldn't be touched, and some even said they could never make such a decision. There's got to be an answer, and we're praying the Supreme Court will have one."

In his study at the Rectory, Father Tom Trapasso composed a letter to his twelve hundred parishioners. "The issue is truly complex," he wrote, in carefully penned script because he wanted it to be as personal as possible. "Yet surely there must be a national solution to the dilemma of Karen's situation. There seems to me to be a real contradiction in our constitutional law. In 1974 alone, 892,000 lives were *exterminated* by abortion legally performed in our country. Yet that same Constitution says we cannot *allow* someone like Karen to die in peace. We have some thinking to do. —Father Tom."

He had the handwritten note photocopied and mailed out to all members of his parish. He didn't know whether it helped them.

"But it was good therapy for me," he told Julie.

As Father Tom felt a need to express his concern, so did dozens of other religious leaders and doctors, and ethicists, and attorneys and laymen—around the world. Reaction had been galvanized by Judge Muir's opinion, and the newspapers and TV screens became a public forum for anyone who wanted to speak his mind.

Dr. Christiaan Barnard, the heart-transplant pioneer, was one of the physicians who disputed Judge Muir's ruling. "The hopelessly ill should be allowed to die," he said in South Africa. "Often doctors concentrate too much on keeping a patient alive. It's often a selfish attitude—a matter of feeding the ego of the doctor."

The majority of medical opinion, however, favored the verdict.

Dr. Chase Kimball of Chicago was representative of his profession when he said, "It is the doctor's judgment when to prolong or not to prolong life. A court cannot decide in total detail what a physician is to do." Many doctors admitted that "turning off the machines" is common hospital practice, and expressed sympathy for the Quinlans' plight; "Karen's luck ran out when the doctor put her on the respirator—now maybe, if she's lucky, she'll have cardiac arrest," said Dr. Laurens White of San Francisco.

The community of philosophers and ethicists established themselves firmly in opposition to Judge Muir's decision.

"I think the judge has just missed the point completely," said Rev. John R. Connery, scholar at the Kennedy Center for Bioethics at Georgetown University. "You just can't solve this kind of problem with medicine alone."

Dr. Robert M. Veatch, medical ethics specialist at the Institute of Society, Ethics and Life Sciences, agreed. "Muir's ruling could have a very serious implication that can be dangerously generalized . . . one implication could be that if the decision to stop treatment is purely a medical decision, then presumably a physician could decide to stop treatment on you, even if you or your relatives did not want treatment stopped."

The opinions of theologians were divided. Most Catholic spokesmen in the United States supported the Quinlans and upheld the "extraordinary means" concept approved by the Diocese. But Protestants were of mixed minds and emotions. Ethicist Thomas C. Oden of Drew University was concerned about a precedent that would admit the practice of euthanasia. But a fellow Methodist, Paul

Ramsey of Princeton University, was quoted as taking an opposite view:

"Everybody has reason to fear the onset of euthanasia," Ramsey said, "but it doesn't seem to me that a carefully drawn court opinion would be the wedge toward active killing of terminal patients." Ramsey was afraid the judge's ruling against the Quinlans could set a precedent in favor of nonstop treatment "until patients at long last succeed in dying, despite our machines."

Orthodox Jews morally opposed the Quinlans' right-to-die plea. "According to the Jewish tradition," Rabbi David Glicksman pointed out, "a person does not have a right to die. Mastery over one's own body ends when there is danger to life or health."

In London writer-TV personality Malcolm Muggeridge announced that he, personally, "would want to be allowed to die in peace," and began circulating a document designed to help doctors face the dilemma. At a press conference, seventy-two-year-old Muggeridge said he had signed the statement, which rejects mercy killing but "informs the doctor that I do not wish to be kept alive if I can't be cured."

New right-to-die movements were springing up in Europe and Scandinavia, as a result of the Quinlan case. In Italy, on the contrary, the Quinlan family strengthened the cause of groups fighting for ailing persons' rights to live. And in France, where a celebrated thirty-nine-year-old Frenchman had been maintained in a coma for twenty years, the case was widely discussed: "But the emphasis," reported the Associated Press, "remained on prolonging life."

A Danish journalist, Christian Soondergard, began distributing "life testaments" to citizens of Denmark. Similar to Muggeridge's document, and to the "living wills" which were gaining prominence in the United States, Soondergard's "statement" asked doctors not to prolong life in the event of accident or mortal illness. (Though not legally acceptable, such documents offer moral suasion to physicians.)

In Germany the Quinlan case, like the topic of euthanasia, was a matter that people reportedly found painful. Memories lingered of Hitler's World War II order to terminate seventy thousand "worthless lives"—mostly the crippled and mentally defective.

A syndicated United Features writer named Martin F. Nolan summed up the verbal furor following the Civil Court trial when he wrote:

"Despite Judge Muir's eloquent and justifiable passing of the buck, the State is now a presence at the deathbed. The consideration of life, heretofore restricted to the family unit, has now become the business of mankind."

It also had become the business of individuals who wanted to use "the Karen case" for their own political or personal gain.

On the five o'clock TV news one night, while Mary Ellen was watching,

—they had a woman come on who'd written a book on adoption, and she started analyzing Karen—whom she never met. Obviously she'd only been following the sensational stories about the case, and she was saying that Karen was self-destructive because she never knew her natural mother. She was making all these totally ridiculous statements that weren't true at all, just to sell her book.

You know, it makes you sick.

It's things like that which make me bitter. And John won't even sit and watch these things on television. He won't talk to reporters. He thinks everybody is out to make a name for themselves, off Karen. He hates it.

The guardianship matter still disturbed the Quinlan family.

On November 24, Paul filed a Notice of Motion for Stay of Judgment Appointing Guardian of the Person, and for Substitution of Guardian of the Person. He also filed a supporting affidavit, executed by Joseph Quinlan, in which Joe expressed his objections to Daniel Coburn on three counts:

A. By his statements in connection with the trial, both in court and to the news media, Mr. Coburn has assumed a posture which I feel and believe to be hostile to myself and my family; B. Moreover, Mr. Coburn has repeatedly proposed that my daughter be subjected to experimental or hitherto untried medical procedures;

I and my family can experience only fear and apprehension when we realize that Mr. Coburn, through his Court-appointed office, might be in a position to influence the type of treatment administered to Karen Ann; C. Finally, Mr. Coburn has never made any attempt to contact or communicate with us in any way. His silence has only increased our mistrust and misgivings.

Two days after the filing of these papers, the New Jersey Attorney General, William Hyland, wrote a letter to Judge Muir, advising that "the State of New Jersey will not oppose the application by Mr. Armstrong for reconsideration of the appointment of Daniel R. Coburn as Guardian of the person of Karen Quinlan.

"While from a technical standpoint the State's standing to become involved in this application may be of limited nature," Hyland wrote, "I nonetheless feel compelled to address the Court on the subject and to urge that, given all of the facts and circumstances, the wishes of the family be given strong consideration.

"I feel that this is not only a consideration to which the Quinlan family is entitled, but also that compliance with their wishes will make for a less emotional atmosphere within which the issues of the appeals may be resolved.

"My suggestion is not intended to reflect in any way upon Mr. Coburn who, in my judgment, has conducted himself with competence and dedication throughout the proceeding," the Attorney General added.

On December 9, Judge Muir met again with Joe and Julie, Mary Ellen, and John.

He reiterated his belief that Daniel Coburn was a capable man and an appropriate choice to be Karen's guardian. The Quinlan family repeated their firm objections.

The following day, Coburn resigned as Karen's guardian, and Judge Muir appointed a Boonton, New Jersey, attorney to replace him.

The new guardian, Thomas R. Curtin, announced: "I intend to be in touch with the Quinlan family at once, and to remain in contact with them at least weekly, to prevent the misunderstandings which marked the earlier guardianship."

On resigning, Daniel Coburn announced that although he was proffering his resignation, he would continue in the case—acting as attorney for the new guardian, Mr. Curtin.

Chapter 19

PROBE "BEATING" OF COMA GIRL. The headline was bannered across the front page of the tabloid *New York Post* on December 16.

Under the by-line of Lindsay Miller, and a date line of Rock Island, Illinois, the story speculated:

> Karen Ann Quinlan may have been the victim of a beating before falling into a coma eight months ago, according to legal papers to be filed here today.
>
> A New Jersey grand jury is investigating the possibility that she was assaulted sometime before she entered a Newton, N.J. Hospital. Papers were filed in Rock Island County Court, as New Jersey authorities attempted to compel a key witness to return to New Jersey.
>
> He is William Zywot, 22, with Karen the night she fell into a coma, now living in Silvis, Ill.

This sensational news shot across the country like a shock wave.

The following day, December 17, William Zywot was flown to Trenton, New Jersey, by state investigators acting under orders of Attorney General Hyland.

He was questioned for several hours, then released and returned to his home.

Attorney General Hyland hastily called a press conference, because of the publicity that had been engendered by the Zywot visit, and said that the purpose of the probe was "to determine whether or not the coma could be related to an 'egg-shaped bump' on Miss Quinlan's head."

Joe Quinlan was so shaken that he could scarcely eat, or even speak logically. Not to Julie, or to the children; certainly not to friends.

—It was so incredible to me. All of the doctors knew that there was nothing to that little bump on Karen's head. At the trial, Morse had described the brain scan he took, after we noticed the bump, and he testified that the scan was normal. He said that there could not have been any trauma caused by an injury. After that, seven other doctors had testified the same way—said Karen's coma couldn't have been caused by a fall, or by foul play.

Well, Hyland was right there in the courtroom. He heard all that evidence. So why did he keep on with this? He kept saying that he didn't want to hurt us, and that he wasn't investigating Karen's "life style."

All Christians are taught to turn the other cheek, but it was impossible this time. Because he wasn't hitting us. He was hitting someone who couldn't speak, either to defend herself or forgive him.

News of the grand jury probe was revealed on precisely the same day that the briefs were filed for the Supreme Court hearing.

Paul and Jim had just concluded nearly two weeks in New York City, shuttling back and forth between the Shearman & Sterling law office and the printing house of Charles P. Young, which had contributed the services of its staff—on a three-shift daily basis—to print the complex brief in time to meet the deadline set by the New Jersey Supreme Court.

Paul remembers that he and Jim were driving through the Lincoln Tunnel toward New Jersey—"totally exhausted, because I had spent the two previous nights sleeping on a small couch in the conference room of Charles P. Young."

—As we drove toward Trenton, Jim was slumped in the back seat of the car trying to sleep, and I was thinking about how he had been through all this. In my exhaustion, I was almost euphoric—thinking about the generosity of Jim and his law firm, and Charles Young

—how all of them had worked so compassionately, sharing the monumental work of preparing the pleadings that I would, within an hour, be able to turn over to the Court. All these feelings of gratitude were surging through me and I felt so pleased with the world—and then I turned on the radio for some music, and that's when I heard it.

At first the news of the grand jury probe didn't quite register in my mind, then suddenly it registered. I turned up the sound on the radio. And when I fully understood what the newscaster was saying, I was irate. I called, "Jim—wake up! Listen to this. You won't believe it." All the rest of the way to Trenton, we discussed it. The whole investigation seemed unreal.

And the timing of that news couldn't have been more abominable.

Here we were, on our way to file briefs for the litigation of this most important tragic case—and the grand jury sensationalism had taken society's attention away from the arguments that were being advanced. It only served to cloud the issues.

On the evening of December 18, with the newspapers still headlining the New Jersey grand jury investigation, a reporter called at the Quinlan home, and John Quinlan answered the doorbell.

"Hello, is this—oh, are you John Quinlan?"
John hurled the door closed in his face.

On Saturday, December 20, Julie awakened feeling ill.

—It came on so suddenly—I felt I couldn't breathe. I had pains across my chest. I was afraid I was having a heart attack, so finally I had to tell Joe that he'd better call his doctor, Monroe Mufson.

It was snowing hard, and I remember thinking as we drove through that storm, "I'm going to die. Right here in the car. I'm not going to last long enough to see the doctor."

But we made it, of course, and Dr. Mufson quickly diagnosed my symptoms as nerves. I didn't know nerves could do such cruel tricks to your mind and your body.

He gave me a prescription for the tranquilizer Librium, and told me I should try to relax and avoid reading the newspapers for a while.

I did what he said, but I had never had a tranquilizer in my life before, and they made me feel drugged. A really awful feeling. So after three days, I gave up the Librium and went back to drinking tea and an occasional glass of wine to relax. And I was all right. I still have that bottle of Librium up in the medicine chest, to remind me that I'm not about to die. That a person can take whatever they throw at you.

The same day that Julie suffered her psychosomatic attack, Father Tom Trapasso sat down at his oak desk in the Rectory and angrily punched out a letter. An open letter of protest against the inquiry, which he addressed to Tim O'Brien of the Newark *Star-Ledger,* a reporter he had viewed the past several weeks as being exceptionally sensitive to him and to the Quinlan family.

On Sunday, December 21, O'Brien wrote a story, incorporating the letter, under the headline, "ANGRY" PRIEST CRITICIZES PROBE OF KAREN'S BRUISES. The story began:

—Rev. Thomas Trapasso, describing himself as Karen Ann Quinlan's "friend and pastor," yesterday lashed out against what he called attempts "to prosecute this 70-pound comatose girl for some crime."

Referring to the published reports of an investigation by the State Attorney General's Office into a possible criminal cause of the coma, Father Tom said, "The pain and anguish of those I love become *my* pain and anguish. I now have become angry, but I'm not sure toward whom my anger should be directed.

"Should it [my anger] be toward the Attorney General who was quoted as saying he had 'no reason to believe there was criminality involved'? Yet he has not to date questioned or even contacted the doctors who were most intimately involved in Karen's treatment. These same doctors at no time seriously considered that Karen's treatment was due to a trauma.

"Should my anger be directed toward those 'unnamed police officers' who stated to the press they were investigating a 'possible connection' of Karen Ann with an unsavory local character? Why were they talking to the press at all? My concept of an investigation always meant the utmost secrecy and discretion. Do they want to prosecute this 70-pound comatose girl for some crime?

"Should my anger be directed toward some of the people of the press whose zeal to 'get the scoop' causes them to forget all human compassion and sensitivity? Some have not reported news. They have gossiped. Innuendo and hearsay have characterized this whole fiasco.

"Should I be angry with some people whose prurient curiosity about the private lives of other people creates a market for the type of press that is willing to pander to their curiosity?

"All I know," concluded Father Tom Trapasso, "is that Tuesday I went to the hospital, and I cried a little bit for Karen."

Attorney General Hyland, the white-haired chief legal authority of New Jersey, reacted indignantly but privately to Father Tom's letter. In a letter to the priest, Hyland maintained that his probe was valid, and necessary.

Hyland denied that any of his officers had contributed information which led to the story which appeared in the *New York Post,* and said that "despicable story" resulted purely from reporter Miller's own investigative reporting. Hyland said that a sense of duty had caused him to make an investigation into the cause of Karen's condition: "I had an obligation to satisfy myself that she was not the victim of some heretofore undetected foul play," he wrote. "If what we have done has created greater anguish for the Quinlans, I think you must know that this would trouble me. But sparing them that anguish would neither have satisfied my duty, nor if indeed someone has committed a criminal act, can the overlooking of that act be excused even out of a sense of compassion for the family."

The Attorney General concluded his letter to Father Tom: "I do not intend to respond publicly to your remarks, for to do so would only add to the controversy that I think all of us want to avoid."

The letter was dated December 23, 1975.

At approximately 11:45 that same night, Julie received a phone call from John, who earlier in the evening had gone out with a friend.

"Mom," he said, "I'm sleeping over at Mike's."

"Oh, John, don't do that," Julie said. "Come on home."

"No, I'd better stay at Mike's."

"Why?"

"We've had too much to drink."

Julie didn't want to argue with that. She had warned him, when he first began to drive, that the most dangerous thing he could do was to drive after he'd been drinking. "In that case, John, by all means stay there," she said wearily. "What's the phone number, in case we need you?"

There was a long pause. Then John said, "Well, I've got to tell you—I'm not really at Mike's house."

"Where are you?"

"I'm in a police station in Dover."

"Oh, John—what happened?"

"I was in a bar, and a fight broke out. . . ."

The anger in young John Quinlan had been building up for months. It finally had erupted in a preholiday barroom brawl.

Julie understood.

—He was just ready for a scrap. And for a while, it made him all the angrier—that he was caught up in a fight that he hadn't even started. But John was all right.

You know, everyone reacts differently to crises. Joe holds his emotions inside until they hurt. I cry. But John is consumed with anger. He wants to get at the truth and straighten things out the simple way, the straightforward way and, in his eyes, honest way.

Karen and John were always alike that way. They have no pretenses. Face the problem and do something—get it over with. If Karen could wake up now and see what is happening, she would fight all the way for her brother.

Although this was the first Christmas without Karen, and in spite of John's unfortunate escapade, Julie was determined to celebrate the holiday.

—I thought it was more important than ever to observe the traditions. To have a big tree, and trim it with the same ornaments we have stored away since Karen was a baby. To exchange gifts and honor the birth of our Lord.

I thought, for one day we must try to be happy together. Except for the memories, I think we succeeded.

On Christmas Eve we went to midnight mass at Our Lady of the Lake, as we always did. Mary Ellen brought a boy friend, Eddie Wallace, and John brought his new girl, Barbara Rodick. Paul came with Maria, who had baked a delicious plum pudding for us. After mass, we all joined Father Tom in the Rectory for wine and a light supper, and Father Tom gave me a terrarium. It was a lovely, large one, filled with tiny evergreens, and he said, "It has life, Julie. That's what is important now."

On Christmas Day we had a family dinner and the exchange of presents, and there was enough surface gaiety to get us through the afternoon. Then late in the day we drove to the hospital to see Karen. We took her a dozen roses. She loves roses.

When we were home again, I couldn't help myself. I went up to my closet and pulled out the plum-colored velvet suit that Karen gave me for Christmas last year, and as I looked at it, a hundred thoughts and memories rushed through my mind. It's a beautiful suit. I hung it back in the closet and wondered if I would ever be able to force myself to wear it again.

Christmas is always difficult, when someone you love is not with you.

We knew that, but at least we tried. And we did well. No one broke down.

One of our New Year's resolutions was to catch up with the mail.

There were at least five thousand letters from all over the world which had come to us since the trial, and once again we went through the emotional experience of reading each one of them.

There were a large number from people who had lost loved ones. Several people wrote to us saying they wished that they had made the same decision we had, ten or fifteen years ago. They had relatives who had been helpless, or on a respirator, for that long a period and there was no hope, but there was nothing to be done except to go on, living day by day. One chaplain, a Baptist minister from Georgia, said that he totally agreed with us because there are not enough machines to keep people living artificially forever. He wrote that he had a vision of hospitals filled up with nobody except patients on machines.

Of course there were many people who didn't agree with us.

Some of the magazines and newspapers had referred to Karen as "sleeping beauty," and this was the concept in many people's minds. They thought she was in some kind of fairy tale coma and might come out of it. A man in New England wrote that he was convinced that Karen had a rare kind of sleeping sickness. Another person in California suggested that the doctors should keep Karen in a suspended state while research moves on. He was sure someday there will be a way to regenerate brain tissues; he said if we just wait, maybe it will be possible to regrow her brain tissues from a single cell.

Then there was a twenty-one-year-old boy named Guy Treadway, who had been in a coma for a month and came out of it. He didn't just write to us—he came to New Jersey and held a press conference to describe what his experience had been. He said being in a coma "was like Utopia." He said once he was in it, he didn't want to come out because it was so peaceful, and he thought Karen ought to be forced to come back.

We heard many, many stories like that. The newspapers were printing them all the time—about people who had been in comas and revived. And all of these people were well-meaning, like the faith healers. They really wanted to help. But they just didn't know what the doctors knew and we knew, that Karen couldn't get better.

I would read these letters every night, and then the next day I would go in and see Karen. She just seemed to be becoming progressively smaller and smaller, and there was a new complication. The bottom part of her face, her whole lower jaw, had begun to recede, so that she was continually biting into her lower lip with the upper teeth. There were indentations in her lip, where the teeth had dug in, and sometimes they would bleed profusely.

When this shifting of Karen's jaw had started, back in November, you could hardly notice it. But it progressed very quickly, just as her body had curled up quickly. So when Dr. Morse called in a dental hygiene specialist, he took one look at Karen and ordered that she be treated with massive doses of penicillin. She had staph infection; her mouth was loaded with the infection. It was so serious, he said, that there was no possible way he could treat the teeth under the circumstances. He said she would not survive treatment.

So he ordered intensive oral hygiene care and heavy doses of penicillin, and he devised a clear plastic plate that fits over the top of her mouth—goes way back into the roof of her mouth—to keep her from biting her lip.

Oh God, how Karen fights that. She hates it, gags on it, tries to spit the thing out.

It is terribly upsetting to see your daughter like that, fighting so hard against what everyone is doing to her. And you can't do anything, while she whips her head around and struggles so wildly, except stand there and watch.

With the Supreme Court hearing scheduled for January 26, Paul Armstrong and Jim Crowley flew to Washington, D.C., to consult with a group of renowned scholars at the Kennedy Institute, Center for Bioethics, at Georgetown University.

For four days, from January 9 through 12, Paul and Jim held intensive dialogue with the priests, physicians, lawyers, and ethicists on the moral, constitutional, and religious issues which formed the heart of the Quinlan plea.

Father John R. Connery and Father Richard A. McCormick, both Christian ethicists, hammered out questions, the answers to which could be decisive before the Supreme Court.

FATHER CONNERY: Mr. Armstrong, can you draw a distinction between allowing to die and actively advancing death?

PAUL: The Catholic moral tradition, as enunciated by Pope Pius XII, certainly recognizes this distinction. Thus it is possible to advance: 1) that state interference with an individual exercising the right to make this decision in accord with his religious belief would constitute a violation of the First Amendment of the Constitution, and 2) if an individual, in accord with the guarantees of the Constitutional Right of Privacy, chooses to make this decision, absent a contrary state interest, the decision to suspend extraordinary medical measures in a terminally ill situation should be vindicated by the Courts. It is also important to point out that it is not the suspension of futile medical measures which causes death, but the pre-existing terminal illness that would yield the demise of the individual.

FATHER MCCORMICK: All right. How will the granting of this relief affect the elderly—or retarded individuals?

PAUL: The fact of "terminal illness" is the key to this question. The Quinlan request is that futile medical measures administered to a terminally ill patient be suspended, in accord with the wishes of the patient.

CONNERY: How do we know what Karen's wishes are, since she is incompetent?

PAUL: Karen's mother, sister, brother, and friends have testified that she would not wish to be artificially sustained. Even if this testimony is found legally insufficient—we contend that those closest to the patient, those who love and care for the person, are in the best position to exercise that right for an incompetent patient.

MCCORMICK: Does not your request to suspend the life support systems in effect constitute euthanasia?

PAUL: Here, the requested relief is the suspension of "extraordinary means of care and treatment," which as his Holiness Pope Pius pointed out, members of the Catholic Church are under no moral obligation to submit to. As Bishop Casey has said, in a statement adopted and filed by the New Jersey Catholic Conference, "The failure to supply the ordinary means of preserving life is equivalent to euthanasia." But neither physician nor patient is obliged to use "extraordinary means."

After the week in Washington, Paul and Jim conferred with Dr. Robert Veatch of the Institute of Society, Ethics and Life Sciences, an ethical think tank in New York.

At the end of these seminars, Paul felt "our minds were well honed for the task ahead."

—But my physical condition was disastrous. Before the trip to Washington I had been ill and finding it difficult to breathe. Thinking I was suffering from severe bronchitis, a childhood ailment I've never altogether outgrown, I had visited the Emergency Room at Morristown Memorial Hospital. X rays were taken and three different doctors studied them. If I hadn't been so sick, I'd have felt flattered. All three physicians explained I had "walking pneumonia," and ordered penicillin and bed rest.

I had taken the penicillin, but the bed rest was out of the question in Washington, of course. So by the time I came back to New Jersey I had a raging fever and had to return to the hospital. This time the doctors prescribed tetracycline and ordered me to bed. I obeyed them for one day, rehearsing the case in bed with tea and tetracycline, and began to improve. I knew I couldn't take any more chances with Joe and Julia's future at stake.

On the day before the Supreme Court hearing, Maria and I—with Jim and Mary Jo and their infant son—checked into the Nassau Inn in Princeton, so we would be close to Trenton and could get a solid night of sleep before rising early for the hearing.

Ironically, I didn't sleep at all. After dinner, Jim and I went in to the inn's meeting room, which was set up with a podium and a public address system for a plumbers' convention which was to start the next day. We reviewed our arguments until 1:30 A.M., after which I sat up in bed and again reviewed the presentation until 3:45. When I finally turned out the light, I continued to argue the case in my mind until 7:15—time to get up and shower.

Maria took one look at me and apparently guessed what had happened.

"I hope you won the case," she said. She smiled at me, standing behind my shoulder and looking through the mirror while I shaved.

I did a lot of silent praying on the drive to Trenton.

Chapter 20

Joe and Julia Quinlan, with Maria Armstrong and Father Quinlan, were ushered into the back row of the mahogany-paneled Supreme Court chambers. They wanted to be as inconspicuous as possible.

The press filled the center twenty rows, and at the front of the courtroom was the same case of attorneys who had appeared at the civil trial: Armstrong, with Crowley beside him, for the plaintiff; Ralph Porzio for the doctors; Theodore Einhorn for St. Clare's; Attorney General William Hyland and Prosecutor Donald Collester for the state and county; and Daniel Coburn, now representing the new guardian, Thomas Curtin.

A court stenographer sat at the left front of the chambers. It had been decided that the proceedings would be tape-recorded rather than stenotyped. As a result, the voices of individual Supreme Court justices often could not be verified. Consequently, in transcribing the historic debate, the stenographer identified, by name, only the Chief Justice and witnesses. Questions and observations by the six associate judges generally were attributed simply to "The Court."

Promptly at 9 A.M., the seven Supreme Court justices silently filed into the room in their black robes and took seats at a massive bench, raised two steps above the courtroom floor.

At the center was the Chief Justice, Richard J. Hughes, a former governor of New Jersey, a Catholic and father of eleven children. He was flanked on one side by Justices Morris Pashman, Mark Sullivan, and Milton Conford; on the other by Sidney Schreiber, Worral Mountain, and Robert L. Clifford.

"The Court will hear argument in case A-116, in the matter of Karen Quinlan," the Chief Justice announced briskly. "Mr. Armstrong . . ."

From the brusque beginning of the rousing four-hour session which was to follow, it was apparent to Paul that these men were eager to solve the philosophical enigma he was posing. "They all had keen intellects, were fully versed in the law and the facts of this tragic case, and harbored a profound and compassionate commitment toward its just resolution."

Judge Schreiber was the first challenger:

"As a preliminary matter, Mr. Armstrong, do you concede that this young woman is alive?" he asked.

"That's correct," Paul said.

SCHREIBER: And you are not asking this court to change the common law definition of death? Even though she's in a persistent vegetative state, as I understand?

PAUL: That's correct.

THE COURT: Specifically then, Mr. Armstrong, what *do* you ask this Court to do?

PAUL: We're asking first that the Court determine whether or not an individual can exercise, persuant to his constitutional rights, this type of action. If the Court deems it licit, I feel that—

THE COURT: Now wait. It would seem to me there's nothing to prevent your clients from talking to the doctors about terminating the situation. Now you're asking the Court to declare that if they do ask the doctors to terminate this situation, no adverse criminal or civil consequences will attach?

PAUL: That's one aspect of it. I think—

THE COURT: And are you asking the Court to declare anything else?

PAUL: Only to recognize that the individuals have a constitutional right to make this type of decision.

THE COURT: You're not asking the Court to order the doctors to terminate the apparatus?

PAUL: Absolutely not. We're not asking this Court to order the doctors to do anything which they may feel contrary to their beliefs.

THE COURT: Well, it goes beyond that—because the doctor has taken the position that he will not medically authorize that action. Aren't you really asking us to overrule the doctor's decision?

PAUL: No. I believe a fair categorization of the doctor's testimony is that while he feels that he may be incapable of doing it, there are others who would not feel incapable of doing it.

THE COURT: What will you do—bring in a third [physician] who will say that he agrees with what you want him to do? Is that what you're saying to us?

PAUL: We will do what is normally done in a physician-patient relationship. That is, if the doctor and the patient are at loggerheads, we would request that these particular physicians resign and ask to bring in another physician.

THE COURT: Well, has your client asked these doctors to get off the case?

PAUL: No, he has not.

THE COURT: Well, I don't follow you then. If you haven't asked the doctors to get off the case, why are you here at all?

Paul explained that he hoped the Court would provide "guidelines." He felt physicians wanted those guidelines, to help them make decisions to terminate life-supporting equipment.

THE COURT: Are you not also asking that if the physicians accede to the parents' request, it will be without any adverse consequences to those physicians?

PAUL: That's correct.

Chief Justice Hughes leaned forward. "Mr. Armstrong, doesn't it come down to this," he said, "the long and short of it being that you ask the Court to declare the law to be—there having been no precedent in any part of the common law that I can figure—that the Court is to declare now that if the doctors stop this procedure and cause death that it will not result in any civil or criminal sanctions as to such doctors, or indeed as to such family members?"

Paul affirmed.

"So that, in effect," Hughes continued, "you're asking the Court to make new law."

PAUL: On these facts, that's correct.

HUGHES: To make new law. On these facts. Without

legislation. In that case, Mr. Armstrong, wouldn't the Court be legislating?

PAUL: No, Your Honor. It would be reflecting the majesty of the evolution of common law, as it has since its inception in England. I genuinely think that the Court is fully competent to address itself to these types of problems. . . .

THE COURT: What is your response, Mr. Armstrong, to those who argue that there is always the possibility of that miracle drug, or the miracle remedy, which may come to pass between the date that once decides the person should die and the date that the person perhaps would normally have died with the supportive measure? What is your response to that fact that we should concern ourselves with that possibility?

PAUL: As a broad general principle, that's fine. However, that was investigated for close to nine months by the family in concert with Drs. Morse and Javed, to find out the existence of any research that could alleviate the particular irreparable brain damage suffered by Karen. It was found that there is none, nor was any advanced—

THE COURT: Miracles don't come about that way. They just wake up one morning and someone says we have a Salk vaccine. They didn't give warnings beforehand. There it was. Why is it so impossible that this could come to pass?

PAUL: Basically, Mr. Justice, those miracles come about as a result of Ford Foundation grants for about a million and a half dollars. There are no grants doing research to alleviate irreparable brain damage.

THE COURT: What if someone were to accidentally just come across something which does the trick?

PAUL: Well, then we'd all be better off for it.

THE COURT: Including Miss Quinlan.

PAUL: Most importantly Miss Quinlan.

JUSTICE MORRIS PASHMAN: Do you agree that it is common practice in most hospitals that labels are assigned in certain cases—d.n.c. [do not code], d.n.r. [do not resuscitate]. Is that right?

PAUL: What you're referring to, Justice, is the concept of judicious neglect.

THE COURT: You seem to say that this is a medical

question, and at the same time you say that the family
and the doctor should make the decision.

PAUL: It's a medical question to this point: The nature of the decision to be made by a physician is this,
that he can give you a diagnosis; he can ask you as the
individual what do you wish to do with your body, especially in the circumstances where you are terminally
ill and the treatment that he advances is of no value to
you. The physician can say: Mr. Justice, what would
you do? Not: I am going to employ this type of medical
treatment regardless of what your particular views may
be on the subject.

Chief Justice Hughes suggested that Paul consider a hypothetical case:

"Let us say some patient, [another] Karen, were
brought in terribly burned, suffering terrible pain, obviously terminally ill. And the doctor, in his judgment, decided
not to apply the life support respirator. . . . I'm talking
about a totally futile case where it is obvious from the
doctor's experience and medical knowledge that this patient is either going to die tomorrow or three months from
tomorrow, after suffering very bitter pain. If he makes
that medical decision, can you conceive that he would be
responsible to the law?"

Paul did not hesitate.

"If he didn't do it in consort with either the family or
the individual," he replied, "I think he should be."

The Chief Justice called on James Crowley, who briefly
elucidated the First Amendment's "free exercise of religion" argument:

"We submit that the Quinlans' decision has a valid claim
to constitutional protection, not only because it is an
exercise of the right of privacy, but also because it is an
effectuation of their religious beliefs," Jim told the Court.

"The testimony, of Mr. Quinlan's pastor, and the hospital chaplain, the papal allocution admitted into evidence,
and the official teaching of the Catholic Church contained in the statement of Bishop Casey—which all the
Roman Catholic bishops of this state have seconded and
which they, as friends of this Court, have laid before you
—make it clear that the course of action chosen by Mr.

Quinlan is actively supported by his Church and is a concrete effectuation of its teachings."

Daniel Coburn was the next attorney called before the justices and, to the surprise of the Court and the lawyers, he began his testimony by urging the Supreme Court to consider the adoption of a "new definition of death."

The Court: "Mr. Coburn. Everybody having agreed that this incompetent is not dead by any thus far accepted definition—you feel we nevertheless should make it part of the opinion?"

"Yes," Coburn said. "That was a request that I also made of Judge Muir, that the definition of death obviously is of critical importance in this case." As present New Jersey law stands, "a person is alive as long as they are breathing and the heart is beating." Under those prevalent laws, Coburn explained, "what we have now is nothing. And while the standard of 'brain death' is probably insufficient, or will be insufficient in two years, it certainly is better than nothing. Right now, I think there's just mass confusion."

Attorney General Hyland quickly dissented with Coburn's opinion: "I would very much oppose any effort on the part of this court to define death," he said. "There is no record from which this court could go into the technical aspects of a definition of death under 1976 standards, as opposed to what we all know was so comparatively easy in the past." Hyland emphasized, "You would feel the pulse, put your ear or stethoscope on the chest of an individual. And if there was no heart and no pulse and no respiration, there was death. The medical profession has made some effort to establish criteria in such studies as the ad hoc committee in Harvard in 1968—and so we have a particular kind of a physical condition: brain death criteria." But any further attempt to define death now, in an era of scientific advances, he said, "would fossilize with the growth of the medical profession."

Justice Pashman looked at Hyland thoughtfully and said, "But, General, really doesn't the horror of continued pseudo life cry out for some type of handling, some type of treatment by a court to perhaps eliminate that situation, or diminish the impact of that situation?"

HYLAND: I'm not really persuaded, Justice Pashman, by that kind of emotional concern. I recognize that life has a great many burdens, a great many pains and anguish.

PASHMAN: I didn't say emotion when I'm talking about truly a horrible existence. That's not emotion. That's a fact, in given cases.

Hyland insisted that the Supreme Court "should deal with just this case before it. And if you're going to go beyond what the issues that have been briefed and presented are, then the case should be remanded to the trial court again. . . ."

PASHMAN: And if we stay with the trial court disposition, General, what have we contributed to this whole problem?

HYLAND: The problem probably should not have been in court, Justice Pashman.

PASHMAN: I agree with you overwhelmingly about that—that it doesn't belong here, it should never have been started. But it was started. And it is here. Now, usually we try to contribute something toward a solution. I guess that's our primary and ultimate function here. . . .

Donald Collester was called, and Chief Justice Hughes posed another hypothetical question.

HUGHES: Mr. Prosecutor, would you assume something for me? Supposing that Dr. Morse, on the night Karen Quinlan was received in that hospital, knew all that he knows now about her condition and prognosis, and he decided, with the consent of her father and mother, not to apply the life-sustaining apparatus. Would you think of prosecuting him in that case?

COLLESTER: I don't think so. No. I wouldn't have a case at all, obviously.

HUGHES: What's the essential difference between a decision *not to connect* the apparatus, and a decision to *disconnect* the apparatus? Is there any real difference —in logic?

COLLESTER: Yes. I think there is. First of all, we get into the act and omission dichotomy where here I don't think it is really applicable. It's hard to think of something more of an act than literally pulling out a plug, to use an odious phrase associated with this case.

HUGHES: Well, let me make it easier for you. Supposing that a fuse blew out and the doctor said, "Don't bother restoring that fuse."

COLLESTER: I think he's still got the same problem in terms of exposure.

THE COURT: Or, say, he didn't replace an empty oxygen tent?

COLLESTER: I think under our law right now, there would be exposure to criminal liability prosecution.

THE COURT: You just rebel at the concept, apparently, of affirmatively—as you put it—pulling this plug, as opposed to all the other measures which ultimately bring about the same result. And that is death.

COLLESTER: The criminal law has, as one of its basic functions, a deterrent. I also think the law of homicide is relatively clear.

THE COURT: Do you condone the Chief's hypothetical case—[that is] at the time she was brought into the hospital, if the doctor is determined not to use the supportive measures, you see nothing wrong?

COLLESTER: It would be my opinion that, at that point, a duty had not as yet taken charge. Once the doctor, together with the parents, had determined that in order to preserve this woman's life—once that decision had been made—the duty attaches, and therefore the consequences, both criminal and civil, attach thereafter.

THE COURT: I don't understand that.

Chief Justice Hughes stepped in quickly: "All right, suppose, Prosecutor, that the life-giving machine, the respirator, became inoperative sooner or later and the question came up in discussion with Mr. and Mrs. Quinlan about a new respirator. Would they then be able to say 'Oh no, let's not carry this on any further'? You wouldn't have a disconnection there. You wouldn't have an affirmative act there."

"You *would* have," insisted Collester, "an affirmative cessation of treatment which was being afforded in accordance with standard medical practice. I think my feeling would be under that hypothetical, Chief Justice, that it would not be permissible within the scope of criminal law."

Hughes frowned. "The difference seems a little flimsy to me," he said.

"Supposing," the Chief Justice went on, "that the technologists were able to say that this life sustaining is going to work—this artificial breathing—for fifty years. We can keep her alive for fifty years. Would that make any difference to you?"

"Of course," Collester replied. "It would disturb me greatly. However, the law as it now exists would seem to indicate that it would have to be continued."

The same hypothetical prognosis was posed by the Chief Justice to Ralph Porzio: "Do we just blindly turn away and allow these things to continue . . . life support for years?"

Porzio replied firmly, "Yes. I would say so because in the long run we've got to look at this from the standpoint of the entire society. There may be a small percentage in our society that are going along like this, but in the interests of the whole, I think we've got to do it."

THE COURT: Mr. Porzio, I was wondering why your clients are resisting the order that the plaintiffs seek here? It's an order which, if granted, can do no harm. It can only give them protection. In other words, the order would not force them—either of them—to participate in life discontinuance. It would simply say that if they decided to do so, in consultation with the parents, they would have no liability. Why should they object to that?

PORZIO: Well, it gets back to—it gets back to the question of the prognosis. And in giving—talking about the prognosis, I'll only talk about what's in the record.

THE COURT: Now wait. Are you being responsive to my questions? I don't think you are. Why should they object to the Court granting the relief that the plaintiffs are asking for here, since that relief would have no adverse effect upon them?

PORZIO: Simply because there is a duty on their part. They are still the treating physicians.

THE COURT: The relief the plaintiff seeks would not

compel them to do anything they didn't want to do. It would simply say that if they did accede, in their judgment, to the plaintiff's desire, they would have no liability.

PORZIO: And the doctors get a chance to step out of the picture?

THE COURT: Of course . . . There will be nothing compulsory against them if the Court granted the plaintiffs relief.

After several more questions, from Chief Justice Hughes and other members of the Court probing to ascertain the doctors' reasoning, Porzio said: "Speaking—speaking for my client—speaking for my client, these two doctors, they would be happy to get off this case at any time, except that they feel that they have a responsibility until somebody comes in here and substitutes. Now as far as I know, Mr. and Mrs. Quinlan have not suggested to them that they get somebody else, but I'm quite sure—and I know this from talking to them—that if it wasn't for Mr. and Mrs. Quinlan, they would be happy to get off this case and let someone else step into it.

"Now the other thing that I wanted to point out is that the doctors here, I think, have some responsibility. There is, I believe, a responsibility on their part which the medical profession has given them, and this has been recognized, and they are carrying out that responsibility in accordance with prevailing standards. And considering all of these factors, it would seem to me that they should be permitted to go on."

There was a concluding appearance by Theodore Einhorn, on behalf of his client, St. Clare's Hospital.

THE COURT: Mr. Einhorn, I'm asking you the same question I asked Mr. Porzio. Why does your client resist a judgment which could only exculpate your client and not inculpate them?

EINHORN: It's the decision of my client that, from a philosophical point of view, they are opposed to the Court injecting itself into the relationship of the patient and the doctor; and the Court making a decision, so to speak, as to who shall live and who shall die.

THE COURT: Well, except that that's not what the plaintiffs are asking for. The plaintiffs are asking only for a determination by the Court that if they go to the doctor and ask that the apparatus be turned off, and if the doctor agrees to do that, nobody is liable. Now that leaves it still within the doctor's prerogative to refuse to be a party to it. In other words, you can't be hurt by the judgment they seek. You can only be benefited by it.

EINHORN: . . . I omitted one very important factor which I think I should have made reference to. Namely, that in addition to the hospital's philosophical objection to the Court intervening into the relationship, there is a very real and a very pressing duty: namely, the duty that Miss Quinlan was and—excuse me—is alive; and the hospital concedes its duty, its primary duty, is to give care and treatment to her as a patient, especially in view of the fact that it is the opinion of the physicians not to terminate the particular apparatus.

"All right," said Chief Justice Hughes. "Thank you very much, Mr. Einhorn. Now that completes our list. Mr. Armstrong, do you have anything further?"

Paul rose and said, "I would just simply like to thank you and express the gratitude of the Quinlan family for the expeditious scheduling of the hearing of this appeal."

"Mr. Armstrong," said the Chief Justice, rising wearily from his chair, "I think the members of the Court, although we haven't particularly discussed this, would want me to express a similar gratitude to all counsel who have worked so hard and briefed this matter so well.

"It's a puzzling and a tragic and a very difficult case.

"We'll reserve decision."

Chapter 21

There would be two months and four days of waiting, while the Supreme Court justices weighed and analyzed the arguments of case A-116, in the matter of Karen Ann Quinlan.

Joe's optimism following the hearing was fragile and, looking back on February and March of 1976, he knows it might have fallen apart "if we'd known the decision would take as long as it did":

—But being ignorant was the same as being lucky, and for a long time we just went along, feeling the announcement might come any day—not impatient, willing to wait. We needed the time to be quiet.

The press was leaving us alone pretty much, and for the first time since all of this began I could sit down and really think about the meaning of all this that was happening. At night after Julie and the children went to bed, I would stretch out in the family room and think about Karen, and wonder why God let her go on like this. I knew He must have some kind of plan, and I prayed over and over that He'd let me in on it. And very gradually the whole thing began to come through to me.

Thirty-one years ago I was in the 84th Infantry Division and we had taken a little town in Germany. I think the name was Sterling. When we pulled into this town, our outfit was completely cut off from the other units by the German troops. They were all around us, and every night these enemy soldiers would counter-attack and try to infiltrate us during the dark. That's the reason I had a great fear of darkness for years after I came out of the service. Stealthy sounds, rustles, crackling noises. You can hear them way out in the street sometimes, once you've been frightened by them. I guess that's why I'm still a light sleeper.

One night, during this period, I was ordered to go on guard duty to watch over approximately twenty enemy soldiers we'd captured the night before. There were two of us on guard. The other man was a full-blooded American Indian.

I was grateful I had him with me, instead of one of the other young wet-behind-the-ears privates like myself. Still, I was only nineteen so I didn't feel exactly at ease.

When we reached the site we were to guard, the prisoners were all sitting on the ground leaning against the wall of an old stone building. The Indian and I didn't talk, we just concentrated. It was his first guard duty, too, and he could have been as uneasy as I was. Then all at once a very large, very fat major came out of the house that we were using as a temporary headquarters—and he called out to us and said he had just got word that the enemy was going to pull a counterattack that night.

"If that happens, soldier," he said to me, "I don't want any of these so-and-sos running around loose."

"No, sir," I said, looking at the Indian. He looked like he could handle the prisoners in the emergency. At least, I hoped he could.

But then this major said, just to make sure we knew exactly what he meant, "I want you to kill every one of them, rather than letting them run around in the dark."

I couldn't believe what he was saying. He was asking me to be a firing squad!

He said, "Did you understand me, Private?" And I said, "Yes, sir."

When he left and went back into the house, the other guard didn't say anything to me, and I just couldn't talk to him. I was afraid he might say, "All right, this is what we have to do." And I couldn't face that.

This was the first time I had faced this question of morality. Is it moral to kill unarmed prisoners?

Many thoughts ran through my mind. I knew that in wartime, to refuse an order means facing court-martial. In a war theater, you can be shot on the spot. An officer could just pull out his gun, as an example

to the rest of the men, to keep the other men in line—
and shoot someone like me. He has this power, in
wartime, under fire.

The Indian went over and sat down on a fence, with
his automatic rifle across his knees, but I had to walk.
I walked back and forth, to give myself something to
do. I was praying so hard my lips were moving as much
as my feet.

But I knew one thing right away: I couldn't do it.
I could never do it. I'd die first.

Just before dawn, two other young men came on
guard duty to relieve us. Now I had to face another
decision. Should I tell them what the major had said,
and transfer my moral problem to them? No—I
couldn't do that, either.

I said, "The major says we may have a counterattack.
If we do, don't let these prisoners run around loose.
Those are the major's orders." Then I got out of there
as fast as I could.

As it turned out, a few minutes later the Germans did
counterattack—and our replacement hustled every one
of those prisoners down into the basement of a nearby
building, where they spent the night. They were all safe.

And that major, who had given the orders—during
this counterattack, a stray bullet penetrated the house
where he was standing, and it bounced off a wall and
hit him.

I couldn't help thinking that God's hand was in that.

Shortly after that experience I was walking across an
open trail with another young private. We were deeply engrossed in conversation, so close that we almost
touched each other. All of a sudden—I could picture it
afterward—a sniper saw us. Two targets out there in
the open. He sighted on one and pulled the trigger, and
he killed this fellow beside me. Right in the middle of
our conversation. The boy was talking at the time, and
we fell to the ground together and the last sound he
made just went on and on, getting weaker and weaker,
till it stopped.

I was lying right alongside him and listening to this
until the last breath was gone, and all I could think of
was "God, why was I spared? Why is he dead, not me?"

And then, only a few days later, a third thing hap-

pened that helped eventually to form my character, and
that will have a telling effect on me all my life.

It was during the Battle of the Bulge, and there was
a lot of noise and excitement and I was scared and mad
at the same time, because the Germans began firing
88-mm artillery shells at us and there just was no place
to run and escape. And all of a sudden, I heard one
coming and I headed for the ground, but that shell hit
the ground in front of me and bounced up and, on the
way up, it caught me. I wasn't the only one—there
were a lot of other fellows around, screaming, and I
started cursing and yelling and praying all in the same
breath. My arm was blown right off.

I didn't feel any pain. But I was convinced I was
going to die, and I remember the prayer was just "No,
Lord, not now, not here!" I kept screaming that over
and over. I was scared, and had had no life to live yet.
You can face death when you've done something with
your life. I've raised a family now, and I would never
plead and beg with God. The next time I face death,
it'll just be time. But then, I felt so far from home
and my family and my mother, and I just cried out "No,
Lord, not now, not here!" until a young officer came
along and grabbed my good arm and said, "Come on,
let's get the hell out of here!"

Those experiences in the war, where God had spared
me—they had to be more than a coincidence. Looking
back, I feel that God was testing me, and sparing me,
for a role in some larger plan.

I began to believe, very strongly, that Karen is
part of the plan. And that when we made the decision
to let Karen die in peace, maybe it just wasn't good
enough for us to have made it alone. Maybe God
wanted everyone to make it, the whole community of
doctors and lawyers and everyone.

I really think that He is using us, running this whole
thing. And now when the Supreme Court makes their
decision, maybe Karen at last will be able to pass into
the loving hands of the Lord. Because He wouldn't
punish anyone—especially someone He's using.

I had a feeling of deep relief when I figured it all
out. I thought soon she will be with Him, and be happy
always. Which is everything.

On February 25 in Trenton, Attorney General William Hyland announced that his office had ended its grand jury investigation into the cause of Karen Quinlan's illness.

The investigation, he stated, had "failed to establish that foul play was the cause of the coma."

Julia was surprised at her own lack of emotion. Perhaps, she thought, time had dulled her anger.

"I couldn't laugh and I couldn't cry. It had hurt us so. Yet, now that Karen had been vindicated, what I felt was only numbness."

Two nights later, New Jersey's most influential newspaper, the Newark *Star-Ledger*, published an editorial under the heading "More Agony":

> One more tragic dimension of the Karen Ann Quinlan case—the investigation by the State Attorney General into the circumstances surrounding the collapse of the unfortunate young woman—has been completed, with the conclusion that her comatose condition was not induced by a physical assault.
>
> But the intervention of the Attorney General into possible criminal culpability raises some troubling issues, not the least of which is that the state's chief enforcement officer saw fit to supersede the authority of local authorities and the county prosecutor.
>
> The notoriety of the Quinlan case is in itself disheartening, along with the anguish of her parents who have found themselves embroiled in a legal controversy over whether extraordinary medical efforts are justified in maintaining life when there is no reasonable hope for survival.
>
> As if the the agony of their daughter's long suffering and the legal wrangling over the constitutional complexities were not enough to bear, Mr. and Mrs. Quinlan were subjected to the additional anxieties involving what the Quinlans' pastor described as "false images of Karen."
>
> There is no question that any unusual circumstances should have been investigated. But it was a matter to be routinely handled by local police and the county prosecutor, without the undue attention generated by the personal intervention of the Attorney General.

From a humane statement, the investigation only served to sensationalize the case—and added to the suffering of already long-grieving parents who would prefer that their daughter die with "dignity and grace."

Joe and Julie wanted an end to the continually painful speculation about Karen's coma.

At Paul's suggestion, the Quinlan family engaged the services of the country's foremost expert in forensic pathology, Dr. Milton Helpern, to oversee an autopsy when their daughter died.

The former New York City medical examiner, Dr. Helpern made it clear that he could only observe; the autopsy, by law, would be conducted by New Jersey pathologists.

Joe Quinlan said, "We may find out, eventually, what Karen dies from. But I don't know if they will ever find the cause of the original coma—unless it was something that left permanent scars, like a tumor.

"I'm sure," he said, "that Karen is the only one who could tell us what really happened."

Karen's twenty-second birthday was March 29. For days beforehand, Julie planned how to observe it. They would take her a dozen roses. It wasn't enough.

—Last year on her twenty-first birthday, we'd had a big, happy family party with all the cousins, and a couple of Karen's friends, and it was great fun. After dinner, Karen had driven in to New York to see *Pippin*, which she loved. It was such a beautiful day, and I knew when we remembered that all of us would have a very hard time getting through this birthday.

The answer finally came to me. We'd have a mass for Karen. We filled the family room with flowers, and invited the immediate family, and the cousins and aunts and uncles, a few friends, and five of the nurses from ICU, and Paul and Maria, of course. I managed to work so hard on the arrangements that the day went by quickly, but while I was waiting for the guests to arrive I became very nervous. The strain of wondering for nine weeks about what the Court would say, combined with the birthday—I guess it was understandable.

It was a bitterly cold night, and when Father Tom came through the door, I guess he could see right away that I was upset. He just smiled down at me and, without saying a word, he reached out and wrapped his arms around my shoulders and, even though his coat was ice cold, I hung onto him and felt incredibly warm.

After that, I was all right. And it was a beautiful mass, concelebrated by Father Tom and Father Quinlan and Father Pat from the hospital.

Father Tom's message that night was:

—We are waiting for a human being who is dying. Waiting is the best way to show our faith. God never gives us things immediately.

Why doesn't God take Karen? I don't know. I only know that twenty-two years ago a child was born who will probably in some way change the world. Her name will go down in history. God did have a plan. Karen's been involved with life and death from the time she was born.

She's precious to God. He is with her.

The next day, as though Father Tom's message on "waiting" had triggered a response in the courthouse at Trenton, Supreme Court Justice Richard Hughes sent an announcement to the attorneys in the Quinlan case that the opinion was written. It would be ready for distribution the following morning, March 31.

Paul drove immediately to the Quinlans' home to discuss strategy and logistics; whichever way the opinion would go, he didn't want the family subjected to the media mayhem that had followed the Civil Court trial.

After a few minutes of discussion, it was decided that Joe, Julie, Father Tom, and Father Quinlan would leave Landing before dawn, to elude the media, and would drive to Princeton.

They would go to the Nassau Inn, on the Princeton University campus, and that is where they would await the news—privately, away from the press. Father Tom would request of the manager a private area, with a phone, where they could receive Paul's call when the decision became known. (The plan was followed the next day, with the manager of the inn offering his private suite of offices, equipped with a conference phone, for the Quinlans' use.)

With all the plans made, and the decision imminent, Joe was painfully reminded of his chronic hernia:

—All of the optimism I had been feeling a couple of months before seemed to slide away, and my stomach began churning. I've always had the highest regard for the Chief Justice, Mr. Hughes. I heard him speak several times when he was governor, and afterward, and he seemed like a very human man.

But we'd been disappointed so many times before that now I wasn't sure of anything or anybody any more. And the last rumor we had heard—we heard a hundred rumors a day, it seems—the last rumor was that every single judge on the Supreme Court had a different idea. That each of them was writing a separate opinion—some of them against us, but the majority in our favor.

Well, if that rumor was true, I wondered where it would leave us.

I asked Paul, "If the judges all take a different stand, what do we do?"

Paul said to disregard the whole thing. He said he had heard about twelve other rumors that sounded more sensible to him.

The fact was that Paul Armstrong, on the night before the decision, had no idea what to anticipate.

"I knew there was a genuine concern among the justices, and I knew that they had clearly understood the arguments we were advancing. But whether or not they agreed with those arguments, we hadn't an inkling."

In the predawn darkness of March 31, Joe and Julie, Father Tom, and Father Quinlan sped to Princeton.

At 10 A.M. Paul and Jim walked into the Supreme

Court Building in Trenton and were ushered into a clerk's office, along with Prosecutor Collester, Deputy Attorney General Baime, and the guardian, Curtin.

It was crowded and noisy and, to Paul at that moment, unendurable. He couldn't face the most important decision in his life in this atmosphere. The court clerk, Steven Townsend, had come into the office with an armload of manuscripts—copies of the 59-page opinion by Chief Justice Hughes—and Paul reached out and touched his arm.

"Steve, could we go to someplace more private," he asked. "With a phone, preferably, so we could call Mr. and Mrs. Quinlan?"

The clerk didn't hesitate. He handed Paul and Jim a copy of the opinion, then quickly led them out a door, through a corridor, into a large, baronial study. It had a fireplace at one end, a long counsel table at the other, and Paul and Jim recognized it as the Supreme Court's own inner chamber.

Paul slid weakly into the Chief Justice's high-backed chair and, like one who cannot wait for the end of a mystery novel, he flipped the pages of the decision to page 58. Swiftly he read that, and then page 59. Then 57, working backward.

As he read, he wept.

The Supreme Court had decreed that Joseph Quinlan should be guardian of his daughter, Karen Ann.

It concluded that Karen's "right of privacy may be asserted on her behalf by him."

Whatever Joseph Quinlan should decide to do regarding his daughter "should be accepted by society, the overwhelming majority of whose members would, we think, in similar circumstances exercise such a choice in the same way for themselves or for those closest to them."

The Court eliminated any criminal liability for removing the life supports:

"We believe, first, that the ensuing death would not be homicide but rather expiration from existing natural causes.

"Secondly, even if it were to be regarded as homicide, it would not be unlawful."

The opinion stated further that if Karen Quinlan's attending physicians concluded there is no hope for her emergence from coma, they were to consult with an "ethics committee," to be established by the hospital.

If that committee agreed with the prognosis, the support system could be withdrawn.

And, should the doctors decline to remove the apparatus—said the Court—then Joseph Quinlan, as guardian, could find another doctor who would consent to do so.

As soon as he could recover his composure, Paul telephoned the Nassau Inn. The switchboard operator, expecting the call, promptly switched it to the conference phone in the manager's suite.

Neither Joe nor Julie could remember who, in their small party, picked up the receiver.

But Julie could never forget the conversation that followed:

—Paul's first words were "Our prayers have been answered." He sounded excited, grateful. He said, "The Court has ruled in our favor."

None of us could speak. Then Father Tom said, "God bless you, Paul."

Joe asked, "How did they vote? How many were in our favor?"

Paul paused. I heard him ask Jim for an envelope. Then he said, "Unanimous in their compassion, Joe—it's unanimous!"

When he said that, all four of us fell into each other's arms, embracing and kissing—Father Tom and Father Quinlan and Joe and I—and I began crying, and I remember Joe managed to pull out a handkerchief and start dabbing my cheeks. In those few moments, I don't believe any of us really could comprehend fully what had happened. We were in awe, and deeply emotional, and we all just clung together as though we could never let go.

And in the background over the phone, I heard Paul saying that we should wait at the inn. That we should wait for him and Jim, and they would come and get us and we'd all go home together, and while he was talking his voice went scratchy and broke, and I knew then that Paul was weeping, too.

Late that day, a press conference was held at the Our Lady of the Lake Grammar School in Mount Arlington, attended by more than one hundred members of the media, and telecast live by the three major networks.

Julie, tearful through portions of the conference, said, "We are grateful to the Supreme Court. I can't say—we can't use the words 'glad' or 'happy' to describe our reaction, because we may be losing our daughter."

Joe, too, described his feelings of thankfulness that Karen could now be returned to a natural state.

Father Tom added his agreement, but noted wistfully, "I think we would be more comfortable now if nature would take its course first, before the court decision has to be implemented."

At the conclusion of the ninety-minute press session, Paul Armstrong thanked the media "for your solicitude and consolation during the ordeal this family has been through."

Paul was resolved, and in his mind convinced, that this would be the last press conference to which Joe and Julie would be submitted.

From now on, through the implementation of the decision, it truly must be a private family matter.

When the reporters and cameramen had left, the Quinlan family, with their priests and their attorneys, drove to the church Rectory for a quiet supper and a discussion of the court decision and day's events.

With considerable embarrassment, Joe confessed the skepticism he had felt the night before. "I should never have doubted," he said, "a man of Dick Hughes's high principles."

While the others were talking, Julie remembers being "overwhelmed by sadness":

—It was a purely selfish sadness brought on by the sudden realization that soon we were going to be left alone here, without Karen. That we would not be able to kiss her good night. I didn't want to talk to Joe about it. I could tell from his face that he was enduring his own private thoughts.

But, late in the evening, I took Paul aside. I didn't know how to tell him about my feelings, so I asked, "How do you feel—I mean, how do you feel about all of this?"

And Paul, who always knows so much of what I am thinking, said, "Julie, that opinion was the kindest piece of judicial writing that's ever been presented. How do I feel?" Paul said. "That it's a very grave responsibility. And that now it's incumbent on us to accept it."

The way Paul said it returned my perspective.

Everything fell back into place.

After the family left the Rectory, Father Tom Trapasso sat alone for a while, pondering what had happened.

He had been concerned about the outcome of the Supreme Court hearing. But the wording of the decision eased his mind.

—I had been worried about the whole issue because I had learned, in talking to people, and in my reading, that "extraordinary means" is such a flexible word to most people.

I was concerned that it would be interpreted as euthanasia, which could lead to a lessening of concern for human life.

But the way the decision was worded, I really believe that people of good will could not misuse it. No one could use it to condone active euthanasia, based on this decision.

The difference between the spirit of the law and the letter of the law—I knew that what is always possible is that people could interpret it as an erosion of concern for life and for the sick. But no law can protect against that—except the law of the human heart.

Chapter 22

Joseph Quinlan was convinced "this was the will of God." It was a confirmation of The Plan, and the Supreme Court was carrying it out.

Joe resolved, however, to be patient with Dr. Morse.

"I know how he must be feeling now," Joe told Julie. "He has a different problem here. He has to decide now either to follow orders or to resign. I feel almost sorry for him. We'll give him a few days to make up his mind."

There was no comment from Dr. Morse, or from the hospital. St. Clare's declined to meet with the media, and even their public relations spokesman, Larry Stern, refused to discuss the court opinion.

Outside of silent St. Clare's, however, the nation's medical community expressed reactions to the decision, and they ranged from strong affirmation to stern criticism.

Dr. John Stapleton, medical director of Georgetown University Hospital, said in Washington that the Court's opinion was "realistic." He said the matter of handling the question is "in accord with what we would generally practice. The ethical principles under which we operate do not impose an obligation on either the physician or the family to sustain life by extraordinary means. And I think that is what the Court is saying."

The American Medical Association, predictably, disagreed. Through its legal counsel, B. J. Anderson, the AMA said the ruling appeared to require physicians to undergo an unecessary review by ethics committees "before making decisions" which are now made all across the country every day. "A treating physician is certainly able to determine whether a patient is in a terminal condition," commented Miss Anderson. "If he is unsure of anything, the doctor can ask for consultation with another doctor. Most hospitals don't have 'Ethics Committees.'"

The committee concept also bothered Dr. McCarthy DeMere of Memphis, a physician and lawyer who had headed the American Bar Association committee which had written a legal definition of brain death in 1969. "It will delay transplants for days, while these ethics committees make decisions," he said, reportedly with anger.

While the more conservative doctors disputed the opinion, Chief Justice Hughes commented placidly, "I have no qualms or doubts about it. I thought of nothing else for two months, and I feel quite comfortable with the decision."

On April 3 the former temporary guardian, Thomas Curtin, visited Karen in Intensive Care.

Upon emerging, he told reporters, who were now on a

twenty-four-hour watch outside the hospital, "I went to say good-by to Karen. I know it may sound cornball, but I came to know her, in a way, as a breathing person. It's an emotional thing to think of her life ending."

The public and the media, like Thomas Curtin, presumed that Karen Quinlan's fate had been court-ordained and that her death was imminent.

During the Civil Court trial, Dr. Morse had testified that he would not remove the respirator from Karen, even if ordered by the Court to do so.

Was he now reconsidering that adamant stance? Was he discussing his current difficult posture with the hospital administration, or with peers such as Dr. Bender? Was he contemplating the most feasible procedure for resigning as Karen's physician?

The Quinlan family had no way of knowing.

There was another vital imponderable, which Paul Armstrong carefully explained to Joe and Julie: "Any or all of the parties involved could decide to appeal the decision to the United States Supreme Court."

Before attempting to implement the decision, therefore, Paul contacted the attorneys for the hospital and the doctors, as well as the Attorney General, county prosecutor, and the former guardian, and requested written confirmation of their intentions.

Within a week, he was advised by letter that none of the parties involved would seek a high review of the New Jersey Supreme Court decision.

The last judicial hurdle resolved, Paul called a meeting with attorneys Einhorn and Porzio.

It was decided by the three lawyers that—in view of the fact that the Court had returned the matter to the family and physicians—it would now be appropriate for the Quinlans to meet with Drs. Morse and Javed. Privately, without legal counsel.

On April 8 Julie telephoned Dr. Morse and asked if she and Joe could meet with him.

She felt his reaction was unusual:

—He seemed to be surprised that we would want to see him. He suggested that he would be at the hospital for the next hour, if we wanted to drop in.

Joe and Mary Ellen and I rushed over—it was 6:30 in the evening—and Dr. Morse and Dr. Javed met us in the hospital chaplain's conference room.

Dr. Morse was smiling and friendly, as though nothing at all had happened. And it seemed that, in his mind, nothing had.

When we asked him when and how he was planning to implement the Supreme Court's decision, Dr. Morse's answer really astonished us.

He said he had not read the decision. And that, in any case, it wouldn't make any difference. He said that he and Dr. Javed intended to continue to use the EEG. They said that the EEG readings on Karen would dictate when the respirator would be removed.

I couldn't speak. Joe was more in control.

Joe said, "Does that mean you are going to ignore the Supreme Court? You're not going to do anything?"

Morse said it meant that he intended to continue to follow his concept of what is standard medical practice.

"You know," he said, "this is something I will have to live with the rest of my life."

I couldn't just stand and take that. I cried, "Well, it's something that *we* must live with for the rest of our lives too, Doctor. And she is our daughter. That's the whole point that you seem to have missed all along. It's never happened to you, seeing your child hooked up to all these things that are not helping her. That is what we have to live with, and Karen has to live with."

Dr. Morse didn't speak, and I looked at Joe for help.

"Doctor," Joe said, managing to remain very quiet, "I would like to say that, at this point, we understand that conceivably *all* treatment of Karen is extraordinary. That means the antibiotics and the food and the respirator. However, we personally have moral problems with our conscience, with regard to the food and the antibiotics. We have problems with it now, and we realize we would have more problems with it ten years from now. Because we know what would happen if they were taken away—we know that Karen would die. So we are not asking for the elimination of these other two things. What we are asking for is simply the same thing that we asked for all along. And that is the removal of the respirator."

It didn't seem to make much of an impression on Dr. Morse. At least, it certainly didn't change his mind.

"In any event," he said, "I'm going to be away for two weeks." He was going to Puerto Rico to take his neurological board examinations, and he told us that he would not consider any change in treatment for Karen whatever until he came back.

"Be patient," he said, and he patted me on the shoulder. "When I come back, we'll talk about it again. Meantime, don't worry about it. We'll work this out."

The meeting was ended on a cool and formal note. We were willing to wait for him to come back.

But it was a frustrating time.

As far as Dr. Morse was concerned, there hadn't even been a Supreme Court decision. He just said, "Trust us."

But we didn't really know what we were supposed to trust him to do.

Dr. Morse flew to Puerto Rico. Since he had ordered nothing attempted in his absence, it was another period of waiting for the Quinlan family.

During Joe's morning visits to Karen, he would attempt to check the medical records, usually left on a table beside his daughter's bed.

—It was a habit I had formed over the many months, to check on Karen's condition—see what kind of night she'd had, whether she was running a fever, and so on. But often, now, I couldn't see the records. Sometimes the nurses would see me coming in, and from across the room I could see them just casually pick up that clipboard and take it away.

Once or twice, I would ask the nurse on duty why she removed the records, and the answer would always be something to the effect that those reports were only for the doctors.

I would try not to be annoyed, or at least not to show it. So I'd smile and say something like, "But I'm not the patient. I'm the father and guardian, you know." Then, depending on which nurse it was, I'd sometimes get to see the records—and other times I'd just get a grin and a shake of the head.

I could never get angry with the nurses, though. They were just following orders. They were all wonderful to us.

But I sensed that I'd better start keeping my own record of what was happening, or what was *not* happening.

I bought myself a maroon leather loose-leaf notebook and, for the first time in my life, I began keeping a diary.

The first entry in Joe Quinlan's diary is dated April 11, 1976:

It looks like we're not getting anywhere with Morse. We had a meeting with Dr. Korein in his N.Y.C. apartment. Korein says he's been working. He says "I've been in contact with doctors around the country. So far I have three of the country's leading specialists standing by, and I will head a team of consultants under a doctor licensed to practice in New Jersey—to take over the case in event of treating physicians' dismissal or resignation.

APRIL 24: 11:30 meeting with Korein at Bellevue Hosp. He says he spoke with young Dr. Bender, and Bender told him to recommend patience with Morse. He said allow a reasonable length of time, "approximately two weeks." Bender says we should tell Morse we have confidence in him. Let Morse do things his own way, and if we give him plenty of leeway, Bender thinks he is capable of making a decision. Korein says "You have to understand all the newspapers in the country are looking over his shoulder now. Don't push him."

APRIL 26: 11 A.M. meeting, Morse and Javed, St. Clare's. We informed doctors of our feelings, that we have faith in their judgment, when the time comes. We will allow them to try their way, and will co-operate. Doctors promise to keep us informed. (Reasonable length of time, again.)

APRIL 29: Karen removed from respirator for approx. one hour.

APRIL 30: Karen removed from respirator one hour.

MAY 1: Drs. Morse and Javed at hospital. Javed encouraged. Next week will tell the story.

MAY 4/5/6: Karen off for 2 hours.

MAY 7: Not off.

MAY 8: 9:30 at St. Clare's; Morse and Javed. Two hours off respirator was most. "We will try harder next week."

MAY 10: Dr. Javed, St. Clare's. Staff too busy to remove respirator this day.

MAY 11–13: Not off respirator. Reason: temperature up to 102 degrees. Antibiotics continuously, from 5/8 to 5/13. Doubt now whether drs. can carry out our wishes.

MAY 14: Nothing going on. Nothing. Hard to understand this.

Late in the second week of May—nearly six weeks after the Supreme Court had decreed the right to remove the respirator—Julie discovered that not only was Karen still dependent on the machine, her technological supports were being expanded.

—I was taking my mother out for a Mother's Day dinner, and on the way to the restaurant we stopped in to see Karen. My parents would visit Karen almost every day—but this particular evening was extraordinary.

As we walked into Intensive Care, I saw a big machine I had never seen before. It was sitting on a table at the foot of Karen's bed.

"What is that?" I asked, and the nurses said, "Karen has been running a fever, and Dr. Morse had that brought in. It's a body temperature control machine."

I couldn't believe what I was hearing. I had to take out my glasses and read the instructions before I was convinced. It just seemed so cruel and unfair to me.

That night I thought my mother was going into shock. Not because of the machine—because it was the first time she had seen Karen without the bedclothes covering her body. They had her uncovered, because of this new machine, and Mama could see what I never thought she would have to see—Karen's little figure, shrunken and twisted in a position that seems inhuman, with a blanket stuck between the legs so the bones don't cut into the flesh, and the gauze pads between her toes to keep them from bruising each other, and the bedsores that go so deep you can see the hipbone exposed. And my mother was just standing there, with her mouth open but not saying a word. Karen was always her favorite, and she just stood there with a hand on Karen's shoulder, not moving, not speaking, not hearing. She was so transfixed with grief that I finally had to pull my mother by the arm to get her out of the hospital.

That night I knew we couldn't wait any longer.

There is a point where even a doctor has got to face reality and say, Why are we doing all of this? Is it for Karen? It's not helping Karen. There is a time when you must say, This is it, we've done everything possible. It's time to let her go.

When I got home about ten o'clock, I told Joe what I had seen. I almost regretted it. He had been working himself up to this all along.

I thought he might be ill, the way he looked. But my husband is a remarkable man, such a good person that he couldn't live with himself if he did anything that would hurt someone else.

I was ready to call Dr. Morse and have a showdown, but although Joe was in a terrible state of despair— there was no color in his face—all he said was, "I think we should call in another doctor to consult with Morse. I think we've gone along with him long enough."

Joe telephoned Dr. Andrew Bender to ask if, once again, he would consult with Dr. Morse. He would have preferred to call on Dr. Korein, but knew "that would just irritate Morse, and that wouldn't help." Dr. Bender indicated that he would be a consultant, if Dr. Morse should ask for him to come in.

Then Julie telephoned Dr. Javed at his office.

She remembers her frustration at the events which followed:

—I asked Javed, "Why hasn't Karen been off the respirator this week?" I knew what the answer would probably be, but I wanted him to confirm it, and he did.

He said, "Because she has another infection."

He sounded so weary that I almost felt pity for him when he added, "Dr. Morse won't permit it, and he is in charge."

Then I called Dr. Morse and said I wanted to see him as soon as possible, and he said he would be at the hospital for another hour or so and that I could come up and meet him there.

So once again, it was time for a confrontation—each of us being polite and each of us determined that this must be the last encounter. The problem had to be resolved.

I said, "Dr. Morse, why did you bring in this body temperature control machine for Karen?" Trying to sound reasonable, but I could hear a shrill edge to my voice that I hated.

"Because she has a fever. This is the quickest way to bring it down." So cool, so rational.

"She is terminal, Dr. Morse. You don't do that to someone in her condition."

"I have tried to explain to you, I am following medical protocol."

He looked at me sternly. "Now, Julie, I am treating Karen the same way I would treat any other patient. No difference whatsoever. I'm giving her exactly the same care that I'm giving the woman in the next bed, who is also in a coma."

I said, "Yes, of course. You're giving Karen, who has been in a coma for thirteen months—you are giving her the same treatment as a patient who was brought in two days ago."

"Yes."

"And if you take her off the respirator—and you find she isn't able to make it on her own—you will put her back on?"

"I will."

"For how long will you continue to do that?"

"For as long as it takes. Forever."

So now this was the end of it. There was nothing more to say. I knew it, it was all futile, and yet I couldn't stop. "Why? Why? What has this all been about? The trials? The right of privacy? The Supreme Court decision? Our daughter's condition is hopeless, and you say you will never let her go?"

"Now, Julie—"

I stood up. I felt I had to get out of this room instantly or I would crumble. Disintegrate.

Morse reached for my arm. "Now—now, don't leave. Let's talk about it." I heard him, and I turned, and slowly I came back and sat down. Like an obedient child. So instinctive, following doctor's orders.

But all he wanted was more time to explain—again —that he was "only following standard medical protocol." Over and over, "standard medical protocol, standard medical protocol."

I pushed my fists into the arms of the chair and raised myself up, feeling my face burning, and I said, "I can't take this any longer," and left the room.

Waves of anger seemed to push me down the hall, the elevator, across the lobby, and outside where I could breathe again in the cold wind. I felt that I would never sit in on a meeting at this hospital again.

Joe's diary for May 13: "Meeting with Dr. Morse, St. Clare's. Reluctantly he will call in Dr. Bender as consultant. But stressed that he is in charge of case. Used those words 'medical protocol' five times."

MAY 14: Phone call from Morse. Extremely angry because I had called Dr. Bender without his knowledge. Says "You broke the breach." What breach? Medical protocol again.

MAY 15: Will draft a letter to Drs. Morse and Javed, stating our wishes and giving them until Monday, May 17, to come up with a plan we agree with, to be submitted to the Hospital Ethics Committee for their approval—or we will be forced to obtain other treating physicians.

MAY 16: Draw up letter, "privileged and confidential," to doctors, reminding them of the Supreme Court decision and urging them to join with us in formulating a mutually acceptable plan for implementing it, to be submitted to the hospital's Ethics Committee. If they are unable to do so, we will honor their right to resign as Karen's primary physicians—but "earnestly request" they remain on case as consultants for orderly transfer of medical responsibility. I will deliver letters to doctors' message boxes at 6:30 A.M. tomorrow.

MAY 17: Letter out. Delivered to message boxes on my way to see Karen. Telephone call to my office from Morse; Javed on extension. They received the letters. Dr. Javed says he intends to remove respirator today for at least 8 hours, maybe more. Dr. Javed asks for more time to make a "serious" attempt. He is confident he can wean Karen. Dr. Morse starts to interrupt, to say something. Javed says, "Please, Doctor, don't interrupt—let me finish. I feel if given a little more time I can wean her, and then my services will no longer be required and I will step off the case gracefully."

Meeting later at hospital, with Bender and Morse. Dr. Bender backs Dr. Morse 100%. If he were in charge, would do same thing. Recommends we stick with Dr. Morse. Feels Karen will be off respirator in a couple of days, and in a private room. And eventually in a hospital for chronic care, where he feels she will probably die.

MAY 18: 8 P.M., Morse, Javed, and hospital administrators, including Sister Urban. Meeting at hospital. Guardian [J. Quinlan] blew his cool. . . .

The meeting of Tuesday night, May 18, was the corrosive climax of a year of misunderstandings and building resentments between the doctors and the hospital, and the Quinlan family, and their attorneys.

It was held in the St. Clare's conference room. Representing St. Clare's were not only Drs. Morse and Javed with their lawyer Ralph Porzio, but also Administrator Courey, hospital attorney Einhorn, and, for the first time at any of the meetings, the president of St. Clare's Board of Trustees, Sister Mary Urban.

Seated at the rear of the large room was the public relations man whom the hospital had hired when it learned the Quinlans would seek legal advice—Larry Stern.

Looking back on the scene that faced him as he walked into the conference room at 8 P.M., Joe confesses, "I am very slow to become angry and, after I do become angry,

I am very slow to show it. But that night I was extremely frustrated. It was like a bad dream. Right from the beginning, there were fireworks."

Paul Armstrong opened the session by demanding to know why the public relations man, Larry Stern, was permitted at the meeting.

He was needed, Administrator Courey said.

"For what purpose?"

The hospital intended to issue a joint press release, in behalf of all parties, regarding Karen Quinlan's status. Stern would write it.

Paul reacted sharply. "Oh no. That is not the purpose of this meeting," he said. "It has always been our commitment to preserve the element of privacy, especially as it attaches to a meeting between doctors and family. Unless Mr. Stern removes himself from this room," Paul threatened, "my clients and I will be forced to leave."

After several minutes of angry discussion, Larry Stern reluctantly left the conference room.

Paul then reminded the assembled group that nearly two months had passed since the Supreme Court announced its decision.

"March thirty-first was the decision," he said. "Now it is May eighteenth, and nobody at this hospital has made any serious move toward honoring the request of the Quinlan family, made within the context of the court ruling.

"Therefore, we are here this evening to request the following actions, within the context of the Court's guidelines, for which we fought extremely hard.

"Number one, we request that this hospital form an ethics committee. Two—that the doctors develop a medical plan to implement the Quinlans' request for the removal of the respirator. Three—we ask that this appropriate information be submitted to your Ethics Committee for its review and consideration.

"As you can see," Paul went on firmly, "we intend to follow the recommendations of the Supreme Court to the letter. If you refuse, or chose not to do so, or if you have any reservations about it, we will honor your right not to participate.

"But if you *do* have any moral reservations, please let us know now, so that we can bring in a team of eminent physicians who will assume the responsibility for implementing the decision. In that case, we would hope that Dr. Morse and Dr. Javed will remain on the case as consultants to ensure an orderly transfer of the medical responsibilities."

While Paul was speaking, Joe Quinlan had been observing the faces of the doctors and the hospital personnel. He could see that "every one of them was tense":

—And we were, too. I could sense a coming outburst, and it came almost immediately.

Paul put the question to everybody there: "Do you have objections to carrying out the court decision, and if so, please tell us now."

Dr. Javed spoke up. "Are you asking us to suspend all treatment? The antibiotics and food—as well as the respirator?"

That annoyed me. We had talked about that several times before. "Doctor, I've told you·more than once how I feel about the antibiotics and the food. All we're asking for, and all we've ever asked for, is the removal of the respirator."

Then Sister Urban looked directly at Paul and said, "Speaking on behalf of the Board of Trustees of St. Clare's—twenty-one people, and I know how each of them feels about this—I would like to say that we are a small community hospital, and we feel that it is morally incorrect."

I was frustrated. "Morally incorrect, Sister?" I said. "Didn't you read Bishop Casey's statement supporting our position?"

"Yes, Mr. Quinlan," she said, "I read Bishop Casey's statement. But there are other bishops in the Church who disagree with him."

"But don't you realize," I said, "that this is the Bishop who sets the policy for the churches in this Diocese? And your hospital happens to be in this Diocese, too. Doesn't that mean something?"

She looked me straight in the eye then, and she said, "You have to understand our position, Mr. Quinlan. In this hospital we don't kill people."

"We're not asking you to *kill* anyone!" I was furious

and I stood up, because I couldn't sit down and take that. "It should be obvious to anyone—to anyone—that the respirator is artificial. That's what this whole thing's about!"

Sister Urban was very calm. All business. "Our position is that we will not do it."

That's when I blew up. "Ten months ago," I said, and my voice wasn't soft, "you turned a meeting over to your lawyer. You were interested in the law—wanted everything by the law. Your lawyer stated the law to me, and he told me what I must do—go to court, and so forth.

"Now we've been through this. We've gone through all the courts, and finally we have a decision in our favor. We've had our name dragged through newspapers all over the country and in many parts of the world, and we're at the point now where our nerves are shot." I was excited, looking right at her, and my face must have been very red, and I said, "And now you have the audacity to tell me, after ten months, that it's morally against the hospital policy? Ten months after going through all this, you have the nerve to tell me that? Why didn't you tell me ten months ago? I would have taken Karen out of this hospital immediately."

Suddenly everything went quiet. Nobody said anything. Everybody was looking at me.

Then Sister Urban spoke again. And she just repeated herself.

"I'm sorry," she said, "but the Board of Trustees feels that we cannot morally do it."

I saw Julie push back her chair, and Paul was sliding some papers into his brief case, and I knew it was finished.

I said, "I don't think any of you understand this court decision at all." And we all walked out of the meeting.

The deteriorating relationship between Joe and Julia Quinlan and Karen's doctors might have ended there.

Julie was certain that it had:

—I was angry, and very worried about Joe, because I had never seen him this angry. I was afraid he might have a stroke. As we walked away from the conference room, I instinctively held onto his arm, more for his support than my own.

But before we reached the end of the corridor, Dr. Morse and Dr. Javed came after us, and Dr. Morse said, "Could we speak to you alone?"

Joe stopped short. We all did.

"We'd like to continue our attempt to wean Karen," Dr. Javed said.

"What makes you think you'll be successful now?" Joe asked. Joe must have felt he'd been through this so many times. "You said it was impossible to wean her."

Javed said, "I think I can wean her this time, and then we'll move her into a private room. Then you can transfer her out to some other facility."

"But keep in mind," Morse spoke up again, "if she needs the respirator, I'll put her back on it."

It all seemed so futile. Yet, if they succeeded, it could resolve it all.

In any case, it was our last alternative to bringing in outside doctors.

They went to the ICU to say good night to Karen, and then drove home together—Joe and Julie and Paul.

Mary Ellen and John were waiting, and while Julie brewed tea, Paul and Joe advised them what had happened at the meeting.

They began becoming excited and angry too, and in the middle of the conversation, Julie sat down wearily.

"I don't think I want to discuss this any more," she said. "I think I will go upstairs and I'm going to slam a few doors. And then I'll cry myself to sleep."

The next day, when Father Tom was given an account of the meeting, he was "deeply disturbed by this new phase we seemed to have entered":

—Up to this time, everything had been very noble, to use Paul's favorite word. But the hospital had backed Joe and Julie into a position of having to fight for implementation of the decision. The inaction of the doctors had forced two very human, loving people to act in a harsh manner that was totally unlike them.

I thought if the hospital had only leveled with Joe and Julie at the beginning, this never would have happened. If they had said "Win, lose, or draw, we won't let Karen die in this hospital," I could have understood it. Image is very important to hospitals; they don't exist to suspend treatment of patients. With all the publicity, I could well imagine some poor soul up in Rockaway saying, "That's the hospital where they—let you go."

But now we had this disastrous confrontation that was turning everyone inside out, and the irony is that the hospital and doctors had used all their technology to save Karen—and in the process had lost sight of the human aspect, which is what saving lives is all about.

This poor girl is the prize example of what modern medicine can do to sustain life. And now no one wanted her.

Chapter 23

The MA-1 respirator is a gray boxlike console measuring approximately three feet deep, two feet wide, and waist-high to a nurse of average height. A plastic tube emerges from its side, coils upward into a pumping container, then curls down and connects into a plastic cuff which is taped to the surgical opening just above Karen's breastbone.

The sophisticated machine is computer-programmed to dispense a specified volume of air with each breath the patient takes; when the patient does not breathe voluntarily, the MA-1 clicks into assistive service, pumping pure oxygen through the tube and into the tracheotomy in precisely the needed amount for proper ventilation of Karen's lungs.

From the beginning of her coma, Karen Quinlan's

breathing had been sporadic and there was no indication
that it might stabilize into a normal pattern without the aid
of the MA-1. She would breathe spontaneously during her
"awake cycles," but her respiration was usually rapid and
shallow, occasionally broken by deep gasps of hyperventi-
lation, at which time deep moaning sounds could be
heard issuing from her throat.

Blood-gas tests indicated that, during her voluntary
breathing periods, the oxygen did not penetrate deep into
the lower portion of her lungs.

In her "sleep cycles," Karen simply ceased to breathe
on her own, and at those times the respirator would click
into action, promptly pumping sterilized air through the
tube in precisely the necessary amount to properly ventilate her lungs.

The imponderables, as Dr. Javed seriously set about to
wean his patient from this technological marvel of sustenance, were several:

First and most obvious, without the assistance of the
MA-1, would Karen simply stop breathing in her sleep
and die? Or would the operative portion of her brain stem
respond to the innate instinct for survival, forcing her to
gasp for air and finally adapt and stabilize the breathing
process?

Even with spontaneous breathing, would her inhalations
be so shallow that she would suffer further anoxia, result-
ing in still further brain damage? Might she then, quickly,
progress to a point of legal brain death?

In her rigid fetal position, would insufficient ventilation
of the so-called "deep space" deep in the lungs result in
pneumonia—an illness that would almost certainly cause
death in a patient so severely debilitated?

Or would the physical strain of striving for air bring
about cardiac arrest?

These were questions that no doctor could answer with
any degree of certainty.

Most of the physicians who had examined Karen did
not even choose to speculate on what would happen to
Karen if the respirator were removed.

But shortly before the weaning attempt was seriously
begun, Dr. Julius Korein told the Quinlans what *could*
happen.

In late April, at a meeting with Joe, Julie, Paul, and
Maria in his Manhattan apartment, Dr. Korein said it

was his feeling that, should Dr. Javed succeed in weaning Karen off the respirator, she might live for some time.

"How long?" Joe asked.

"For days, weeks, and possibly longer," the neurologist said.

"I thought—" began Joe. "Well, everybody had the impression that if she is off the respirator, she'd just pass away."

Dr. Korein shook his head. "I personally have had patients in similar circumstances who have lived for several years. And I've heard of some comatose patients living for ten years," he said. "I think you should be prepared for that. Don't be surprised if it happens."

Dr. Javed began the weaning effort quietly on May 15, with nurses standing by, making notations at ten-minute intervals, and ready to reinstate the respirator instantly if Karen should appear to be in danger of succumbing.

Javed's scrawled daily medical reports record the surprising swiftness of the procedure. (Samples of the nurses' notes are abbreviated below each of the pulmonary internist's observations.)

MAY 15: Off MA-1 for 4 hrs. Did well; will continue weaning process. J. [for Javed]
[Nurses] Regular breathing pattern with sleep cycle. Pulse rate down to 60, then proceeded to hyperventilate, and pulse went to 78. Restless period, with deep sighs. Returned to MA-1.

MAY 16: Off respirator for 4 hrs. Tolerated well. Will up this period off MA-1 to 8 to 12 hrs. tomorrow. J.
Off MA-1, 7 A.M. Sleep cycle, with little movement. Later—restless with scream like motions. Sleep cycle with occasional restless period. Put back on MA-1, 11:05.

On the morning of May 17 the doctors received the letter from Joseph and Julia Quinlan urging that they comply with the Supreme Court guidelines. That day the hospital called a meeting between the doctors, the administration, and the Quinlan family, to be held the following evening. Dr. Javed's notes for that day indicate the beginning of a more determined effort to wean Karen from the respirator.

MAY 17: Off respirator 7 hrs. Doing Well. J.
Color pale. Off MA-1, 8:30. Remains quiet. Respirations remain regular. Awake 10:10, moving head and arching back. Periods shallow breathing. 6:30, respirations irregular and shallow at times. Corrects herself.

MAY 18: Off MA-1 for 12 hrs. Did well. J.
Pt. repositioned. Sleeping cycle. Pt. restless and suctioned for thick yellow secretions. Restless period. Sleeping, in no apparent distress.

MAY 19: Tolerating period off MA-1 very well. Stable. Will keep her off as long as there is no sign of respiratory insufficiency. Lungs are clear. J.
Pt.'s respiration rate went down to zero, 1:30 A.M. until she was stimulated to start her own respirations again. EEG done. Pt. restless, but no respiratory distress noted.

MAY 21: Off MA-1 over 48 hrs. J.
Pt. clean and positioned. Pt. awake and calm. No distress.

MAY 22: Doing very well without MA-1. Lungs are clear. J.
Pt. resting comfortably. Color good. Restful evening. Respiration even and full most of the time.

So it was done.

The media was not informed. Reporters, most of whom expected a swift and fatal climax to the Karen Quinlan story, found themselves behind a no-comment barrier as solid as the brick walls of St. Clare's.

Paul's answer to all queries was a statement couched in the kind of language which the press now viewed as typical, eloquent Armstrongese:

—All medical care and treatment presently being administered to Karen Quinlan falls within the area of physician-patient privilege. The Supreme Court has based its decision on the Constitutional Right of Privacy, and wisely and justly returned those administrations to the doctors and the family, within the context of the sacred realm of privacy.

This period was recalled later by Jim Crowley as "a time when Paul realized that he wouldn't endear himself to the press, but that didn't matter to him at all. Paul's actions were motivated by the highest ethical commitment, and it made him completely single-minded. In his mind, this was a delicate and private matter. And he would do anything for the larger goal, which he considered to be the honor of Karen and the family. He would do anything, including going into penury, for this cause."

With no hard news to report, the media resorted to its own resourcefulness and speculation. . . . There was a rift between the Quinlans and Karen's doctors. . . . New doctors were being sought to take over Karen's care and implement the decision. . . . Nursing homes around the state of New Jersey were being urged to accept the girl in the coma. . . . And the most appropriate headline of all, in the Newark *Star-Ledger,* was KAREN'S CASE TANGLED IN WEB OF CONFUSION.

All of these speculations were valid.

By the last week in May, in spite of all efforts at privacy, the news of Karen's successful weaning inevitably reached the public.

The impact of the truth that Karen could now breathe on her own was diminished by the rumors that had preceded it, and the media had already moved on to the latest problems: When would the patient be moved to another health facility? Where would it be? Who were the doctors who would take over her treatment? And, most importantly, to what extent would they be willing to go to let her "die with dignity"?

When the public gradually absorbed the reality that Karen Quinlan would survive, their reactions were emotional and varied.

Some felt her ability to breathe on her own was evidence of what they had suspected: that she might survive.

Others felt sympathy for the Quinlans, feeling that now the family dilemma was only beginning.

In Florida, where he read the news, Tommy Flynn experienced an emotion close to elation. "She showed them all," he thought. "The weakness people were trying to find in her, the slander and muckraking, everything they tried to throw at her—Karen lived through it. She proved to everybody she is worthy of distinction. Otherwise she'd have died, and maybe that's how it was supposed to come about. Maybe now she can just go in peace."

And Joseph Quinlan met with Father Tom. He was trying to assess, in his own mind, the meaning of what was happening to them now:

—We were all convinced that morally it was right—to get Karen off the machine. And now she was off, and I couldn't help but wonder, what could God be using her for now? You would think her suffering would be over now, and it was still going on.

Father Tom was comforting. He said, "If Karen had died immediately, who is to say how you would feel about that?"

I thought about it. "I didn't want her to die," I said. "I just wanted her put back in her natural state, and leave her to the Lord."

"Yes," Father Tom said. "Ten years from now you might have had second thoughts, if she had died right away. That is was just the respirator that kept her alive. Now we know that it's not that. The respirator had nothing to do with it. There must be another reason."

He just kept throwing out thoughts to me like that, and I stopped questioning. You can't question God's motives. People are discussing death openly now. Maybe that's the reason He's kept her alive. Less and less people are fearing death today, because of Karen. Whatever His purpose is, I know if the Lord wants her to live in a natural state, she'll live. If He wants her to die, she'll die.

The objective now was to transfer Karen to a private room in St. Clare's—and then to find another facility to which she could be moved, and another doctor, licensed in New Jersey, who would be willing to assume the responsibility for her care.

For Julie the experience began a new form of frustration:

—Dr. Morse told us that we could move Karen to a private room, but only if we could supply round-the-clock nurses for her while she was there. He said that now she would be considered a "chronic care" patient and that the hospital did not have either facilities or nurses for that kind of patient.

This came as a new surprise. I thought, "He's just putting up every kind of road block to keep Karen there in the ICU. But there seemed to be no way to fight it. We'd just have to get our own nurses. Joe and Mary Ellen and I took turns on the phone, calling people to see if they knew of any nurses who'd be willing to come in on a moment's notice. It had to be very quickly, because Morse stressed how scarce private rooms are. So if we didn't take the one that was now available, perhaps we'd have had to wait for days for another.

The first nurse we phoned was Geri [Geraldine] Lofgren, a friend of ours in town. Geri has a new baby, about six months old, and of course I didn't think she could take on a job herself but I knew she'd be acquainted with other nurses who might fill in. But Geri said her husband could take care of the baby, and she wanted to take a shift. And she called Marge Leonard, a wonderful girl, and a few other friends. Father Tom asked for volunteer nurses at Sunday mass, but it was really Geri who brought the girls in. One by one, she found them, and we had a crew of nurses who came in for eight-hour shifts to help us. And not one of them would take any pay for her services. Geri was horrified when I even mentioned money. She said, "Would you please stop talking like that? You do it for love, and if it's love you don't take money." When somebody asked Marge who was paying her for this work, she laughed and said, "It's the Lord who's payin' me."

So by May 22, in the early afternoon, we had enough nurses lined up that Dr. Morse said it was all right to move Karen out of Intensive Care and into Room 248. It was only a few yards down the corridor from the ICU, because he still felt that if an emergency arose, he'd rush her back and put her on the respirator again.

That afternoon, as they wheeled our daughter's bed out of that big door and across the hall into the little cubicle of a private room, Karen looked peaceful.

She still had the guard outside the door, and she had all of the dangling bottles around her bed, and the nasal-gastric feeding tube in her nostrils, and the tube into her bladder. They also added that electric heart monitor—and a breathing monitor, to check her respiration. And there was another sort of hose now, resting on her tracheotomy, connected to a container of distilled and sterilized air—and this distilled air leaked out and formed a white, misty vapor around the bed. That room looked like a dream world, almost surrealistic, with the fog seeming to hang over her body. And they made it clear that the ICU nurses would stop in often, to keep a watchful eye on Karen.

So it really wasn't that much different from the way it had been before, except for the most vital thing. At least Karen was away from that great gray machine.

For the next two weeks, we scarcely knew where we were from one day to the next. We rushed around from one sanatorium and nursing home to another, looking for a place to transfer Karen.

All of the places had waiting lists. Or rules against admitting comatose patients. It wasn't only Joe and I and Paul who were searching. Mrs. Cors at St. Clare's was on the phone checking out various chronic care hospitals. Even Bishop Casey himself was trying to help us. It seemed as though nobody could take her in.

It was difficult not to be bitter.

It would be so nice to know that somewhere there was a hospital which would really care about Karen so much that they would want her. Even with the publicity. That they would open up their hearts and take her in.

The thought was always in the back of my mind that maybe we would have to bring Karen home. It didn't seem possible. It would be terrible for all of us trying to sleep in the same house, hearing her moans, and the doctors and nurses coming and going. But I realized I might have to do it, as a last resort.

One day, when I couldn't think of any other way, I mentioned it to Paul. "Do you think we should bring her home?"

Paul said, "Oh no, Julie—don't even think about it." He said he still had faith that we would find doctors and an institution with the courage to accept the responsibility of treating and caring for Karen.

One day we saw a story about a Dr. Fennelly who had been interviewed by the local newspapers and had said he favored the Supreme Court decision. I read the story aloud, "Dr. Joseph Fennelly of Madison said it was his personal opinion that as a result of the decision, 'Society is now in the position to share the thinking and decision making of shutting off a life support machine. Too often, the problem of life and death have been suppressed and repressed. I am delighted.' "

We were sitting at the Rectory. Joe, Father Tom, Paul, and I. And we were discussing this Dr. Fennelly, who was listed as the chairman of the Humanities Committee for the Morris County Medical Society—and wondering if perhaps he would be willing to help us—when Father Quinlan walked in.

I said, "Look at this, Father Q. Here's a doctor who has spoken up in our favor."

Father Quinlan glanced at the article and said, "Say! This is my doctor."

"You mean—you actually know him?"

Father Quinlan said, "Yes, I know him. But not as well as he knows my stomach. He's a really good man."

We all started talking at once. "He's already on record as approving the court decision." "He was on the Humanities Committee." "Do you suppose he'd help us?" I asked Father Quinlan.

Without a word in response, Father Quinlan went to the phone and dialed Madison.

"Dr. Fennelly? Father Quinlan. I'd like to see you sometime today if I could. Well, I know. Maybe later? Sure, I understand that. Well, yes, it is—it is sort of an emergency. Tomorrow at three? Okay, thanks."

They were to meet in the emergency room at Morristown Memorial Hospital the next day at three o'clock, and all that day and night and the next afternoon, Joe and I were in suspense, wondering what Dr. Fennelly would say when Father Q. talked to him about us.

I was in the family room at about 5:20 that next afternoon when Father Quinlan came ambling through the door, that bashful grin of his spread clear across his face, trying to look casual. He said, "Well, I think Dr.

Fennelly might take on the case. Can you and Joe and Paul go with me to his office tonight at eight o'clock?"

We were there at 7:45, to be sure we didn't keep him waiting. Joe, Paul, Father Quinlan, and I. When Dr. Fennelly came into his waiting room, I could only pray that he was our man. And I felt that he was. He was extremely sympathetic—but not soft or wavering. Totally self-assured and in control.

"I'd like to help you," he said, "but if I do, I am concerned that the case be handled as privately and professionally as possible."

He said that he would accept the responsibility for Karen's treatment but only if he could find a committee of other doctors to assist him. No one doctor, with a large number of private patients, could possibly oversee Karen's care alone.

Dr. Fennelly told us that he felt the medical profession helped to bring about this problem. "And it's up to us in the medical profession," he said, "to resolve it."

We had never thought about that before. But I guess it would be true.

Then he said he would begin a search immediately for other physicians to assist. And later that same evening, he telephoned Paul and said that already—it had only been a couple of hours after our meeting—he had contacted seven New Jersey doctors who were ready and willing to help us.

While Paul was still on the phone talking to him, I confessed to Joe and Father Quinlan that I had felt an almost irresistible urge at the meeting to run over and hug and kiss him.

Father Quinlan said, "You should have. He's the kind of human being—he'd have understood and loved it."

Then Paul hung up and turned around and said, "Dr. Fennelly wants us to come to his office for another meeting tomorrow night. He'll have all the other doctors there to talk to us."

At the meeting the next evening, we came to realize the significance of this assignment to Dr. Fennelly, and to the other doctors who had agreed to become involved.

Not only were the other physicians present, but also there was the claims manager of Chubb & Son, the large medical malpractice insuring company, and an attorney for Chubb & Son.

It was all extremely businesslike. After the introductions, all of the doctors adjourned to another room with the insurer and his lawyer and Paul. They were closeted there for a while—I don't know how long, but to Joe and me, it seemed forever. When finally they came out, the doctors, one by one, assured us that they would help by taking over Karen's treatment, whenever we found a new facility to which she could be transferred.

As we were about to leave, Dr. Fennelly told us that the names of his fellow physicians were to be withheld.

"In light of the world media attention," he said, "we all feel it better that they be anonymous."

That night, as we drove home, we felt the same faith in our fellow man that we had felt right after the Supreme Court decision.

It occurred to us that the number seven truly is lucky.

Seven justices of the Supreme Court had shown us the way to go. And now seven doctors had stepped forward to help us. It was a wonderful, wonderful coincidence.

Dr. Joseph Fennelly wasted no time. He promptly called a press conference and announced that he and a voluntary group of New Jersey physicians were standing by to assist the Quinlans. He expressed his hope that a chronic care or nursing home facility would soon "open its doors to the unfortunate Miss Quinlan."

Publicly chiding the entire medical community, hoping to prod their collective consciences, Fennelly told reporters that it seemed the state of New Jersey's hospitals and doctors "are too afraid of their medical skins" to act humanely.

St. Clare's was pressing Joe and Julie to find another institution for Karen, because rooms at the hospital were in short supply.

However, it seemed that every facility in the state of New Jersey had its private reasons for not admitting Karen Quinlan.

"We are not a chronic care institution," some said. "Our charter forbids the acceptance of comatose patients," others reported. Homes for the aged had regulations written into their charters against admitting persons under sixty years.

Joseph Quinlan was too busy—with his office work, with visiting Karen, and the constant telephoning to keep a schedule of volunteer private nurses functioning—to join the search for a place that would take his daughter. But Julie, Father Tom, and Paul devoted most of their time, now, to visiting institutions and pleading with them to accept her.

Even Dr. Robert Morse entered the search, as did Bishop Casey, both men telephoning facilities which conceivably could take in Karen. It had been two weeks since she had been sequestered in the $185-a-day private room Number 248, and there were increasing pressures upon the doctor to free that space for other patients.

A total of twenty-two New Jersey institutions expressed sympathy and regret but found it impossible to admit Karen Ann Quinlan. The specter of the publicity involved undoubtedly affected their decisions, but was never mentioned. Every facility maintained it had other reasons, ranging from rules of charter to insufficient staff and equipment.

Meanwhile, the newspaper, radio, and TV reporters, trying to cover all the possibilities of an imminent move by the world's most famous patient, were researching all of the private and state- or county-operated nursing homes and therapy centers, prying for news in the media blackout.

By late May, their attention had focused on the Morris View Nursing Home, a spacious and modern institution operated by Morris County in a pastoral location approximately twelve miles from St. Clare's.

Joe Quinlan could not understand why all the newspapers seemed to conclude that Morris View might accept Karen. "They had already turned down our request at least two months before. They said they couldn't accept comatose patients—it was impossible. We had no reason to think they would change their rules."

Nevertheless, at a private meeting of the Board of Trustees of the Morris View Nursing Home on June 3, 1976, in an unusual "reversal of policy," the board voted unanimously to amend its long-standing rule against accepting comatose patients.

They would gladly accept Karen.

Paul Armstrong and the Quinlans met with the home's medical director, Dr. Richard Watson, who would be directly responsible for Karen's care. They liked the forthright, pipe-smoking, quiet-spoken physician immediately.

Julie recalled later, "He said exactly what he thought. He talked everything out with us completely openly. He seemed a strong, unwavering man, but sympathetic, and he agreed with us that Karen would have excellent care, but that in her case no heroic treatment should be necessary."

Joe and Julie, Paul, and Father Tom were requested to meet with an Ethics Committee, which the nursing home ultimately formed, consistent with the Supreme Court ruling. That meeting established the nusing home's intention to comply strictly and faithfully with the Court's directives in the matter of Karen Quinlan. Morris View and Dr. Watson subsequently announced that "aggressive treatment of any acute problem is inappropriate—as is readmission to a hospital."

Chapter 24

Dr. Richard Watson—lean, wry, mid-forties, an internist who divided his time between a private practice and directorship of Morris View—had been firmly opposed to admitting Karen Ann Quinlan.

—The principal reason was that, over the preceding three months, we had turned down three other applications for patients in coma. Technically and mechanically, we weren't well equipped to take care of patients who could do nothing for themselves. Under the circumstances, when word came through to us that St. Clare's Hospital wanted to send Miss Quinlan here, our feeling was that we couldn't take care of her any more than we could the others. And that if we admitted her, then we'd have to admit the others.

There were other problems, aside from lack of equipment and nurses for a coma unit. One was security. Morris View is an open place—no end rooms. You can get into the halls from one end or the other, or even through the basement up the middle.

Still another factor, a personal one. I had followed the story in the newspapers, and I was sympathetic with absolutely nobody involved in the Quinlan case, except the patient herself. I was slightly cynical about their positions. I thought everybody concerned—the doctors, the hospital, the family—was completely, unnecessarily, getting themselves painted off into ideological corners by their own quotations, and were by now so protective of their own egos and their own legal aspects that nothing positive could ever happen.

Under the circumstances, after meeting with the staff a few times, I said no.

I thought that was the end of it, but one rainy morning early in May a couple of doctors from Medicaid in Trenton drove up to see me, and they did what I considered to be a bit of arm-twisting. That clinched it in my mind—never! But Medicaid was tough. The fellow in charge at their New Jersey headquarters told me on the phone that he could force us to take this patient, and that raised a few bristles in the back of my neck, and I replied, "Well, maybe you can—but you'll have to do it."

Then Dr. Morse telephoned me. He said he was only calling to tell me what his thoughts were—that he felt it entirely appropriate for Karen to be transferred to a nursing home. He said it was long past the time of there being any hope that she could be helped, in a purely medical sense. Dr. Morse also mentioned that a county home, like ours, would be more appropriate than a private institution, because of the accessibility to county assistance in terms of security.

"However," Dr. Morse said, "I will certainly understand if you say no." And then he assured me that he would happily continue to take the total responsibility for Karen, as long as anyone wished him to. He didn't want me in any way to get the idea that he was trying to get a touchy problem off his hands.

Dr. Morse's phone call disarmed Dr. Watson. He wondered why the neurologist had taken such a strong stand
against elimination of the respirator, a widespread practice in hospitals in the case of hopeless cases. Dr. Watson
himself had disconnected a respirator on a dying patient in
a hospital many years before.

—We had a patient who was an obvious brain death,
flat EEG, five days after a massive intracranial hemorrhage, supported by a respirator. I was making rounds
with four other doctors—medical students—nurses, and
a social worker. When we came to this patient, I looked
at the group and said, "It's almost immoral to keep up
this treatment." Everyone sort of nodded and I asked,
"Okay, how many of you think this life should be maintained the way it is?" and no hands went up. "Well,
how many think it's wrong to turn this respirator off
for a few minutes and see if there's any sign of spontaneous life?" Nobody thought it would be wrong to do
that. So I just turned it off.

After about five minutes, there was no more heart
or pulse. We were lucky that time. It is unlikely,
but it's possible, that there could have been struggling
and convulsions. But this was relatively simple.

I feel strongly that, in that case, turning off the
respirator was the right thing.

I cannot see going in with a gun in hand and pulling
the trigger on a hopeless patient, although I can understand why relatives have done that when they can no
longer bear the agony or the financial expense. I can't
see pulling out a feeding tube either, because that is
not a nice way to die, starving and wasting away over
a period of weeks. It is not a "dignified" way to go. It's
something like putting a pillow over somebody's head, cutting them off from something the body is meant to have.

But over the years, almost every doctor has probably played at least some part in the demise of a patient who was hopeless, who was in pain, with the
family's consent. That's because it is the doctor who
should take the heat for letting someone die. It's not
fair to make a family, alone, come to that decision,
because no matter how strongly they feel that it's the
right thing, it is painful for them. Afterward, some peo-

ple are always going to feel guilty. Imagine the relative of someone in a coma who makes the decision to let the patient die, and then they read in a newspaper about a person who's been in a coma for three weeks, or three months or three years, and now is out riding a bicycle. That relative is going to feel guilty. So it's up to the doctor to take the pressure.

Dr. Watson, wondering why Dr. Morse had refused to accept that pressure in the matter of Karen Quinlan, decided to visit St. Clare's and call on him. And on her.

Though he had seen many patients in coma, Dr. Watson was unprepared for the sight of Karen Quinlan:

—She was so twisted that I couldn't even conceive the pain she would feel if she were to regain consciousness. One could only imagine the feeling if one would take a foot, twist it around a couple of times, and then tie it in that position, curled backward.

I thought about people who have strokes, who have only a little tightening and some use of their extremities—they often get severe pains just from that degree of contraction. Karen, with her heels tight up against the buttocks forming pressure ulcers—I just can't visualize that kind of pain. I realized, from seeing the way Karen's muscles were so severely contracted, that it was an unsalvageable situation.

Then I talked to Dr. Morse.

He had not told anyone in the media how he felt, or why he had declined to remove the respirator, and I think he will hold his silence. He believes he does not have a right to discuss a patient who cannot give her approval of what he is going to say.

In general, what seemed to happen to Dr. Morse was a concern that turning off the respirator for Karen Ann might result in a rather gruesome death scene. Turning it off, he felt, was not going to result in a three- or four-minute ordeal—it might be prolonged. And he said he was worried about the feelings and reactions of some of the family, especially the younger ones. He thought it would be unpleasant, and that they might not soon forget it.

That was coupled, apparently, with the very strong belief on Dr. Morse's part that she would probably die any day, in any case.

Now, I don't know if somebody may have given him a legal opinion along the way. The legal climate these days is such that doctors worry. The more people within a hospital who get interested in a case, or a patient, the more things come to the surface. As a doctor, he felt that the decision had to come from him, rather than some mandate from outside, from a nonmedical source. He couldn't live with that. And he made a casual remark about Karen herself. He maintained that he'd never taken care of a patient that long that he hadn't talked to, and he still found himself wondering about her. What she really would want him to do. She is dead in many ways, he said, but she is still breathing. And, when all was said and done, she was his patient and this had considerable meaning to him.

I came away with an understanding of his view. I don't know what might have happened if the Quinlans had not been forced to go to court, but I do know that the legalities made it even harder for a doctor like Morse. When someone said, "Okay, you're all clear now—turn off the respirator," that made it more difficult.

Doctors don't like to feel they have a gun at their heads.

After hearing Dr. Morse's views, Richard Watson knew he should meet the Quinlans.

—The rumors and speculations had built up in the newspapers, to such a pitch that it looked like no business would ever be done again in Morris County if it weren't decided what was to happen to Karen Quinlan. It was dominating life at the nursing home, with constant meetings back and forth between me and the staff, reviewing our guidelines and policies. It just looked to me like we had to do something—it didn't make much difference what. I met with Mr. and Mrs. Quinlan and their attorney, Paul Armstrong.

I wanted to find out their feelings about this thing, and their expectations.

After I met them, I found I was completely sympathetic to them, as I had been to Dr. Morse. That was the strange part. I had been reading the papers and was cynical about all the people involved in this and yet, after meeting them, it was impossible not to like all of them.

There were no loudmouthed types. They were all good people. And the feelings of Mr. and Mrs. Quinlan, and of the hospital personnel, turned out to be considerably less antagonistic, when stated in person, than appeared to be the case from the stories I'd been reading. Given the nice personalities involved, I thought that if perhaps the Quinlans very early had been a bit more explicit in their demands, and if Dr. Morse and St. Clare's had given a little more thought to the matter —then none of this needed to have happened. Because they were all working for the same goal. That was the irony.

In the end, my impression of the entire matter to all of the people involved was that this was like a Greek tragedy—where things happened to people, completely beyond their control, without their knowledge, and they were carried away by tides in different directions.

None of them willed it, but Fate sort of developed the tragedy in a manner that led to their being on opposite sides, all wanting the same thing, but swept apart by tides so strong that nobody could effectively function the way that, basically, they wanted to.

Sad.

On June 3, in a secret, hastily called meeting, the board of Morris View Nursing Home, with its administrator, legal adviser, and medical director, Richard Watson, voted to amend its long-standing rule against admitting comatose patients.

The key to the reversal of policy was Dr. Watson's assurance that "everybody is in complete agreement, and has so stated, that this was going to be the final stop for Karen, that all previous prognoses agree there will be no recovery, that we will do the nursing care, but nothing dramatic will be attempted."

This understanding was crucial. As Dr. Watson explained it, "We sympathized with St. Clare's Hospital's position, that Miss Quinlan is taking up a prime bed occupied by someone who doesn't belong there any longer because she is now a chronic care patient.

"On the other hand, Medicaid covers all hospital costs —but when a patient gets to a nursing home, Medicaid doesn't necessarily recognize a need for extra nurses, or extra care. So the only way to be fair to the Morris County taxpayer was to have everyone agree that no extra measures, and no extra personnel, would be needed to take care of Karen Quinlan."

It was agreed that Karen Ann would be treated with a "general medical and nursing care routine." And subsequently, throughout her terminal residence at Morris View, those simple procedures would be followed:

DIET: A commercially packaged tube feeding formula (powder) mixed in distilled water, fed via nasogastric tube, to be replaced (because of discoloration and tendency to become blocked) every forty-eight hours.

NURSING PROCEDURES: Position changed every two hours in order to equalize skin pressure points and lung secretion. Skin breakdown treated with a gastric antacid and tincture of Merthiolate. A soothing lotion applied to skin folds every shift; bedclothes changed frequently, vital signs checked daily, and as frequently as every hour if there is indication of change in status.

RESPIRATORY MANAGEMENT: Tracheostomy area cleansed and covered with antibiotic ointment at least every eight-hour shift. Trachea suction as needed for the removal of excessive secretions. Patient to breathe room air, with no external mechanical assistance, but air is humidified by machine delivering water vapor through a tube connected to tracheostomy.

BLADDER is drained by an indwelling Foley catheter; into catheter tube is drained an irrigation solution containing small amount of antibiotic ("neosporin"), to prevent crystal formation and retard growth of bacteria.

MEDICATION: Dilantin, an anticonvulsant: 50 mgs. every eight hours via nasogastric tube. Potassium io-

dine, five drops every eight hours via NG tube; an ex-
pectorant, tending to loosen trachael secretions.

It was a relatively simple medical program, actually re-
quiring less medication and care than that offered many of
the relatively healthy elderly patients at Morris View
Nursing Home. It should not unduly burden the county
taxpayers.

At the quiet meeting, the board of Morris View agreed
that an ethics committee, required by the Supreme Court
decision, would be promptly named.

Dr. Watson, now knowing Karen's condition, felt that
her death, when it came, would likely be sudden.

He did not specifically discuss his prognosis with the
nursing home Board of Directors that day. But later he
said:

—When she dies, it probably is going to be without
time for a committee to act, because things happen
quickly to people in her condition.

She could have sudden, overwhelming pneumonia. It
would be a little fever that suddenly becomes 105°,
with overwhelming pneumonia. With a chest that's only
partially ventilated because she isn't doing anything that
requires full, normal respiration, and an ineffective
cough, any question of treatment would become academic.

People who are completely immobile, like Karen, also
tend to form clots in their veins, especially in the legs;
these get loose and sail upstream and settle in the lungs.
It could start as phlebitis, but very often that condition
is not recognizable until after the clot migrates.

Karen could have a period of difficult irregular
breathing, which could lead to one millimeter less oxygen pressure in the blood than she could survive on.

Bleeding ulcer—brain-damaged people are suscepti-
ble to massive gastric ulceration. And when they bleed,
they bleed heavily.

A great many things might happen to Karen Quinlan that are not capable of early recognition. By the
time we knew what was going on, it could be many
minutes too late.

By agreement with the Morris County Sheriff's Office, her room would be guarded by armed deputies, twenty-four hours a day, for as long as she lived. (This security measure, against frequent intrusion attempts by the media, the curious, sometimes medically disturbed, and religious zealots, would ultimately be the most costly single factor in maintaining Karen Quinlan, costing county taxpayers an average of $4,199 a month.)

The time of her transfer would be decided by St. Clare's Hospital, in conjunction and co-operation with Joseph and Julia Quinlan, their lawyer, Paul Armstrong, and the safety expert who would meticulously engineer the move, Morris County Sheriff John Fox.

Dr. Joseph Fennelly was no longer needed.

He promptly issued a statement, withdrawing the services of his volunteer staff of seven physicians. "We never were intended to be a roving squad," he said. "We were going to provide the necessary care for Karen if it could not be found among the indigenous staffs. But the staff at Morris View Nursing Home, under a rather courageous Dr. Watson, intends to follow through and do what is needed.

"Therefore, our services will probably not be necessary."

And Paul Armstrong dictated to his wife, Maria, seven letters to the physicians who had volunteered anonymously to help.

"Dear Doctor," Paul wrote, "This momentary respite from the demands of this tragic case affords me the opportunity to extend to you the profound gratitude of the Quinlan family and myself for your courageous and compassionate bestowal of your professional and humane art. It is such an effort that lends nobility to the endeavors of man."

These letters were mailed to Drs. Daniel J. Carlin of Chatham; John Valeri, Basking Ridge; Benjamin Weissglass, Morristown; Oscar R. Kruesi, Bernardsville; Arthur N. Hoagland, Florham Park; Donald P. Burt, Morristown; and, of course, Dr. Fennelly.

Paul wished he could write individual letters to each of these men, whom he considered to be genuine heroes of their profession, but there was too little time.

The transfer of Karen Quinlan from St. Clare's Hospital to Morris View Nursing Home was scheduled to take place on June 9—six days after the home had agreed to accept her.

Absolute secrecy was essential.

Paul realized the all but insurmountable difficulties involved in trying to keep the maneuver quiet.

—Throughout all the two months since the Supreme Court ruling, there had never been a single item of news released through us, through me or Joe and Julie. Yet, somehow the media was always kept in touch with what was happening.

Some of their stories were pure speculation, and others were the result of solid investigative research. But much of the solid news seemed to come out of thin air. While I answered questions with my persistent reply about this being a time for absolute privacy, the media too often knew exactly what was going on.

This presented us with a frustrating and potentially dangerous situation as we attempted to plan the transfer. If word should leak out that Karen was being moved, it could present an extremely serious danger to Karen.

Joe and Julie were tense now. Well, we all were. I spent two full days with Sheriff Fox, who planned the effort skillfully because he knew, perhaps better than anyone else, that the security problems would be incredibly difficult. He had been caught in the middle during the trial, between the press and the zealots—and it had instilled in him an entirely appropriate fear of what could happen if the time of the transfer should become known.

We notified Attorney General Hyland's office, and Prosecutor Collester, of our plan. There would be sixteen sheriff's officers assigned to the transfer—half of them posted at St. Clare's to serve as guards and escorts during the twenty-minute drive to the nursing home, and the other eight men stationed inside and outside of Morris View to protect Karen on arrival.

It was decided that we wouldn't use one of the St. Clare's ambulances, because the media would be expecting that.

Father John Quinlan was captain of the Jefferson

Township Volunteer Ambulance Squad, and he offered to provide the ambulance. We all thought that might effectively throw the press off the scent—seeing an ambulance from another town.

Everything seemed to be precisely arranged—but then, the day before the move, we had one last contretemps with St. Clare's.

Sheriff Fox wanted the transfer to take place as late at night as possible for maximum security. Of course, we concurred. But the administrators at the hospital insisted that Karen be moved earlier in the day. Their reasoning, which seemed to us a bit unusual, was that if she were moved after nightfall there wouldn't be an available physician to travel in the ambulance with her.

As far as we were concerned that was out of the question. The sheriff argued with them, warning that transferring Karen during daylight hours—especially during visiting hours—would not only infringe on her privacy but invite actual mishap.

They were adamant.

Through most of the day, we were on the phone five or six times with the hospital, reminding them that there would be photographers out there willing to go to extreme lengths to get Karen's picture, and therefore, there was very real physical danger involved in the mob scene that could develop if we moved her under daylight conditions.

Finally, I reminded them that if they persisted in this illogical plan against the recommendation of our expert on safety, Sheriff Fox—and if, as a result, something happened to Karen or any member of the staff, or the press, or even helpless visitors caught in the melee—it would be totally their responsibility.

At last, they deferred to our judgment. But still, they wouldn't move her as late as midnight, which Sheriff Fox felt would be the safest hour for the transfer. St. Clare's compromised on a time just after nightfall.

We geared up to move at nine o'clock the night of Wednesday, June 9.

Chapter 25

It was a hot, oppressive night. Hazy and still, with far-off flashes of heat lightning; temperature lingering in the nineties even after the sun went down.

At 8:30 Joe and Julie drove to St. Clare's Hospital. Mary Ellen and John stayed at home, to avoid rousing suspicion. Joe parked the brown Buick at the rear of the hospital, near the emergency entrance. The location was part of the secrecy plan, and Joe thought it would be effective.

—This was our usual parking place when we'd come to see Karen after dinner. We didn't want anyone to think this night was any different from any other. It was pitch-black in the parking area, and when Julie and I climbed out of the car, we both had a feeling that there were eyes on us.

Julie said, very softly, "Maybe it's my imagination again, but I feel we're being watched."

I just nodded and lit up a cigarette. Then I took her elbow and moved her along, trying to be casual.

As we crossed the circular drive toward the door, there was movement in a panel truck parked nearby, and a flashbulb went off. So they were there, and they probably knew something unusual was happening, but they weren't showing themselves.

We pretended not to notice the flash and walked through the emergency doors. It was quiet inside, as it usually is. We took the elevator up to the second floor, and there didn't seem to be any activity there either. That seemed a little eerie to me. Probably because I was so restless inside, myself, I felt there should be all kinds of activity. But it was still early. My stomach was jumping, and I kept wishing it was all over, that Karen had been safely moved already.

When we walked past the security guard into Room 248, we were relieved to find Karen was quite calm. She wasn't asleep. Her eyes were open. But she wasn't moving about, and she wasn't grimacing, and a great rush of gratitude came over me. She was co-operating, making it easier for us.

You never know how she will be when you visit, and when she is having a difficult time and she's moving around a lot, then it is difficult for us, too. Julie can never bear to leave her as long as her head is moving around and she seems to be suffering, but this night she was so quiet—so fragile and so still—as though she knew. I wondered if they had given her an extra dose of Dilantin, which is the anticonvulsant drug they give Karen continuously to control her spasms, and I thought of asking the head nurse, Laurie Miller, about that. But what would be the use? Once when I asked Laurie about the Dilantin, she said, "I really can't tell you, Mr. Quinlan." And I said, "That's all right—nobody ever tells me anything." Afterward, I felt sorry. I'd put her on the spot, and she was only following the doctor's orders. I thought his orders not to tell me anything were all wrong, but I didn't want to take out my feelings on her.

We had a few minutes alone with Karen. I took my Cursillo crucifix, which always hung over her bed no matter what room she was in, and the picture of Our Blessed Mother, and the rosary beads and green scapulas that had hung over the head of her bed right from day one. I wanted to be sure they got safely to her new room at the nursing home.

Then, all of a sudden, there was a lot going on. Everybody was rushing around and getting excited. Mrs. Rovinski came into the room and said, "The press has been tipped off, I'm afraid. I think it would be best if you leave first, before the ambulance comes. Would you mind? I think it's the best way to get her out safely."

Of course we didn't mind.

Julie leaned over and kissed Karen, and her eyes filled up, and I knew what she was thinking. That maybe this would be the last time we'd see her alive. There was no reason to think Karen would die on the way to Morris View—but no one could know. She was still "critical." And she hadn't been out of a hospital bed for nearly fourteen months.

We pulled ourselves away. Just as we left the room, at about 8:45, to drive to the nursing home so we would be waiting when she came, I saw Bert from the sheriff's office come striding up the corridor. Then two interns came hurrying toward the room with a stretcher. So we knew that Father Quinlan must be there, and everything was ready to go on schedule. And as we walked down the hall, I remember thinking at last this will be the end of our problems with St. Clare's. We have finally, finally, almost freed our daughter.

Father John Quinlan had been told to have the ambulance outside a private, rarely used entrance of St. Clare's Hospital at 8:45.

Just before he left the Rectory to pick up the ambulance, Father Quinlan received a phone call from Sheriff Fox.

—I was already nervous, to say the least, but when Sheriff Fox called I could have slipped through the floor. He said, "Don't say anything to anybody, Father, but we've just had a threat on Karen's life."

I decided right then that I was not going to drive the ambulance—another man from the Emergency Squad, Augie Wister, could do that—I wanted to ride in the back with Karen. The sheriff said we'd also have an armed guard inside with us, along with a nurse and doctor—a respirator therapist. The sheriff also told me the press was camped out at the emergency entrance of St. Clare's, so I should be sure they didn't see me. He didn't have to tell me twice; I'm not comfortable around the press at all.

At 8:45 Augie and I drove around a circuitous route to the private entrance, which is hidden by trees and is used only by the nuns from a health resort next to the hospital. We parked, and I picked up the metal ambulance stretcher and rushed in fast. On the second floor, I was met by the interns and the guards and the nurse, Laurie.

Nobody said much. There wasn't any need to talk.

We just had to act quickly. I went in the room to put Karen, very carefully, onto the stretcher. There was nothing to it. She was quiet, and so light that it was like handling a sleeping little child.

The hospital had all the hallways cleared, and there were armed sheriff's men by the elevators and by the doors, and almost before I realized what was happening we had Karen's stretcher down the hall, down the elevator, out the private door, and into the van.

I had pulled the ambulance curtains closed and put adhesive tape at the bottom. Then I'd stuffed towels around the sides, to make doubly sure that no one could get a camera shot through any slits anywhere. So there was no light from the outside at all, but we had a dim light overhead, and the nurse adjusted the bottles that fed Karen, and the therapist was there with oxygen in case it was needed, and Augie started up the engine, and we took off.

It was a smooth ride, but we really sped fast. We were bound and determined to put miles between us and St. Clare's, and between us and anybody who was threatening her.

I kept looking at her and thinking, "It's kind of all over now, Karen." She was fairly restful, and I kept my eyes on her, and once she became very restless all of a sudden and all I could think then was "Karen, don't die going over there!" And then I prayed a lot, and she seemed to calm down.

I knew we were well covered. I knew the sheriff was driving his car in front of us, and another sheriff's car was behind us, and we were taking the back roads and that, if something should happen like a road block, or if she looked like she was dying, then there were alternate plans to take her elsewhere—to Morristown Memorial Hospital. But still, I just about had a nervous breakdown because she was right now my responsibility. This was Joe and Julie's child, and John and Mary Ellen's sister—and here I was, with all my human emotions and weaknesses, with their most precious possession.

All of a sudden, I could hear rain starting to beat against the windows, and my automatic reaction was "Oh no!"—and then I thought hey, wait a minute,

this is great. Rain on camera lenses doesn't go too well.
And I remember saying, "Good, good, God, keep that
rain comin'!"

Then there was a flash of light so powerful that you
could see it through the curtains and the towels, and
all of us looked up, except Karen, and the ambulance
suddenly stopped. I didn't know whether that flash of
light was from a camera or lightning, but the next minute I heard someone outside wrestling with the ambulance door and asking, "Ready in there?" and I knew
we had made it safely.

Reporters and photographers were clustered outside the
nursing home entrance, focusing powerful arc lights on the
action as the ambulance sped up the circular driveway,
stopped short, then backed up to the heavy glass front
doors.

But the flash of light which had pierced the shrouded
windows around Karen was a sizzling, crackling streak of
lightning, which was followed instantly by a curtain of
torrential rain.

The media, racing forward for a prized picture, were
momentarily blinded by the lightning bolt, then inundated
by the sudden rain.

Inside Morris View, where she had been waiting beside
Joe and Father Tom, Julia Quinlan had seen the ambulance back toward the entrance, had caught a glimpse of
sheriff's men dashing out to open its door and rescue Kar-
en. She had begun to run across the lobby toward her
daughter when the lightning exploded.

"Suddenly the lights sputtered and went out," she remembers, "and the fire doors automatically clanged shut
and locked. I could hear someone crying 'Don't worry,'
and another saying 'Don't panic,' and all I could think was
'Karen's out there! Somebody get Karen—she's locked
outside!' "

The blackout lasted only a few seconds. The lights
flashed on again. And simultaneously the huge doors
swung open, at the exact moment the stretcher was being
hoisted from the back of the ambulance into the hands
of sheriff's deputies waiting below. And Karen, a small
mound covered by a white sheet on the stretcher bed,
was whisked instantly through the glass doors and wheeled

swiftly and silently across the large lobby and into a waiting elevator.

Joe, Julie, and Father Tom hurried after her, along with
nurse Laurie Miller and Dr. Richard Watson, who had
been standing by, fascinatedly watching the drama.

They all crammed into the large, brightly lighted elevator and held it open for Paul Armstrong and Jim
Crowley, who had ridden to Morris View in the sheriff's
car and now were dashing across the lobby. While the
frustrated press corps cowered outside in the downpour,
Paul moved quickly into the elevator, inhaled deeply, and
smiled at Julie. He said, "The Deity helped again."

Gently they lifted Karen's twisted, rigid body from the
stretcher, and placed her on a water bed in a private
room on the second floor. A spacious 8×10-foot room, it
was painted a sunny yellow and looked out on tall trees
she would never see.

Laurie Miller, the nurse from St. Clare's ICU who had
supervised Karen's care for nearly fourteen months, went
into the room ahead of the family, to attach the tubes
and the bottles, and to brief Dr. Watson, and, presumably,
to say good-by.

Joe, standing outside in the hall waiting, wondered how
the nurse felt now. "All of the girls had become so fond of
Karen. They had lived with her, talked to her, sung to
her, and taken such tender care. They would talk to her
as though she were a baby. 'Good morning, Karen, how
are you feeling today? Okay, Karen, we're going to give
you a bath now.' They were wonderful. I imagined it must
be difficult for them, to know they wouldn't be seeing
her any more, and I resolved we would invite them to
visit her, anytime they could get away."

Ten minutes later, Laurie emerged from the room and
walked directly to Julie, who was standing alone in the
corridor outside. Both women looked at each other, and
each had tears in her eyes, and Laurie murmured, "She
looks peaceful." Then the nurse turned slowly and began
to walk toward the elevator.

Joe, seeing her go, hurried after to thank her—"You
nurses have been beautiful," he said. She nodded, and as
she turned away Joe Quinlan wanted to say more. "I
thought about everything, even about the doctors—if the

doctors had been there, I would have thanked them, too, at that moment; I would have said, 'You were good to Karen, you did the best you could for her.' All these emotions filled up in me, and I wanted to let them out, but it was too late. Laurie was gone."

Dr. Watson came out of Karen's room.

"It's okay. You can go in now."

Julie led, followed by Joe. Father Tom moved to the foot of the bed, and Paul and Jim leaned against the door, not wanting to intrude.

Karen was awake, moving her head lazily from side to side, her eyes seemingly glancing at objects and figures, then moving on. Julie kissed her cheek, a ritual performed hundreds of times before. "It's a nice room, honey," she said.

Joe looked around for a tissue. Karen was perspiring. He found a box of tissues on a corner table and used one to stroke the dampness from his daughter's forehead. Then he carefully propped the picture of the Holy Mother on a shelf directly above the bed. Searching for a hook or nail from which to hang his crucifix, and finding none, Joe asked Julie if she had anything that would help him hang the crucifix. Julie searched in the coin purse in her bag and found a safety pin. He opened it, slid the pin through the ring on the top of the crucifix and reached up and attached it to a chain on a light above Karen's bed.

After a few minutes, Karen's head slowed its restless movement, and her eyes closed.

Julie stepped back, and Father Tom moved forward, leaned over Karen, and whispered a prayer. It was inaudible.

"What did you say, Father?"

"I just commended her to the Lord. I prayed that her life will have been worthwhile," the priest replied.

When finally Karen slept, they left the room. Joe and Julie, Father Tom and Paul. They said good night to the sheriff's deputy who was sitting beside a wooden table outside the door. One of the girls at the nurses' station, twenty feet down the broad corridor from Karen's room, asked cheerfully, "Will we see you tomorrow?"

"We'll be here early," Joe said. Julie smiled.

Down the elevator, across the lobby, dimly lighted because it was past eleven o'clock, and out the glass doors.

The rain had ended, as had the long fight.

A few reporters appeared out of the shadows. There was no pushing now, no desperation. Everyone seemed weary, subdued, deadlines passed, perceiving a story almost concluded. Paul whispered to Joe, "Why don't you two go on to the car. I'll speak with them."

To the reporters, Paul Armstrong said, "As you know, the Supreme Court decision was wisely premised on the right of privacy. Any information concerning the care and treatment of Karen, from this point on, falls within the sacred realm of family privacy."

"Is that all?"

"That's it," Paul said. "There will be no more news to report."

A traumatic phase of their lives was finished. Julia Quinlan realized that, as she slid into the front seat of the car. There would be no more legalities, confrontations, press conferences; no more pleading or weeping out of anger and frustration.

—I felt almost exhilarated—for Karen. She was liberated now, from the machines she would have hated. And she had done something that I think benefited the whole world, and I thought she would have liked that. Been proud of that, because helping people was her way. And I kept thinking, "You're free, honey."

Then all at once I just wanted to go home to my other children and hold onto them. If anything ever happened to Mary Ellen or John, I knew that would be the end of me. Suddenly I couldn't think of dying any more, I had to live. Make it up to the children. I looked at Joe and said, "Let's get going, honey. The kids will wonder what happened to us."

Joe nodded, and turned the key in the ignition.

As he backed out of the parking lot, he heard Julie talking with more animation than she had shown in months.

She said it was a lovely room they'd put Karen in, wasn't it?

Joe agreed.

She said she had an idea. She was going to buy some pretty nylon nightgowns for Karen, and she would split them up the back and hem them—"I can finally do something for her with my own hands, Joe, for the first time in more than a year," she said. So excited.

Joe liked that idea.

Julie seemed optimistic—the worst was over, and now, for the sake of the children, they should try to live a normal life again.

Joe Quinlan decided not to tell her, right at this moment, what he was thinking. Maybe later.

"I didn't want Karen to die," Joe had explained weeks before. "I just wanted her back in her natural state. If God wants her to live in a natural state, she'll live. If He wants her to die, she'll die." Joe had said that and he had meant it, and tonight Karen was where she should be. Now she was in God's hands, and there was nothing more that he or Julie or anyone else could do to change anything. Their struggle was finished, the ordeal was finished, everything was finished except the waiting, visiting, seeing her every morning, every night.

Then one day, even the waiting and visiting would end.

And Joseph Quinlan, driving home that night in June, forced himself to face the truth that there would be a world without Karen, and that for him, and for Julie, "emptiness may be harder to deal with than anything else."

Chapter 26

In late August 1976, Mary Ellen Quinlan was searching through a bureau drawer in Karen's room and discovered, folded and tucked away in the back of it, a sheet of loose-leaf notebook paper.

At the top of the yellowed page was a date: two months and one week before the fateful coma.

Below that date, carefully printed in ink, were six lines which may have been Karen Ann Quinlan's last poem.

> *January 7, 1975*
>
> *the constant struggle with submission*
> > *is tiring*
> *this so-called strength I've gained*
> > *is just another heavy load,*
> *I wish to curl myself into a Fetal rose*
> > *and rest in the eternal womb awhile.*

Appendixes

Appendix A

THE POSITION OF THE BISHOP
OF PATERSON
ON THE USE OF EXTRAORDINARY MEANS
TO SUSTAIN
THE LIFE OF KAREN ANN QUINLAN

"It is in the face of death that the riddle of human existence becomes most acute."[1] These words of the Second Vatican Council have a special meaning to the family of Karen Ann Quinlan and, indeed, to a host of people who have come to know about her tragic condition. Her parents have made a painful and difficult decision, to request the discontinuance of the means sustaining the continuation of her life; it is a decision which elicits the sympathy and concern of many people and which now demands the attention of the courts. It has been with the competent advice of their pastor, the Rev. Thomas J. Trapasso, that the family has made this decision, and it is incumbent upon me, as Bishop of Paterson, to comment on the moral correctness of that decision in the light of the Catholic Church's teachings.

I.
BASIC ASSUMPTIONS

1. *The Bishop of Paterson has the authority and competence to present the Church's teachings in this matter.*
The local bishop has both the responsibility and the right to witness to the divine and Catholic faith by proclaiming the teaching of the Church as it is held and taught by Peter's successors and his fellow bishops; and

he has a similar responsibility and right to apply that teaching in a particular instance as a matter of faith and morals to be held and practiced by the people he serves.[2]

A primary office of the bishop as pastor of souls in the diocese committed to his care by the Church's supreme authority is to be within the territory of his competence the principal dispenser of the mysteries of God and the one called upon to teach them with the authority of Christ.[3]

It is with this authority and competence that I, as Bishop of Paterson, accept the responsibility and right to apply the teachings of the Catholic Church to the request for permission to discontinue the use of a respirator as an extraordinary means of sustaining the life of Karen Ann Quinlan, which request is made by her loving parents and our beloved brother and sister in Christ, Joseph and Julia Quinlan, faithful members of the Parish of Our Lady of the Lake, Mount Arlington, New Jersey, within the Diocese of Paterson.

2. *Karen Ann Quinlan is alive.*

The verification of the fact of death in a particular case cannot be deduced from any religious or moral principle, and, under this aspect, does not fall within the competence of the Church.[4] Therefore, we appeal to the traditional medical standards for determining death; by these standards, Karen Ann Quinlan is assumed to be alive. The same assumption is deduced from the proposed standards of the "Ad Hoc Committee of the Harvard Medical School to Examine the Definition of Brain Death," in their report issued in 1968.[5] In this case, then, from the viewpoint of the Church, the "brain death" issue is a secondary one.

3. *What is being requested by Joseph and Julia Quinlan is not euthanasia.*

Karen Ann Quinlan's parents have requested the termination of a medical procedure which is an extraordinary means of treatment. The *Ethical and Religious Directives for Catholic Health Care Facilities,* approved in November 1971 at the annual meetings of the National Conference of Catholic Bishops, states: "The failure to supply the ordinary means of preserving life is equivalent to euthanasia."[6] It also states: "Neither the physician nor the patient is obliged to use extraordinary means."[7] Since the Bishops in these directives forbid *all* forms of euthanasia, they thus teach that non-use of extraordinary means does not constitute euthanasia. Pope Pius XII in discussing the case of a patient in deep unconsciousness, a case, moreover, considered hopeless in the opinion of the competent doctor, said that the discontinuance of a respirator as an extraordinary means is not to be considered euthanasia in any way. "There is not involved here a case of direct disposal of the life of a patient, nor of euthanasia in any way; this would never be licit."[8]

Euthanasia or "mercy killing" may be described as the deliberate and direct causing of the painless death of a human being who is helpless or who, for whatever reason, is deemed unable to live a so-called meaningful life. The Church teaches that: "Euthanasia is immoral and unlawful because it is intrinsically evil and entails a direct violation of man's right to life and God's supreme dominion over His creatures."[9] A person does have the ethical right to die peacefully and doctors and family do have the ethical right to allow such a death to happen in accord with the presumed will of the patient, when there is no reasonable hope for some recovery. However, there is never a right to take the life of a patient or to comply with a family or patient's request that the patient be allowed to take his own life. This would be contrary to divine law and contrary to the obligation of the state and society in general to uphold and defend the right to life from direct attack.

4. *The possibility of God's intervention in the recovery of health is not and cannot be precluded.*

God's intervention in human life takes many forms. He can do all things. He can and does work through His creation, and, in particular, through the knowledge and expertise of His people. These are interventions in accord with nature. For this reason we pray for those who undergo surgery and medical treatment. He can and does also work beyond the powers of nature, in which cases He does not need the intervention of man-made machines. He can restore life and health without them.

II.
GENERAL TEACHING OF THE CHURCH ON THE PRESERVATION OF LIFE

Human life is God's great and first gift to each of us. We must love life and work to preserve it. When there is hope for returning a person from the threshold of death to a measure of recovery we should work to preserve God's gift of life.[10]

The Church further teaches that human life does not end with death. "The Church has been taught by divine revelation, and herself firmly teaches, that man has been created by God for a blissful purpose beyond the reach of earthly misery," and, further, "God has called man and still calls him so that with his entire being he might be joined to Him in an endless sharing of a divine life beyond all corruption."[11]

As for the methods to be used in preserving human life, Pope Pius XII has laid down the principle: "Natural reason and Christian morals say that man (and whoever is entrusted with the task of taking care of his fellowman) has the right and the duty in case of serious illness to take the necessary treatment for the preservation of life and health." The Holy Father states further: "But normally one is held to use only ordinary means—according to circumstances of persons, places, times, and culture—that is to say, means that do not involve any grave burden for oneself or another."[12]

The distinction between "ordinary" and "extraordinary" means has been expressed in the 1974 document entitled "Respect Life," prepared by the Family Life Division of the United States Catholic Conference, and issued in the name of the National Conference of Catholic Bishops' Committee for Population and Pro-Life activities:

• Distinguishing between "ordinary" and "extraordinary" means has become commonplace in discussing the obligation to prolong life when a person is irremediably ill and death is certain.
• Citing Pope Pius XII for his assertion of the principle, moralists and ethicians hold that we must take all ordinary means to preserve life, even if there is little hope of recovery. We are not obliged to use

extraordinary means to prolong life when recovery is
no longer possible, although we may do so.

• Ordinary means are described as "all medicines,
treatments and operations which offer a reasonable
hope of benefit for the patient and can be obtained
and used without excessive pain, expense, or other
inconveniences." By extraordinary means are meant
"all medicines, treatments and operations which cannot be obtained or used without excessive pain, expense, or other inconveniences, or which, if used,
would not offer a reasonable hope of benefit."[13]

The "Respect Life" document quoting the Rev. Gerald
Kelly[14] does qualify the elements of pain and expense, but
accepts the over-all criteria as working principles for the
determination as to which means are ordinary and which
means are extraordinary.

Pope Pius XII in his address of November 24, 1957,
to anesthesiologists, quoted above, dealt with a specific
question stated as follows: "Does the anesthesiologist have
the right, or is he bound, in all cases of deep unconsciousness, even in those that are considered to be completely
hopeless in the opinion of the competent doctor, to use
modern artificial respiration apparatus, even against the
will of the family?"[15]

In answering the question the Holy Father makes several points:

1. In ordinary cases the doctor has the right to act in
this manner, but is not bound to do so unless this is the
only way of fulfilling another certain moral duty.

2. The doctor, however, has no right independent of the
patient. He can act only if the patient explicitly or im-
plicitly, directly or indirectly gives him the permission.

3. The treatment as described in the question constitutes extraordinary means of preserving life and so there
is no obligation to use them nor to give the doctor permission to use them.

4. The rights and duties of the family depend on the
presumed will of the unconscious patient if he or she is of
legal age, and the family, too, is bound to use only ordinary means.

5. This case is not to be considered euthanasia in any
way; that would never be licit. The interruption of at-

tempts at resuscitation, even when it causes the arrest of circulation, is not more than an indirect cause of the cessation of life, and we must apply in this case the principle of double effect.

III.
APPLICATION OF THE CHURCH'S TEACHING TO THE CASE OF KAREN ANN QUINLAN

Competent medical testimony has established that Karen Ann Quinlan has no reasonable hope of recovery from her comatose state by the use of any available medical procedures. The continuance of mechanical (cardio-respiratory) supportive measures to sustain continuation of her body functions and her life constitute extraordinary means of treatment. THEREFORE, THE DECISION OF JOSEPH AND JULIA QUINLAN TO REQUEST THE DISCONTINUANCE OF THIS TREATMENT IS, ACCORDING TO THE TEACHINGS OF THE CATHOLIC CHURCH, A MORALLY CORRECT DECISION.

IV.
THE INTERRELATIONSHIP OF THE THREE DISCIPLINES OF THEOLOGY, LAW AND MEDICINE

The right to a natural death is one outstanding area in which the disciplines of theology, medicine and law overlap; or, to put it in another way, it is an area in which these three disciplines convene.

Medicine with its combination of advanced technology and professional ethics is both able and inclined to prolong biological life. Law with its felt obligation to protect the life and freedom of the individual seeks to assure each person's right to live out his human life until its natural and inevitable conclusion. Theology with its acknowledgment of man's dissatisfaction with biological life as the ultimate source of joy, proclaims the individual's call to an endless sharing in a divine life beyond all corruption. It also defends the sacredness of human life and defends it from all direct attacks.

These disciplines do not conflict with one another, but are necessarily conjoined in the application of their principles in a particular instance such as that of Karen Ann Quinlan. Each must in some way acknowledge the other without denying its own competence. The civil law is not expected to assert a belief in eternal life; nor, on the other hand, is it expected to ignore the right of the individual to profess it, and to form and pursue his conscience in accord with that belief. Medical science is not authorized to directly cause natural death; nor, however, is it expected to prevent it when it is inevitable and all hope of a return to an even partial exercise of human life is irreparably lost. Religion is not expected to define biological death; nor, on its part, is it expected to relinquish its responsibility to assist man in the formation and pursuit of a correct conscience as to the acceptance of natural death when science has confirmed its inevitability beyond any hope other than that of preserving biological life in a merely vegetative state.

The common concern of the three disciplines as they focus on the situation of Karen Ann Quinlan is that of life and death. This fact demonstrates the need for theology, medicine and law to develop an even greater interrelationship in an open, continuing and growing dialogue on the profound issues arising from the Biological Revolution, a designation aptly applied to the age in which we live.

V.
CONCERNS FOR THE FUTURE— KAREN ANN QUINLAN'S CASE AS A PRECEDENT

Since many are concerned that the decision in the case of Karen Ann Quinlan will establish a precedent, it is necessary to look beyond the immediate decision regarding this young woman.

What may be the overriding issue in this case is whether society is prepared to distinguish in law and in practice between the non-obligation to use extraordinary means of treatment in cases that are determined by competent medical authority to be hopeless, and euthanasia, so-called mercy killing. Can society understand and accept the distinction between the right to die a natural death peacefully, and the call for a right to take another's life or the life of oneself even for reasons of compassion?

The first alternative may in fact represent the status quo at least in some practicing medical circles, and it does not in itself undermine society's reverence for life. The other alternative—euthanasia, again, even when advocated by compassionately motivated people—does undermine society's reverence for life. This has been the admirable and traditional position of both the State and the medical profession in our country. The taking of life even for allegedly noble motives is a first step toward barbarism. The horrifying euthanasia statutes of Nazi Germany earlier in this very century bear witness to this.

In the present public discussion of the case of Karen Ann Quinlan it has been brought out that responsible people involved in medical care, patients and families have exercised the freedom to terminate or withhold certain treatments as extraordinary means in cases judged to be terminal, i.e. cases which hold no realistic hope for some recovery, in accord with the expressed or implied intentions of the patients themselves. To whatever extent this has been happening it has been without sanction in civil law. Those involved in such actions, however, have ethical and theological literature to guide them in their judgments and actions. Furthermore, such actions have not in themselves undermined society's reverence for the lives of sick and dying people.

It is both possible and necessary for society to have laws and ethical standards which provide freedom for decisions, in accord with the expressed or implied intentions of the patient, to terminate or withhold extraordinary treatment in cases which are judged to be hopeless by competent medical authorities, without at the same time leaving an opening for euthanasia. Indeed, to accomplish this, it may simply be required that courts and legislative bodies recognize the present standards and practices of many people engaged in medical care who have been doing what the parents of Karen Ann Quinlan are requesting authorization to have done for their beloved daughter.

In all of this we pray for God's guidance of our society in its efforts to appreciate the precious gift of human life, and for His blessings upon the family of Karen Ann Quinlan and of all those in similar circumstances who must make their judgments based on mutual love. Finally, we pray for Karen herself that the Lord Who has brought her into the hearts and minds of more people than perhaps she ever dreamed, will bestow on her the happiness which is the goal and purpose of all mankind.

⊹LAWRENCE B. CASEY

Bishop of Paterson

November 1, 1975, Feast of All Saints
Paterson, New Jersey

FRANK J. RODIMER

Chancellor

Notes

1. Con. Vat. II, "The Church Today," par. 18. (This and following translations are in *The Documents of Vatican II*, edited by W. Abbott, The America Press, 1966.)
2. Con. Vat. II, "The Church," par. 25.
3. Cf. Con. Vat. II, "The Bishops' Pastoral Office in the Church," par. 15, and "The Church," par. 25.
4. Address of Pope Pius XII to an International Congress of Anesthesiologists, Nov. 24, 1957. AAS XXXXIX (1957). (Translation from the original French, *The Pope Speaks*, Spring, 1958, Vol. IV, No. 4, pp. 393–98.)
5. Cf. discussion of report "A Definition of Irreversible Coma" in "The Eerie Need to Redefine Death," *America*, Sept. 27, 1975, p. 164.
6. Article 28, "Ethical and Religious Directives for Catholic Health Facilities," Department of Health Affairs, United States Catholic Conference, Washington, D.C. 20005. 1971.
7. Ibid.
8. Address of Pope Pius XII, supra.
9. "Euthanasia," New Catholic Encyclopedia, Vol. V, p. 639, Washington, D.C., 1967.
10. Cf. Chancery Statement, Diocese of Paterson, Sept. 16, 1975, reported in *The Beacon*, Paterson diocesan newspaper, Vol. IX, No. 34 (Sept. 18, 1975), p. 21.

11. Con. Vat. II, "The Church Today," par. 18.
12. Address of Pope Pius XII, supra.
13. "Respect Life," Family Life Division, United States Cath-
    olic Conference, Washington D.C. 20005. 1974.
14. "The Duty to Preserve Life," *Theological Studies*, Vol. XII
    (1951), p. 550.
15. Address of Pope Pius XII, supra.

Appendix B

*Phyllis Battelle is the only member of the media ever
permitted to see Karen. Her impressions, after many visits
to the bedside, are recorded here:*

I first visited Karen in the evening of May 17, 1976, in
the Intensive Care Unit of St. Clare's Hospital. My reaction was not shock or revulsion but deep pity—a feeling of
"Oh, this poor child." She looked like a child. Her body
was a small, rounded mold concealed under a sheet. All
that was exposed were her head and her hands. The hands
were drawn tight over her chest, the wrists sharply cocked
so that the long, white fingers pointed straight downward,
stiff and thin as pencils. Karen's head was in constant
movement, straining back and forth in an erratic, swivel-
ing motion—as though seeking relief from her rigid body.
The eyes, still intensely blue, roved wildly, never quite
focusing, and her mouth closed and opened in a series of
grimaces that gave the impression she was soundlessly crying out in anguish. Her once tawny, sun-streaked hair was
short and curled in damp wisps around her cheeks and
forehead. Her jaw had receded in recent weeks, causing
Karen's upper teeth to bite into her lower lip; as a result,
the teeth had been encased in a protective plastic mold.
She was attached to a series of machines and hanging bottles by a variety of tubes: two thin ones inserted into her
nostrils fed her; another delivered antibiotics directly
into her kidneys; a transparent, hoselike tube was attached to her upper chest, sputtering and gurgling as it

pumped air from a respirator into Karen's lungs. Occasionally, she would emit a low, moaning sound.

In later visits, I saw Karen's body free of the masking sheet. It was emaciated, and seemed totally foreign to her round and still attractive (even when contorted) face. Her knees were pulled up taut against her chest, her legs twisted and entangled together in a posture no healthy being could assume—outside the womb. The towels that padded her knees and the gauze pads separating her toes helped to prevent the contracting limbs from imposing open wounds and bruises upon themselves. Under surgical pads, her bedsores were so deep that the hipbone could be seen beneath.

This is the rigid, irreversible "persistent, vegetative state" in which Karen Quinlan lay. As neurologists have explained, her highly developed "cognitive" brain function had ceased. Only the internal "vegetative" regulators—which control breathing, facial movement, and to some degree body temperature, blood pressure, and heart rate—still functioned.

After the respirator was removed, she appeared more peaceful, for longer periods of time. There is no doubt in my mind that the tracheostomy tube had been an irritant, causing her to strain in an effort to dislodge it. Following the transfer to a water bed at the Morris View Nursing Home, Karen was maintained on anticonvulsant medicine (Dilantin), not so much for her own sake as for those who love her. Dr. Richard Watson explained, "Keeping Karen at rest is an irrelevant point, because she doesn't know what is happening. But one of our goals is avoiding the unpleasant things that occur to other people; we want to keep the people visiting her—and the nurses caring for her—from suffering too many pains."

There have been times when she has seemed close to death, gasping for breath as mucus accumulates in her lungs and she is unable to cough it up because of the cerebral disease. In June 1977 Karen developed pneumonia in just such a crisis and for several days was expected to die, although Dr. Watson refused to give a prognosis. "She has defied too many predictions," he said. After four days of running a fever and struggling for air, Karen Quinlan "miraculously" brought herself back to stable condition, without the aid of antibiotics or other heroic measures.

Joe and Julie Quinlan, to whom daily visits with their daughter are a way of life, see her severely weakened. Most of the time, when they come into the pale yellow room, Karen is lying peaceful and calm, wide awake, staring off into space. They still kiss her, and speak softly to her. Sometimes they will take her hand, if she is sleeping, and move it down to her side. But, relentlessly, it moves slowly back into the rigid fetal posture.

For me, watching Karen's face has been an emotional, rather than a rational, experience. When her face is composed, it is easy to slip into the illogical rationale that Karen really is a "sleeping beauty," as some of the media have imagined her. But when she is awake and grimacing, I found it difficult to believe that Karen did not suffer pain, however primitive. And her original neurologist, Dr. Robert Morse, did not foreclose the possibility of Karen's suffering. "The sensation of pain is a subjective thing," he testified in court. "Yes, she does move. She does feel. What quality she feels these impulses at, God only knows. I don't."

Pain or not, physicians say there is no hope of recovery for Karen. Those arms and legs will never untwine. The mind will never think normally. This is not one of the several other kinds of coma that can respond to medical miracles. And that is why, each time I leave Karen's bedside, I feel a compelling urge to whisper—though I never did, and she wouldn't have heard me if I had—"Go to sleep, Karen. Sleep in peace."

ABOUT PHYLLIS BATTELLE

PHYLLIS BATTELLE, a noted newspaper columnist for King Features Syndicate and feature writer for magazines such as *Good Housekeeping* and *Ladies' Home Journal*, was commissioned by the *Journal* to write an article from Mrs. Quinlan's point of view, which appeared in the September 1976 issue. She is the only journalist whom the Quinlans have allowed to visit Karen in the hospital.